# Power, Reproduction and Gender

# Power, Reproduction and Gender

The inter-generational transfer of knowledge

EDITED BY
WENDY HARCOURT

Zed Books
LONDON AND NEW JERSEY

For Caterina and Nico

*Power, Reproduction and Gender: The inter-generational transfer of knowledge* was first published by Zed Books Ltd, 7 Cynthia Street, London N1 9JF, UK, and 165 First Avenue, Atlantic Highlands, New Jersey 07716, USA, in collaboration with the Society for International Development (SID), in 1997.

Cover designed by Andrew Corbett.
Set in Monotype Ehrhardt by Ewan Smith.
Printed and bound in the United Kingdom by Biddles Ltd, Guildford and King's Lynn.

A catalogue record for this book is available from the British Library.

US CIP data is available from the Library of Congress.

ISBN 1 85649 425 X cased
ISBN 1 85649 426 8 limp

# Contents

# Notes on the contributors

*Richard A. Banibensu* is a senior research fellow of the University of Ghana with extensive experience in participatory research and participatory evaluation. He has carried out research in all the regions of Ghana and in some other African countries, as well as in Britain. He has recently completed a major evaluation of a national programme in development education in Nigeria, using participatory methods. He is currently completing the analysis of an impact evaluation of a population education programme in Ghana.

*Emanuela Calabrini* graduated from the University of Reading, UK with a BA in Italian and international relations and an MA in European studies. She collaborated with WIDE in the follow-up of the Fourth World Conference on Women in Beijing. She is currently working as a researcher with the Society for International Development. Her main fields of interest are women in development, nationalism and peace-keeping, migrants and refugees.

*Brigit Obrist van Eeuwijk* has a PhD in anthropology, sociology and folklore from the University of Basel, Switzerland. She has conducted research in Papua New Guinea, Switzerland, Indonesia and Tanzania, mainly on illness perceptions, health behaviour and users' responses to health services. Since 1987 she has lectured at the University of Basel; her special interest is medical anthropology. Collaboration with colleagues in Tanzania began in 1993, when she became consultant to the Dar es Salaam Urban Health Project, which is supported by the Tanzanian and Swiss governments.

*Professor Miranda Naabia Greenstreet* has been with the Institute of Adult Education, University of Ghana, for over three decades, serving as director for ten of those years. She is chairperson of the Valco Trust Fund and vice-chairperson of the National Population Council of Ghana. She is also president of the Ghana National Council on Adult Education and the West African Distance Education Association, as well as chapter leader of SID. In 1992 Miranda Greenstreet won a National Arts and Culture award in appreciation of her contribution to education and cultural development in Ghana. In March 1995 the University of Ghana conferred on her a Distinguished Meritorious Award for exemplary service and research and for her contribution to the university.

*Wendy Harcourt* is director of gender and development at the Society for International Development (SID), the largest international-membership non-governmental organization, founded in 1957 with headquarters in Rome. She joined SID after receiving her PhD from the Australian National University in 1987. For the last eight years she has edited *Development: Journal of SID*, co-ordinated the SID women in development network and published and lectured widely on gender and economic development, population, reproductive health and sustainable development. Since 1989 she has been a member of the network Women in Development Europe (WIDE) steering group and until 1995 was editor of the WIDE *Bulletin*. In 1994 she edited *Feminist Perspectives on Sustainable Development* (Zed Books) following a collaborative project with the Institute of Social Studies, The Hague. In 1995 she wrote *Alternative Economics from a European Perspective* with Lois Woestman and Louise Grogan and edited, in collaboration with UNESCO, *Cultural Changes in Women's Life Stages*. Both publications were widely distributed in Europe and internationally in preparation for the Fourth World Conference on Women.

*Sandya Hewamanne* is a lecturer in the Department of Sociology at the University of Colombo in Sri Lanka. Currently she is a Fulbright scholar undertaking a masters degree in anthropology at the University of Texas, Austin, USA.

*Verena Hillmann* has been a consultant with Caritas Zurich, Switzerland, since 1991. Her main fields of interest are gender relations, ethnopsychoanalytical approaches to women's life histories, parental influence on children's psychological development, and the changing of family and households during the transition to industrialization. She was a co-researcher on the Swiss contribution to the project 'Sustainability for Future Generations'.

*Cecilia de Mello e Souza* is a psychologist and anthropologist who currently works in the field of reproductive rights and reproductive health. She received her MA and PhD in social anthropology from the University of California in 1993. She is a professor at the EICOS Program (Interdisciplinary Studies on Communities and Social Ecology) of the Federal University of Rio de Janeiro (FURJ) and a consultant at

Citizenship, Studies, Information and Action (CEPIA). She is a member of the International Reproductive Rights Research Action Group (IRRRAG).

*Susan Mlangwa* studied sociology at the University of Dar es Salaam, Tanzania. She conducted a study on coping mechanisms of urban widows in Dar es Salaam and participated in several projects in other parts of Tanzania, namely the Kagera AIDS Research Project and a Women and Development Project of the Mothers' Union of the Anglican Church in Mwanza. Since 1994 she has worked as a research officer under the supervision of the Dar es Salaam Urban Health Project.

*Hans Peter Müller* is currently head of the Department of Anthropology, University of Zurich, Switzerland. He has a PhD in social anthropology. He has done fieldwork in several countries, including Bangladesh, Cameroon, Pakistan, Sri Lanka, Bhutan, Burundi, Guinea-Bissau, Kenya and Nepal. His areas of interest include methodology, peasant societies and social organizations in irrigation systems, development studies, social change, conflicts and migration.

*Khawar Mumtaz* is a graduate of the University of Karachi. Since 1966 she has been a research fellow and journalist and has lectured at various universities in Pakistan on international affairs, environmental studies and women in development. She is currently co-ordinator of Shirkat Gah Women's Resource Centre, Lahore, Pakistan, and project director of women and sustainable development, working with IUCN and SDPI on a joint project on population, environment and responsibility. She has worked extensively with the government of Pakistan and international agencies on environment and women's issues. In the preparations for UNCED in 1992 she wrote chapters on women, population issues, NGOs and national heritage for the Pakistan National Report to UNCED and the chapters on those topics for the National Conservation Strategy of the IUCN.

*Jacqueline Pitanguy* has been deeply involved with Brazilian women's movements for democracy and gender equity. During the 1980s she presided over the National Council for Women's Rights, a federal governmental organization, and in the 1990s she founded Citizenship, Studies, Information and Action (CEPIA), a non-governmental organization based in Rio de Janeiro. CEPIA develops studies and research, advocacy and public education work mainly in the areas of reproductive health, gender violence and human rights. Jacqueline has taught at the

Rio de Janeiro Catholic University and at Rutgers University (USA). She is on the board of several organizations, including the Commission on Citizenship and Reproduction in São Paulo, the Inter-American Dialogue and the UNESCO Institute for Education.

*Fauzia Rauf* is a legal expert and political scientist. Since 1989 she has been engaged in community development with Shirkat Gah. At present she is carrying out research on gender and environmental issues, participatory methodology and sexual and reproductive health.

*Therese Vögeli Sörensen* is a lecturer on methodology at the Institute of Ethnology, University of Zurich, Switzerland, and works in intercultural communication. She is a member of the board for questions concerning migration and culture conflict.

*Elisabetta Vaccaro* graduated from the University of Rome in 1992 with a degree in foreign languages and literature. She has been working for two years as a researcher and editorial assistant on *Development*, the quarterly journal of the Society for International Development, Rome. Her main interests are women and children in development and anthropological and cultural aspects of development.

# Introduction

WENDY HARCOURT

This book has many midwives: the Women's World Congress for a Healthy Planet, Miami, 1991; Planeta Femea, NGO Forum, Rio de Janeiro, 1992; the Society for International Development–WUMEN Roundtable on Women, Environment and Alternatives to Development, The Hague, 1993; the Sustainable Development Policy Institute Seminar on Population, Environment and Responsibility, Islamabad, 1993; the General Assembly of the Network, Women in Development Europe, Madrid, 1994; the International Conference on Population and Development, Cairo, 1994; an international seminar by SID–Unesco on Cultural Changes in Women's Life Stages, Paris, 1995; and finally, a Seminar on Sustainability for Future Generations, Zurich, 1995. As these dates and places indicate, this book belongs first and foremost to the international feminist project that is trying to redefine women's position in the population and sustainable development debate. Women from Tanzania, Ghana, Brazil, Pakistan, Sri Lanka, Italy and Switzerland have come together, as members of the Society for International Development's Women in Development (WID) network, at various times in the preparatory work for these meetings in order to build knowledge and political strategies for change in the area of gender, environment, reproductive rights and alternatives to development. The book comes directly out of research undertaken with funding from the Swiss National Science Foundation[1] to build North–South institutional links in the follow-up to the United Nations Conference on Environment and Development (UNCED).

Like all feminist projects, it is ambitious. It aims to uncover the silences that women maintain over some of the most intimate areas of their lives – sexual activity, family and marital relations – in order to break down the barriers we have surrounding the issues of reproductive behaviour, sexuality and gender relations.

It is also ambitious in inviting women of different ages, cultures and experiences to work supportively together in order to foster an open conversation about the ethical and political dilemmas that publicly discussing reproductive rights, sexuality and gender power-relations brings for feminist researchers and activists. The feminist slogan, 'the personal is political', translated across cultures in research that exposes women's very private lives to the public domain can have unforeseen, sometimes unsettling consequences. Even if all the women involved are researchers and activists committed to going deeper into the problematics of women's lives, in writing the book we found that we were at times uneasy about breaking women's silences. Speaking about taboo areas can unsettle the delicate balance between genders and generations, and create perhaps more uncertainties than empowerment.

The book is based on a series of case studies: adolescents in a suburb in Dar es Salaam, Tanzania; three generations of women from five regions in Ghana; unionized domestic workers in Rio de Janeiro, Brazil; women of eight families in a Punjab village in Pakistan; young married and unmarried women migrating from one village in Sri Lanka to the Middle East or Free Trade Zones; two generations of women in Rome and Cuorgné, Italy; and first-time pregnant women living in Zurich, Switzerland. Each investigates the transfer, within and between generations, of knowledge about reproductive behaviour, looking at when and why women's reproductive and sexual behaviour and attitudes change. The research aims to establish when it is possible to break down the knowledge barriers on sexuality and reproductive health, what could strengthen women's decision-making in the area of reproductive rights and what could be a catalyst to enhance women's self-identity and choice, leading to more equitable relations with men.

The studies look at social, economic and environmental changes in women's lives that lead to changes in the transfer of knowledge of reproductive behaviour and sexuality. Two kinds of change are considered: the first in codes and behaviour related to health and bodily care during the shifts in life cycles, the second in the knowledge of sexuality and reproductive behaviour.

The book aims to contribute to the debate on health, empowerment and reproductive rights, and sexuality and power relations that is part of the international development debate on population and gender relations. It represents a hopeful beginning, to answer large questions about reproduction, power and gender in very different societies. The researchers were careful to look at different women's lives, using participatory methods, which took women as subjects, not objects, of the research, and which respected age, ethnic, class, geographic and cultural differences. We also continually question our own role and responsibilities in conducting research, which, inevitably, will break the zones of silence sometimes constructed by women as strategies in the fight to survive poverty and gender inequities.

Though the same conceptual concerns inspire the research, each chapter has its own unique material, methodology and approach. Chapter 1, by Wendy Harcourt, working at the Society for International Development (SID), introduces the analytical background to the case studies that follow.

Chapter 2 takes a close look at how sexual activity and teenage pregnancy are perceived in contemporary Tanzania. The chapter is based on a detailed series of interviews with teenagers (both girls and boys), their parents and grandparents in a suburb of Dar es Salaam. Brigit Obrist van Eeuwijk and Susan Mlangwa, researchers involved in a collaboration between the University of Basel, the Swiss Tropical Institute and the Dar es Salaam Health Project, find that a once strong sexual ideology has been broken down with the introduction by mass media, modern schools and clinics of new ideas and values. Grandparents no longer play a crucial role and children turn to the media or their peer group for sexual knowledge, with parents acceding responsibility to schools or clinics. They document how traditional ideologies compete with medical ideologies for hegemony, with a decided gap between policy-making based on the medical approach and people's lives. They raise the important question of whether the 'teenage-girl problem' (the high level of teenage pregnancy – 60 per cent of girls at 19 are or have been pregnant) is perceived by the local community as such, or whether it is a Western-imposed 'problem'. As in Ghana, the silences between parent and child are notable, even if the child expresses the wish to have a more open relationship with his/her parent. People express their views more openly if a moral issue is recognized, rather than the need to pass on relevant information on reproductive health, even in the full awareness of teenage sexual activity and the high risk of contracting HIV–AIDS.

Chapter 3, also based on a case study in sub-Saharan Africa, draws on a large demographic study of over 500 Ghanaian women in five areas of Ghana, focusing on the transfer of reproductive knowledge between daughter, mother and grandmother. Miranda N. Greenstreet and R. A. Banibensu, leading a team of researchers from the University of Legon, examine women's understanding of reproductive choice across generations in a country with strong customary allegiance, and poor access to education and family-planning. Women may play a leading economic and social reproductive role, but they have little say in family decision-making, or on their own sexual and reproductive activity. The study finds that modernity has disrupted traditional knowledge-transfer of reproductive health and sexual behaviour, so that grandparents, once so important in educating young people at puberty, are no longer consulted, and birthing rituals involving whole families are now abandoned. But no adequate way of gaining knowledge is replacing old traditions, with family-planning services rarely reaching poor, rural Ghanaian women. Their study records emotionally fraught relations between generations, due to the break-down in tradition, and continuing problems between genders. Modern medical knowledge and ways of approaching sexuality appear to be creating confusion, which women young and old are struggling against in their pursuit of women's rights.

Chapter 4, presented by a women's research group working in a non-governmental organization, CEPIA, based in Rio de Janeiro, looks at the sexual and reproductive experiences of domestic workers in Brazil. As part of a larger study on women, citizenship and reproduction, Jacqueline Pitanguy and Cecilia de Mello e Souza examine the inter-generational transfer of reproductive experiences and decisions among domestic workers in the multi-racial and multi-cultural society of Brazil, the ninth-largest economy in the world. Domestic workers are among the poorest social groups in Brazil, though domestic service absorbs most of the female urban labour force. From girlhood, these women are trained for a life of social reproduction. Motherhood is central to their sense of identity, even if it is often disconnected from biological reproduction. Work dominates these women's lives as does the double moral standard which imposes a deep sense of purity and honour. The study traces the changing perception of feminine identity during the different stages of life. As in the African studies, a silence surrounds the issue of sexuality and, with the exception of some women who have found a strategic way around, the needs of boyfriends and husbands dominate women's reproductive decisions. The medical information available is ambivalent to women's needs, and the inter-generational transfer of knowledge between mother and daughter practically non-existent. These women rely more on the men with whom they are involved and the mass media for knowledge of reproductive health. The latter, particularly under the impact of AIDS, has become an important source of factual information and a source of changing feminine identity.

Chapter 5 takes us to another continent and a different set of cultural constraints, of very poor women living in a flood-prone village, Sun-nakhi, in the Punjab region of Pakistan. Khawar Mumtaz and Fauzia Rauf, of Shirkat Gah, a women's research institute and non-governmental organization based in Lahore, conduct interviews with women in family groups, a delicate task that had to take into account the strong, multi-tiered hierarchy of rural Pakistan, where all women live in *purdah*. They find that breaking silences on such intimate concerns is difficult, particularly as women of different ages do not openly engage in discussions of bodily health or sexual activity, even if women's reproductivity, particularly their ability to bear male children, defines their lives. Transfer of knowledge on menstruation, childbirth and sexual duty is proscribed by a tradition whereby only sisters may speak in private; ultimately, male control over women's bodies is absolute, with violence and abuse common. Modernity reaches these women through their work – sewing slippers – but education and access to health-care remain poor, and the strong patriarchal traditions do not provide adequate knowledge for safe and fulfilling female reproductivity.

Chapter 6 takes us to another group of women workers in Asia: married and unmarried Sri Lankan village migrants to the Middle East and to the locally based Free Trade Zone. The study, undertaken in a collaboration between the Universities of Zurich and Colombo, measures the socio-economic changes in these women's identities, health and well-being, due to their change of environment. Sandya Hewamanne, working with Hans Peter Müller, finds that even if marriage and motherhood continue to be the goal of returning migrant women's lives, their experience outside the village allows them to question their traditionally servile status, and gives them privileged access to information about reproductive health. It also produces conflicts on their return to the village, with the difficulty of reintegration caused by the disruption to family life, and the suspicion that their foreign experience arouses.

Chapter 7 takes us to the North, with a case study in Italy, looking at the changes in the transfer of knowledge on reproductive health, marriage and sexuality for teenagers living in Italy in the 1960s and in the 1990s. Emanuela Calabrini and Elisabetta Vaccaro, researchers working at the Society for International Development, look at teenage girls' and their mothers' different experiences of sexuality and reproductive health. Following an extensive survey on demographic, social and economic changes in Italy, the chapter focuses on the findings of a series of interviews with two generations of Italian women living in the capital, and young women living in a small industrial town in the north. They find surprisingly similar concerns for both age groups, who share a modern and liberal attitude to reproductive issues, notwithstanding the presence of the Pope. The changes in Italian family structure, women's status and education, inspired by the public battles over issues such as abortion and divorce discussed in the first half of the chapter, are reflected in the awareness of reproductive health issues of the women interviewed. But silences exist between generations, about sexuality, and the younger generation does not enjoy a full sense of confidence about life-choices. Confidences on sexuality are exchanged among peers not within the family, and they state that there is a lack of useful information in the media. The authors, young women themselves, would like to see a revival of the public debate on reproductive health and sexuality in Italy, led by the national media, which should also be more aware of international women's issues.

Chapter 8, also based on European women's experience, begins with a survey of the main demographic, social and cultural trends for women in Switzerland. Verena Hillmann and Thérèse Vögeli Sörensen, researchers associated with the Institute of Ethnology, University of Zurich, then take us down a slightly different track from the other chapters. They focus not so much on inter-generational transfer of knowledge on reproductive health but on the related topic of motherhood, in their examination of how women living in Switzerland, one of the world's richest countries, with one of the lowest birth rates, decide to have or not have a child. Their case study is based on detailed interviews with three women entering pregnancy for the first time, in order to bring out the myriad reasons behind the choice for motherhood. They ask in what way – if at all – it is possible to come to a rational and responsible decision to have a child in modern Switzerland. They test out the concept of 'autonomous individual', and in so doing illustrate some of the dilemmas modernity presents for women, and the negotiations women undertake with partners, family and state in order to make a choice for motherhood.

The book concludes with a final chapter by the editor, which draws together the major issues raised by the case studies in order to raise questions for further research and local, national and international-level policy changes for a reproductive health agenda.

As the variety of material covered and the number of women's lives involved in the book attests, this is a rich resource of some of the most difficult and important issues for feminists, whether living in the first or the third world. The book evolves out of shared commitment to a cause, and to some extent by the accident of chance meeting through the networking of the Society for International Development. It therefore does not pretend to be all-inclusive. By no means are all women's lives covered; there are many gaps and silences. For example, no collaborator was found in East Asia, the Pacific, the Middle East, countries of the former Soviet bloc, or Eastern Europe. It is, instead, intended to be a series of questions, ideas, puzzles and contradictions about some women's lives, which we tease out in our lives, research and political activity. We present these cases to the reader in the spirit of feminist research, which does not seek to prescribe definite answers, but aims to open out the apparent confines of women's lives to the possibilities for change.

## Acknowledgements

There are many people whom we need to thank, beginning with the women who participated in all of the case studies. The major institutions that provided financial and logistical support for the international collaboration that made the book possible are: the Swiss National Science Foundation, Berne; the Institute of Ethnology, University of Zurich; the Society for International Development International Secretariat, Rome; Citizenship Studies, Research, Information, Action, Rio de Janeiro; Shirkat Gah, Lahore; the Institute of Adult Education, the University of Ghana, Legon; the Swiss Tropical Institute, Basel; and the Urban Health Project, Dar es Salaam.

As editor, I would particularly like to acknowledge the collaboration of everybody on the project. It has been a great pleasure and important learning experience to work with them. I need to mention the support of the team at the SID Secretariat in particular: Franck Amalric, who provided a sympathetic ear and insightful critique as I completed the final drafts, and Arthur Muliro, who fielded the computer communications when negotiating cyberspace became too complex. Most importantly, a warmly felt personal thank-you to the highly motivated team of two dedicated, intelligent young women, Emanuela Calabrini and Elisabetta Vaccaro, who not only took on a chapter themselves with great gusto, but also managed the proof-reading and preparation of the final text; without their efforts, this book could not have taken its final shape.

We have dedicated this book to Caterina and Nico, two babies born during the project.

## Note

1. Priority Programme Environment, Project No. 5001–41113, 'Sustainability for future generations: the relevance of inter-generational transfer of knowledge for health and population programmes'.

# An analysis of reproductive health: myths, resistance and new knowledge

WENDY HARCOURT

## Introduction

This book has been born out of the involvement of women in the international debates stimulated by three United Nations events: the United Nations Conference on Environment and Development (UN-CED), held in Rio de Janeiro, June 1992; the International Conference on Population and Development (ICPD), held in Cairo, September 1994; and the Fourth World Conference on Women (WCW), held in Beijing, September 1995.

In these events, women's voices were clearly heard in both the official government meetings and in the parallel forums of non-governmental organizations.[1] An international consensus emerged on the need for a radical reform of economic co-operation and development. It included a resounding agreement that gender is a critical conceptual category. In this new consensus, women's needs are to be treated as central, not marginal, to economic and social development.[2] The story of political battles to win such consensus has been told many times in many versions, which we do not need to repeat here (Braidotti *et al*, 1994; DAWN, 1994; Antrobus, 1996; Davis, 1996; WIDE, 1996). What is important to note is that the groundswell of confidence for women at these international events gave them a tremendous visibility and authority, which they had not before enjoyed in the international arena, fostering the sense of hope that feminism, unlike history, is not dead.[3]

The uneasy question, though, for the feminists celebrating women's victories in Rio, Cairo and Beijing, remains whether these milestones at the international level have any connection with the reality of the majority of the world's women – on behalf of whom these victories are scored – living in impoverished rural communities, or in cities. What influence do the flourishing of signatures, the mountains of paper, the festive happenings have for women at the local level, who are dealing with the everyday survival needs of caring for and sustaining their families, their immediate surroundings and their communities? These are women for whom politics and economic affairs are not interesting, at least in the manner in which they are presented to them every day by their fathers, their husbands, the local media or local authorities.

The research on which this book is based tries to make connections between the global and local levels, in the spirit of the UN events and their search for greater justice and equity. The book aims to translate these events' grand designs into local women's reality and perceptions. This proves a hard task conceptually. As feminists, we find ourselves grappling with several difficult questions, none of which can be totally resolved: how can we combine insights from our political activities with our research observations? Are we, because of our feminism, imposing our own views as the only authoritative voices in this exercise? How can we involve poor women as partners and agents, not objects of research? For whom are we doing this research?

I aim, in this chapter, to introduce the reader to some analytical considerations that inform our attempt to connect international visions, feminist commitments and local realities in the area of reproductive health.

## Analytical considerations

Many issues emerged in the long passage between Rio, Cairo and Beijing that throw up exciting new paths for women, new alliances, new ways of understanding and new battles. These stories are well documented in many places by myriad commentators, so that here we do not need to do more than dip into the main conceptual findings that impact on our focal topic of reproductive health.

Our approach is founded on the premise that, though at times it may be politically expedient to talk about 'women' as a universal category,[4] it is most emphatically not so when undertaking our research. First, there are major differences among women's experiences in industrial and agrarian societies (referred to throughout the book as North and South). Second, women's realities can be affected as much by culture, race, class, age and ethnicity as by gender. Many pioneering feminist writings about women, which fired the international debate from Betty Friedan onwards,[5] assume as universal truths assertions that later observers have pointed out are written from Western, middle-class, educated, white and English-speaking perspectives. African Americans and Third World women have challenged the authority of these writers to describe all women's experiences (Nakano et al., 1994). This challenge has been particularly important in relation to the United Nations debates, which are attempting to legislate for all people and all countries. Women contributing to the debates therefore seek to document the wide variety of women's experiences, for example from local community women's struggles against the environment at UNCED, to testimonies of cultural differences in reproductive behaviour at the ICPD, to women's fight to attain recognition of their rights as human rights at the WCW.[6] With the huge collection of stories and data on women to hand, it is now very difficult to speak universally of 'women and environment', 'women and population' or 'women and development'. Instead the specificity of any woman's historical, political, linguistic, economic, cultural, racial, ethnic and class background is demanded when trying to explain her behaviour, needs or ambitions as an actor in these three areas. Our case studies apply this approach in order to contextualize reproductive behaviour in concrete settings in the North and South.

Gender is the term used by feminists to argue that even if we cannot change biological sex,[7] we can aim to change social and cultural behaviour, and the institutions that create them, as the determining factors of gender attributed to each sex. Differences between men and women have been and continue to be interpreted and rationalized as the natural and immutable biological order, rather than as socially or historically determined. We can use the concept of gender to explain the inequalities between men and women individually and socially, in different countries, as based on social and political realities expressed through power relations and social hierarchy, including international relations, age, class, ethnic origin and race. We can do this by looking at each society as a microcosm and trying to understand how women experience gender power-relations. This can be in terms of oppression or of resistance and women's own power. As Teresita de Barbieri remarks when speaking about Latin American women and population programmes:

> forced to perceive themselves and others through bodily difference, women can use the power of their bodies to their own advantage, disobey norms, pretend obedience, not discipline themselves, and resist domination. In fact because women are seen as the primary source of our first identity and of the satisfaction of emotional needs, women are extremely powerful and are directly involved with life and death and people's sense of self-esteem. (de Barbieri, 1993: 85–6)

Gender, self-evidently, is a crucial analytical concept in our attempt to contextualize reproductive behaviour. Gender is about having a particular kind of power over certain capacities of the body as regards sexuality and reproductive health. Gender power operates most forcefully during the reproductive stage of the life cycle, where means for controlling sexuality, reproduction and access to work are situated and function most clearly. But gender power in those stages influences both earlier and later stages in life (de Barbieri, 1993: 85).

In our book's research the concept of life cycle emerges as a key differential in women's lives, one that is rarely factored into an analysis of women's experiences. In defining reproductive health and all its qualifying elements related to environment, development and demography, life cycle, we find, is a major determinant (Harcourt, 1995: 6; see also Katz and Monz, 1993). The important moments in a woman's life cycle – adolescence, menstruation, motherhood and menopause – are not universal experiences; rather, as each case study shows, they are social and cultural constructions grounded in their unique historical and economic settings. Jacqueline Pitanguy and Cecilia de Mello e Souza, in chapter 4, describe it, using the anthropological term, 'classes of age'[8] (see p. 83).

Adolescence is a relatively new life stage in most cultures; even in the West it has a history of only a hundred or so years (Harcourt, 1995: 12). In non-Western cultures exposed to development, it has been introduced, along with other cultural changes, through the process of modernity. As the studies in the book show, it is now a troubling period in many cultures, as young people slip out of the reach of many traditional areas of responsibility during these newly defined years of transition from childhood to adulthood, while not being catered for successfully by the new institutions of the state. For young women in particular, this can have unfortunate consequences, as active sexual lives, unacknowledged by parents or other authorities as valid, can lead to pregnancies, which might prevent them from succeeding in other areas of life. The case studies based in Dar es Salaam and Ghana illustrate this dilemma for a very high percentage of girls in these transitional societies.

Reproductive-age women are in most societies assumed to be mainly involved in marriage and mothering. But this period of life, too, has changed with the impact of modernity, as more women control their fertility rate, for a variety of reasons, which we look into below. In both North and South, women have fewer children, so that their time is taken up less and less with mothering. This opens up potential new ground for women to be more active in the public arena. The case studies document how women are trying to balance new productive responsibilities with the changes in their reproductive lives. There are, of course, many constraints that prevent women from entering traditionally male terrain, and there are indeed many battles to be won, but women are creating new ways to live their lives that take into account the reduction in the demands of motherhood. The irony is that whereas national and international development institutions, whose stated goal is to assist women, still do not see this change, many multinational businesses are already well aware of the possibility of exploiting cheap female labour, now less bound to home and children, and are making good use of it in the globalization process (see below and Bakker, 1994; Sparr, 1994; Aslanbeigui *et al.*, 1994; Vickers, 1991).

Finally, with increasing longevity, the years of menopause are becoming more and more significant periods of women's life cycles, even in some of the poorest countries. The 'third age', as it has been coined by Friedan, is, like adolescence, a troubling time because the usefulness of most women's contribution to community life – as paid-workers and mothers – is presumed finished. There is little place for the wisdom and contribution of the grandmother in the modern age, though, as the cases in the book show, there was ample space in other times in non-Western cultures. Although men too are experiencing this phenomenon of the third age, it is particularly a feminine phenomenon, as women tend to outlive men in all countries (with the exception of five: India, Pakistan, Iran, Maldives and Nepal) (UN, 1995: 87). As few women have reached a position where they can bend the rules (many influential men continue to be publicly engaged well past 65) many perfectly healthy, able women find themselves excluded from mainstream day-to-day life because of the assumption that they are too old or out of date to assist in their families' or communities' well-being. Our research just brushes on this issue, as it still remains largely articulated as a Western phenomenon; very poor communities in the South welcome all hands that can help to sustain families' livelihoods. However, as the case studies from Ghana and Tanzania suggest, grandmothers in these societies, which once revered old women, are also losing respect and power within the family.

As this discussion on the life cycle indicates, the impact of modernity is a major analytical concern when describing women's reproductive rights and health. By modernity we mean the prescription for the modernization of traditional societies. This involves

a fundamental proposition that people in traditional societies should adopt the characteristics of modern societies in order to modernize their social, political and economic institutions. The *raison d'être* behind this is that there are certain characteristics of enterprise, achievement and progress with which the Industrial Revolution has been identified and which subsequently have enabled the USA to provide a model of mass-consumption society. (Spybey, 1992: 21)

Embedded within the concept of modernity is the belief in progress.

Development brought to the Third World the idea that progress was what they needed in order to join the modern world. Indeed, José Maria Sbert argues that progress is more than just an ideal: 'It is modern destiny', and that it is the 'idea of progress that provided the justification for western self-assertion abroad' (Sachs, 1992: 195–6).

As all the case studies illustrate, modernity is an important analytical concept because the specificity of women's concrete realities and definitions of life-cycle categories change over time, and especially in our historical epoch of rapid economic and social change and transition. The case studies look at women at different distances from this modernity, with the Swiss perhaps being the closest (if not in a post-modern age), and the Pakistani the farthest, allowing some scope for measuring the inter-cultural transfer of knowledge (see concluding chapter).

As many of the discussions around UNCED, ICPD and WCW attest, modernity cannot be dismissed as either all bad or all good. Certainly there are those who tend to welcome all aspects of modernity, who maintain faith in modernization theory, as do most development planners, and those who reject the dependency that modernization has produced (Spybey, 1992: 226). They argue that the West, operating a capitalist economic system, has exploited other regions through a process of modernization that has devalued all other traditions (Shiva, 1989; Sachs, 1992; Apffel-Marglin and Marglin, 1990). But from a women's perspective, that debate proves to be of less use, particularly in the field of reproductive rights. The Western emphasis on women's rights, on health and reproductive choice, is welcomed by feminists and, as the case studies of Ghana, Tanzania and Brazil show, also by poor women, who wish to have more say in their lives. But the technologies and institutions set up to deliver health, education and legal services to the South – the transportation of modern Western life – are riddled with traps and contradictions for women, which can be as oppressive as the traditional lives from which they sought to move away. Nor can we say that traditional knowledge systems and cultural behaviour are in themselves oppressive to women and need to be removed wholesale. The loss of traditions in some cultures means a great loss for women's economic and social autonomy (Swantz, 1995). It is a question of looking at each case and understanding where women can benefit from modern life and where the constraints lie. We cannot turn back the clock, but we can aim to take what is good for women from the old and new. This requires careful research that is culturally sensitive and open to other ways of understanding gender relations and reproductive behaviour than the one inscribed in Western sexual ideologies. We hope that this book will prove a contribution to just this type of research.

In the post-development era that some argue we are now living in, globalization is the new form through which progress and modernity are to be attained. We are only beginning to grapple with this phenomenon, which is happening in so many different forms (finance, trade, technology, economic restructuring and communications) at such a rapid pace, causing vast economic, cultural, political and social change.[9] As the work by feminist economists[10] and women activists working on structural adjustment and trade attest (Bakker, 1994; Sparr, 1994), the impact of globalization on many women's lives is complex. On the one hand, the gap between the rich and poor is widening; women are the majority of the poor because structural changes are based on governments withdrawing state support in social services, health and education, blindly assuming that they can rely on women's hidden, unpaid social reproductive work, along with their flexibility to adapt to new situations. Women will adapt because they and their families need to survive. They are also, therefore, entering the new high-tech labour force, because, as mentioned above, women in the South are sought by big multinational corporations looking for cheap, docile labour (Mitter, 1995; Harcourt, 1996b; Huws, 1994; Webster, 1995). This type of work is a mixed blessing, as the Sri Lanka case study illustrates. Women are employed, but at low wages and heavy social costs. The modern global economy impinges on the lives of the Pakistani women living in *purdah* in the remote rural village of Sunnakhi in the form of piece work.

On the other hand, globalization offers some positive advantages for women. The success of women at the three UN conferences mentioned above was due to the availability of global communication technology to women's networks, which were used to great effect by the women's caucuses at the events, and by women networking in 'cyberspace' in between (Davis, 1996; Harcourt, 1996a). The research project on which these studies are based is a product of this global communication revolution – co-ordination and editing have all been conducted by courtesy of 'the Net'. Many questions need to be raised about the domination of these structures on people's time and way of thinking, and how it reflects current economic inequities. We also need to consider why it is 15–30 per cent of women are using the Internet (Schmeiser, 1995; GVU Surveying Team, 1996), as well as to be aware of the North–South bias of the current communication system (Feather, 1994; Carnoy *et al.*, 1993; Panos, 1995). Potentially, however, there is now a technology that could enable women to balance their social reproductive and productive needs to their own benefit.[11]

Another issue needs to be raised, in relation to globalization, that is not so positive for women: the rise of fundamentalism in the face of uncertainty and fears of Western cultural domination.[12] At the ICPD and at the WCW, feminist headway to achieve agreements for reproductive rights was fought all the way by Catholic anti-abortion groups and Islamic fundamentalist groups, and several countries (we should include here the threat to legal abortion in the USA, as well as countries such as Algeria) have repealed progressive laws. At the WCW, women raised the alarm at the rise of fundamentalism and the threat it poses to some of the gains made by the international women's movement in the last 20 years (DAWN, 1994). The Italian study shows that an alarming number of the young teenage women surveyed are against abortion, and the Ghanaian study hints at growing conversions to Islam in some northern regions of Ghana.

## Four myths

Coming out of this history, this book helps to dispel some myths that discussions on women, population, environment and development present.

*Myth one* The first myth to dispel is the conventional view that women in the North, as explored in most detail in the Swiss case study, have complete freedom to choose. The whole debate on reproduction in the North is constructed around the apparent choice of women to have or not have children. Medical science is central to this choice, with highly complex techniques to guide women's entire reproductive lives and to enable infertile women to become mothers. To characterize this 'freedom' as a myth is not to say that modern medical knowledge, health procedures and services are of no use to women. Rather it is to open to question the profoundly gender-insensitive institutions and discourses that determine how the services are delivered. Modern medical discourse operates to produce a series of practices that define and capture the female reproductive body as a medical object to be manipulated and dominated by science and technology, rather than being an enabling or liberating set of practices for women.[13] They are a powerful example of a reductionist view of 'woman', or in this case 'the female body', as universal. The 'health' of the social body (whether the modern industrialized nation has an ageing or young population, whether women produce enough babies for the renewal of the modern state, and so on) is linked directly to the individual reproductive (female) body, removed from women's diverse social, economic and political realities (Phillips, 1992; Hartmann, 1995; Lykke and Braidotti, 1996).

Let us look historically at how this came about. Historians and philosophers have traced the emergence of the modern Western concept of population, as the 'body politic', to be measured and calculated, to the late eighteenth century, with the rise of the Enlightenment and people's interest in studying society as a whole (Foucault, 1986). From its inception, the concept of population is founded on the science of statistics. Hence population was described in mathematical and statistical formulations, and reproductivity became one of the many variables to be aggregated and depicted graphically in order to compare figures on contraception, nutrition and abortion across nation states (Duden, 1992: 148–9). The complexity of the human condition was reduced to figures in a scientific language, which is then brought into public discourse as objective evidence on complex ethical, social, and profoundly human subjects.

A parallel historical development was the focus on the female body as the key to the control and management of population. As Foucault (1986) and others (Sayers, 1982; Rubin Suleiman, 1986; Stanworth, 1987; Jacobus, 1990; Duden, 1993; Eyer, 1992) have pointed out, this has been linked to a sexualization and medicalization of the female body from the late eighteenth century onwards. At the beginning of the nineteenth century, as the social movements for a healthy population became popularized in the eugenics movement (Harcourt, 1987), the female body became subject to medical scrutiny and control (Jacobus, 1990). What was once outside medical interest, the female reproductive process, became the subject of intense medical concern. Women's reproductivity was no longer seen as a natural social event, but put into the terms of a modern medical discourse based on pathology and illness. Female reproductivity became interpreted as a general disorder of femaleness, which needed medical intervention and supervision, not only for the individual patient's health but also for the good of the State. The social, political and economic factors determining an individual woman's reproductive health were obscured by the objectifying, medicalized practice of modern reproductive medicine, which was in the hands of the (largely) male medical profession.

In these historical developments, women's reproductivity is understood, on the one hand, as the key to the health and growth of the population, as objectively measured in population statistics, while, on the other hand, it is in need of close medical supervision, removed from social needs and constraints. In both cases, women as subjects with choices, histories and social, political and economic concerns, rather than as objects of the scientific medical gaze, are missing.

The development of gynaecology and obstetrics as medical specialisms during the twentieth century has led to a high degree of medical intervention in women's lives, with the development of genetic engineering, synthetic contraceptives and manipulation of eggs, sperm and embryos outside the environment of the human body (Stanworth, 1987; Spallone, 1989; Klein, 1989; Eyer, 1992; Duden, 1993). Although these techniques are presented as offering greater choice to women, these choices are predefined in limiting ways, where the female body is seen as a medical object to be experimented on and to be understood by the expert, rather than as a physiological entity belonging to a woman who has a particular economic and social history. Feminist critics have raised the question of what these technologies mean, in terms of the health, safety and choice over reproduction, for women; the 'bodies' on which these new technologies are developed (Stanworth, 1987: 3). Rather than reproductive self-determination which advocates improvement in women's social and economic status, where health and safety are primary concerns, and safe, effective birth control a component of health care services – we have a male-dominated cultural, legal and social system, which defines women by their reproductive role. The point is that there is the illusion of choice for women. In reality, the choices, from contraception to what kind of birth they give, are determined by medical and market demands, and by their own social and cultural context.[14]

Another question to be raised concerns the pervasive ideology of motherhood as women's greatest fulfilment. The point here is not whether women want to become mothers, but the implications of motherhood for women in modern Western society. 'Is mothering women's primary and sole mission and chief source of satisfaction or one of many roles? Is women's fate tied to their biological role in reproduction? Do pregnancy and childbirth put women in a unique position?' (Nakano Glen, 1994: 1). These are complex questions, which require more than the glance we can afford here. In the context of our discussion, Northern women, in order to be 'good' mothers, give away the traditional power of women as mothers. Whatever other role in life they may play, as pregnant women and mothers of new-born children they submit themselves to today's highly medicalized environment.[15] Women are offered a safer pregnancy at the cost of lack of control and self-management. Pregnancy is monitored at every level.

The focus on the medical event of motherhood blurs contradictory messages about women's reproductive role in modern society. On the one hand, women's reproductive role is crucial, and considerable sums of money are spent in advancing medical frontiers, to treat women's health problems, provide female contraception, solve infertility problems, but, on the other hand, women are not being provided with the social services that would allow them to play fulfilled productive and reproductive roles. Rarely do modern state services, policy-planning, or modern environs, transport or housing take into account women's needs as mothers; rather they are systems designed for stereotyped male citizens with life styles organized around their careers. Women are therefore obliged to choose 'male' life styles, internalizing a social devaluation of women's role as mother and house-carer. At the same time, women are expected to take all the responsibility for birth-control and parenting, individually and socially.

Feminists emphasize that we need to decode the interests and power relations in science and technology. Donna Haraway (1990) proposes, as a potentially positive step, and one which we have to face anyway in our present reality, that Western power relations have blurred the boundaries between science and nature, in what she calls our 'cyborg world'. She sees the monstrosities of the cyborg myth, but also a potential for a politics that could provide new ways out of the present relations of domination, and offer fresh sources of power (Haraway, 1990: 205–7). She suggests that in the apparent abstractions of science, and the capturing of the female body, there is also embedded a power of resistance to which people can have access. Haraway argues that people should take up their responsibility for the social relations of science and technology, 'embracing the skillful task of reconstructing the boundaries of daily life, in partial connection with others, in communication with all of our identities', and this means 'both building and destroying machines, identities, categories, relationships, spaces, stories' (Lykke and Braidotti, 1996).

*Myth two* The second myth is that in the South women's needs are central to population and development programmes. The issue here is not so much how to remove the gender-blindness of development policy-makers and thinkers, who have failed to see the link between women's productive and reproductive work,[16] but rather to look at how pre-occupations that are essentially Western have become translated into distorting programmes in the South, in the fields of population and development, women in development, health and education services. As in the North, we need to challenge the reductionist medical approach of these programmes.

In Southern countries, reproduction is discussed in terms of the problem of population growth and the need to contain the worldwide 'population explosion' (Stanworth, 1987; Spallone, 1989; Hynes, 1991; Kabeer, 1994; Duden, 1992; *In Context*, 1992; Correa, 1994). In this argument, 'women's bodies are the primary site of population planners' (Spallone, 1989: 6), and women as subjects and individuals disappear in a morass of figures, which demographers, development and population experts collect in their recommendations to control over-population. In these programmes, the complex realities of men's and women's lives, and their relation to their immediate environment, have been obscured. In most cases, the discourse has been framed as needing technological solutions, which contribute little to the quality of life of the poor women involved.

It is interesting to note that while in the North there is a concern that women are not producing enough children and the search to cure infertility in childless couples is a thriving industry (Oakley, 1994), women in the South are blamed for producing too many babies, increasing the poverty rate and accelerating environmental destruction, thereby preventing the development of their countries. In the four development decades, population programmes have had major support from industrialized countries keen to assist in the depopulation of the over-populated South.[17] National governments, through the support of international programmes, have built up powerful, centrally controlled and run population programmes (Duden, 1992: 154). Though focused on the control of female reproductivity, these programmes put traditional economic development goals before women's needs and choices. The programmes fund and promote medical teams to introduce injectable and oral contraception, and to intervene surgically, in cases where the women involved are commonly ill-informed of the consequences.

The dominant European and American concepts of womanhood and the female body have been challenged by Southern feminists (Sen and Snow, 1994; Correa, 1994; Sen et al., 1994; Phillips, 1992). Motherhood, for example, has quite different meanings in cultures where extended families take joint responsibility for nurturing and caring for children. Pregnancy, childbirth and even health are experienced quite differently from Northern norms in societies where women work long hours in fields or dusty streets, or in the confined environment of purdah.[18] A comparison of the experiences of the women in the Swiss and Italian case studies and the Pakistan study reveals this most starkly. Monitoring pregnant women and infants requires the introduction of technology, which privileges mind over body, quite a foreign concept to people who see pregnancy and childbirth as a social experience, and who do not share the same history of medicalization as women in the North. Medicalizing the female body turns what was treated as an essentially private event into a public activity, where the mother and her family no longer have control over the procedure. This was done through a series of shifts in practice and thought in the North over at least a century. To expect people from different cultural traditions to jump straight into high-tech birth, feeling in control and able to participate and benefit, is both to ignore the many criticisms made by women in the North (Oakley, 1994), and to undermine powerful social and cultural experiences of motherhood. Other ways of dealing with fertility choice, pregnancy and birth are lost as medicalized procedures (sometime crudely applied) are established as modern, and therefore better. Women's self-identity is lost in the normalizing procedure of medical knowledge, and respect for cultural specificities is swept aside.

Sexuality also needs to be looked at more boldly, in a gender- and culturally sensitive way. As the case studies from Italy, Brazil and Sri Lanka show, women's own view of their body and sexuality is beginning to enter the public domain, though it is still shrouded in silences that women themselves find hard to break, a trend noted in all the case studies.

*Myth three* The third myth that we challenge is the 'population-growth problem'. The ICPD reached a rather remarkable consensus, given the many diverse groups involved in the process, that population growth is a major impediment to sustainable development, with an 'unprecedented comprehensive stance of gender issues, women's sexual and reproductive health and reproductive rights' (Amalric and Banuri, 1994: 691). How does this international consensus translate at the local level? As Franck Amalric and Tariq Banuri and others (Hartmann, 1995; Sen and Snow, 1994; Sen *et al.*, 1994) point out, women do not always control their own fertility, owing to pressures from their husbands, extended family, and social and religious traditions. But they argue that the solution of better education, so that a woman might take control over her own body, and so become more health conscious and therefore reduce her fertility is flawed: 'the problem here is bad health, limited education and patriarchy. Population growth is only a consequence of these different factors, not the problem itself' (Amalric and Banuri, 1994: 693).

Instead of talking about population growth, we need to talk about people, politics and power.[19] Within that agenda, we must address the separate issues of women's reproductive health and sexual rights, environment, demography, North–South relations and government policy. If the ultimate goal is to reduce numbers, the temptation is to treat the women and men involved as abstract identities to be managed in such a way as to stop them reproducing. Women's reproductive self-determination needs to be delinked from the 'population problem'. We need to enlarge women's decision-making over their fertility, sexuality and child-rearing options, but women's basic rights – to livelihoods, to a life free of violence and oppression, to safe contraception and legal abortion under broad health care – should be addressed on their own merits, and not as part and parcel of population programmes. Strengthening projects for women's primary health and education and greater awareness of reproductive choice are much more complex development tasks than programmes to reduce the number of a given target population group. The urgent question is: what institutions can we put in place that would provide economic and social justice? What types of policies can be created that would enhance women's access to reproductive and sexual rights and health? The more pertinent questions, on a 'people, power and politics' as opposed to a population agenda, are how to establish women's rights to decision-making over their own fertility, their sexuality and how they bring up their children; how to end the destruction of cultural and physical environments due to unsustainable development and the exploitation of people in dire poverty; how to correct the distortions of the economic growth model that has perpetuated inequitable international trade and financial institutions; and how to establish new local, national and international institutions that would ensure more responsible governance.

*Myth four* The final myth that this book helps to challenge is that sustainable development, as it is officially conceived, can incorporate women's needs.[20] There have been many definitions of sustainable development since the Brundtland Commission first popularized the term. One of the most influential since the Earth Summit in June 1992, when the goals of sustainable development became officially adopted, is the definition made by the United Nations Development Programme (UNDP) Administrator Gus Speth in February 1994:

> Sustainable human development is development that doesn't merely generate growth, but distributes its benefits equitably; it regenerates the environment rather than destroying it; it empowers people rather than marginalizing them; it enlarges their choices and opportunities and provides for people's participation in decisions affecting their lives. Sustainable human development is development that is pro-poor, pro-nature, and pro-women. It stresses growth but growth with employment, growth with environment; growth with empowerment, growth with equity. (Speth, 1994: 2)

Here we have a picture of how the global development project is attempting to adapt to environmental and people's concerns, while staying within the parameters of the traditional focus of development: to achieve economic growth. Women are one of the marginalized groups (like the poor) who need to be brought into focus, and the environment is treated as a factor that needs more care and attention in order to ensure proper development. The assumption is that economic growth is a good thing if enough care is taken not to degrade the environment, and to include the poor and women in the aims of development.

Although the terms 'pro-women' and 'pro-environment' are used, the emphasis on growth, employment and vague mechanisms for re-distribution does not reflect the deep ambivalence that development presents for women. We cannot simply add women and the environment into the equation, because of the inherent gender bias in this con-ceptualization of development. What is missing from the picture is reproductive work in the caring economy, and the intimate relationship between environment, gender and culture. One reason for this is that sustainable development is a macro-level concept, whereas much of the work women do with their families and the environment is best under-stood at a micro-level. Another reason is that sustainable development proposes economic welfare mixed with changes in ecological management as a solution to the problems of development. This does not tackle the issue of major power imbalances within development institutions, which ultimately fail to take into account the very different realities of poor women's productive and reproductive work. By ignoring women's work in the caring economy, and the many socio-cultural factors that impact on people's relation to the environment and the development process, it can perpetuate rather than solve the problems of widespread poverty. What is needed is a different, more holistic approach that can more accurately reflect gender concerns.

Pertinent to our discussion here, the international women's debate has moved from 'equality between men and women' and the 'integration of women in development' to advocacy of social transformation towards a more humane and equitable world and a healthy planet. From an exclusive focus on gender in development, the women's agenda now recognizes the inter-relationship between gender oppression and all other forms of oppression. From a narrow focus on traditional women's issues (education, health, domestic violence, access to credit and land), the concern is now to understand all issues – from environmental and economic justice to social development, human rights and population – from the perspective of women. As Peggy Antrobus (1996) states:

> With its insistence on the link between the personal and the political and with its growing recognition of the linkages between all the structures through which patriarchal domination is expressed – structures of production and gender, religion and governance – feminism has produced the most inclusive analysis of the relationships which have served to perpetuate the marginal-ization of the majority of the world's people. ... The effectiveness of this movement in mobilizing around the global issues of environmental

degradation, human rights, reproductive rights and population, social development and structural adjustment is clear in the documents which have come from international conferences of the past five years.

## New perspectives: reassessing the reproductive health debate

Having set the historical and analytical context for the book, and dispelled some prevalent myths, let us look from a new perspective at reproductive health.

In dispelling these myths we open up the opportunity for more appropriate alliances among women working in the North and the South. In the midst of competing and conflicting ideologies of different power groups (medical doctors, religious groups, men, development institutions and different generations), there is a need for a gender-sensitive approach that tries to find a way for the different actors to meet and work together towards knowledge and accountability. In such an approach, women's differences are acknowledged and therefore all types of women's experiences are valued, disrupting hierarchical presumptions among different cultures North and South. In this new political space (Mouffe, 1993), development does not happen only in the South. The institutions and discourses that oppress women are present in all societies. The neglect of human welfare in the interest of capital, the materialism of market liberalization, and the violence that has emerged with the rise of fundamentalism have an impact on the quality of all women's lives, leading to widespread poverty among women (and men) in both the North and the South (Antrobus, 1996). It is in this breaking of the traditional North–South divide that the international women's movement has found its strength in analysis and advocacy.[21]

In order to contextualize reproductive health, we need to study the complex concrete realities of ordinary people, with their participation. To this end, a more useful approach than 'sustainable development' is 'sustainable livelihoods', which focuses on the micro-level, of people-centred, environmentally aware development.

The concept of 'sustainable livelihoods' is defined as long-term means of living or of supporting life. 'Sustainable livelihoods' takes the reality of the poor people at the margins as the subject for a new agenda for economic, social and environmental research and, ultimately, change. This approach stresses not economic growth and income, but well-being and the quality of life. Robert Chambers at the Institute of Development Studies in Sussex, UK, who first developed this concept, asks us to take into account health, security, self-respect, justice, access to goods and services, family and social life, ceremonies and celebrations, creativity, fun, spiritual experience, love and the pleasures of place, seasons and time of day.[22] Development, in this context, means positive changes in these areas as poor people experience and wish them.

The sustainable-livelihoods agenda is a multifarious and dynamic process, which aims to reverse the North–South patterns of dominance, and to build a reality based on the experience and analysis of those who are either living on the margins or who respect the knowledge and understanding of those on the margins. It also questions the need for economic growth, quite simply because it can destroy livelihoods. The earth's resources are finite, and we are now witnessing the results of the pursuit of modernization and economic growth, undertaken at the expense of the natural resource base and the majority of the world's people. Complementing the micro-level agenda for sustainable livelihood at the macro-level, a politics of self-limitation needs to be established, which would mean differential strategies for rich and poor nations, in order to secure universal rights of ownership, access and use of the common resource base, promote equitable access to economic resources, and ensure access to effective health services for the poor.

The concept of sustainable livelihoods helps us to understand the reality of women's lives because it adopts a holistic approach, takes into account the work of reproduction in the home and community, and reflects the multiple roles in which women are engaged. It also allows us to reject the concept of power as domination and control, and to adopt a concept of power that is the power to act or to empower others (Antrobus, 1996).[23]

## New knowledge and new accountabilities

As we change these institutions and discourses, we are inevitably creating new types of knowledge. This is precisely the aim of the case studies, which take up the realities determining women's reproductive health at the local level in both the North and the South. The case studies aim to explore the redefinition of life-cycle categories in the local contexts of North and South: are adolescence, motherhood, and sexuality given new meanings in these shifts? If so, by whom and why? What are the old and new channels for transfer of reproductive knowledge within and between generations? How and by whom was and is reproductive knowledge transmitted? How can we redefine gender, politics and power in these processes?

In the Southern case studies, the research seeks out the existence of non-Western knowledge systems and other ways of seeing the female body. They aim to bring out the tensions between medical knowledge and traditional knowledge of the body and reproductive behaviour, and the tensions between modernity and traditional codes of knowledge defining feminine identity, sexuality and motherhood, looking at the differences between generations. The two case studies of the North examine changing codes of behaviour in relation to reproductive health and sexuality. The research seeks to uncover some of the ambiguities and tensions women experience in taking control of their reproductive life.

Creating new knowledge also implies the need for new methodologies. As feminist researchers, we attempt to work in partnership with the women with whom we are studying, using participatory methodology, and involving the women in the design of the research wherever possible. The exceptions to this methodological approach are the Ghana case study, which is based on a large-scale demographic survey, and the Italian case study, which is based on a series of questionnaires and interviews. Data collected through traditional political science and demographic means are also applied to amplify the material gathered qualitatively. In all cases, the results are to be shared with the women, and in at least four cases (Switzerland, Pakistan, Brazil and Ghana), the research will continue in order to put into practice some of the recommendations.[24] The women are, therefore, being treated as subjects not objects of the research; the aim is for their voices, expressing their experiences, to come through as well as the researchers' opinions. The women also helped to shape the research questions. Indeed, the whole exercise is a collective undertaking, with the researchers endeavouring to work out their differences in approach, style, and expectations among themselves and their partners in the field. It is also important to state transparently that the research is attempted because of our feminist commitment and political interests, rather than as a purely academic pursuit. It has also been interesting to see that much of the intellectual leadership of the project, even though largely funded by Northern money, comes from the South, reversing traditional stereotypes and reflecting, in microcosm, the shifts in power and direction of the international feminist movement over recent years.

The research is in support of local activity among the community women as well as the researchers' wish to further the international debate. We hope in this way to develop ways to produce knowledge that are based on more interactive methods and a more comprehensive understanding of the social, political, cultural and economic context of the people involved in the study. This new type of knowledge can then be used to indicate and suggest more appropriate life choices for the women involved. We also hope that in this way we show how reproductive health cannot be found in better medical understanding or medical technologies alone, but also in producing knowledge that opens up possibilities for different political and social practices. This discourse moves beyond the present relations of domination to create strategies for political, economic, and social gender justice and equity so that women, in the South and the North, can choose equally with men how and when they enjoy their reproductivity.

As stated in the beginning, it is an ambitious undertaking, one which raises considerable ethical dilemmas. Women who are politically active and conduct research are not neutral actors. We try to avoid the sense of the expert imparting knowledge to poor women unidirectionally, and instead embark on a shared learning process with commonly defined goals, in order to create a space for other forms of knowledge, which Western science and development have displaced (Harding, 1973). In some cases, it proves very difficult to unsettle the power relations invested in scientific and bureaucratic institutions, in which we also have a stake. Particularly when dealing with such intimate concerns that the issue of reproductive health necessarily touches on (family and marital relations, women's sense of worth and honour, taboo topics around sexuality and bodily functions), we infringe private spaces through the mediation of doing research. Given that one of the discoveries of the research is the importance of silences to the women in this domain, we find ourselves questioning how far we can conduct research without heedlessly obtruding into women's lives.

While not being able to resolve all dilemmas, we aim to be aware of the political implications of our research, the potential gains and losses of those in power if we ask certain questions, and therefore the need for us to fight political as well as theoretical battles, if we are to achieve our goals. We also stress that being explicitly political in our research is not to lack rigour in the work we do, but rather to place our research in a larger context, and to see ourselves, as feminist researchers, participating in the transformation of the development agenda. Our research will, we hope, have direct results for the people with whom we are working, and have an impact on our own lives and society. On a personal level, this is a more exciting and rewarding prospect than simply aiming to do a good piece of work for other academics to read. And, on a broader level, in this way we are not instrumentalizing the knowledge of those whose lives we are researching and thereby adding to the subjugation of their lives.

## Acknowledgements

I would like to thank Franck Amalric, Brigit Obrist van Eeuwijk and Verena Hillmann for their helpful comments on an earlier draft of this chapter.

## Notes

1. Women were well organized both at the government meetings and at the NGO events. In a historically unprecedented move, the NGO parallel forums opened up UN Conferences to the impact of civil society which, through this process, came of age as the third actor in development. See Davis (1996) for an interesting personal account of how the women's caucus organized by Women's Environment and Development Organization (WEDO) functioned. Several contributors to this book (Miranda Greenstreet, Wendy Harcourt, Khawar Mumtaz and Jacqueline Pitanguy) were deeply involved in this series of UN events, both as members of the delegations to the ICPD and WCW and as active organizers of and participants in the large women's events at the NGO events. See Harcourt (1996b) for a review of the networking of women working in sustainable development.

2. In relation to the debate on reproductive health specifically, the 1990s have witnessed an intensification in the debates regarding reproductive rights and reproductive health, between governmental and non-governmental sectors of society. The 1994 UN conference in Cairo on population and development introduced a new paradigm at the international level, in which women's perspective and experiences became central. Thus, we feel it is critical that the wide variation in the perspectives and experiences of women become known so that they inform scientific debates across disciplines and the elaboration and implementation of public policies (comment contributed by Cecilia de Mello e Souza and Jacqueline Pitanguy).

3. The reference here is to the famous statement by right-wing economist Francis Fukuyama in 1991, that capitalism had triumphed over socialism with the fall of the Berlin Wall in 1989 and the evident failure of the socialist experiment. Even if not all agreed with this statement it summarizes the strong sense of lost direction particularly felt by the now 'old' left.

4. There is a very interesting and important debate raised in Nussbaum and Glover (1995), which takes up the issue of whether we can talk about women's rights in non-Western development contexts without being culturally insensitive. In that volume, the debate on universality is discussed in terms of ethics, equality and justice as universal principles for all women, whatever their culture.

5. Germaine Greer's *The Female Eunuch* and Shulamith Firestone's *The Dialectic of Sex* are examples of major texts which, after Friedan's classic *The Feminine Mystique*, influenced the Anglo-Saxon world's feminist debate from the early 1970s.

6. As well as papers given at the conferences and data gathered by UN agencies, the newsletters of women's NGOs are an important record of this

documentation; examples are *DAWN Informs, WEDO News and Views, Al-Raida, Oxfam's Links, WIDE Bulletin, The Tribune, ISIS Women in Action, APDC Issues in Gender and Development, AWID News.*

7. Let us leave aside the complex issues of sex changes and how one defines sexual identity.

8. The actual ages when women are considered to be in one of the 'classes' varies from culture to culture as the case studies document, but they are, roughly, the teens, from 20 to 49, and then 50 and over.

9. 'Globalization' is at risk of becoming the new buzz word, like 'sustainable development'. It can give the illusion of describing what is happening, while being devoid of exact meaning. The Society for International Development is now working on the topic in order to try to further the international debate on the different forms of globalization, with a World Conference on the theme 'Which Globalization? Opening Spaces for Civic Engagement' to be held in May 1997. There is also a powerful group, known already for their strong anti-developmentalist stance, beginning to organize against globalization. As founding member Vandana Shiva stated to the US press in November 1995, 'Globalization isn't new: we in the Third World are very familiar with it. We used to call it colonization.' The International Forum on Globalization is an alliance convened in January 1994 by sixty activists, scholars, economists, researchers and writers, in order 'to stimulate new thinking, joint activity and publication in response to the rapidly emerging economic and political arrangement called the global economy' (International Forum on Globalization, 1995). Members include Edward Goldsmith (editor of *The Ecologist*), David Korten (President of the People-Centered Development Forum, Vandana Shiva (writer and green 'star'), and Helena Norberg-Hodge (anthropologist and writer). They are concerned, through their meetings, writings and 'teach-ins', to revitalize local communities, enhance peoples' capacities to exercise democracy and use local resources for local production, and to abandon the paradigm of unlimited economic growth.

10. In very recent years, there is much more being published by feminist economists, for example Nancy Folbre's *Who pays for the kids* (1993), Antonella Picchio's *Social Reproduction and Production* (1993), and the other collections on structural adjustment quoted in this chapter. It is encouraging that this writing is bridging the academic and activist world, so that the writing is pertinent to women trying to tackle everyday issues of globalization and economic injustice. As Manchester economist Diane Elson stated in a speech given in 1995, women need to break the myths of economics in order for economic thinking and policy to begin to answer their needs (WIDE, 1996). Two noteworthy organizations in this context are the International Association for Feminist Economics (IAFFE), which is an international group of largely academic economists, and the more policy-oriented Network Women in Development Europe's Working Group on Alternative Economics and Trade.

11. On a personal note, I managed to be involved with the international preparations for the WSSD and WCW, as well as hold down my job, in the first six months of my daughter's life, with the use of my home computer, modem and internet. I was often breast-feeding or rocking the baby with one hand while

typing out my messages on the other – a living example of Donna Haraway's cyborg! (see p. 18).

12. The network, 'Women Living under Muslim Laws', begun in the early 1980s, has been tracing this rise of fundamentalism internationally from women's (not just popular press) perspectives. Gita Sen and Sonia Correa, writing in *DAWN Informs* 94/5, reported that fundamentalism was one of the most damaging global trends: 'human rights and health were the battlegrounds of the major struggle between women's organizations and religious fundamentalists' (DAWN, 1994: 8).

13. One of the more recent and alarming examples for me, personally, of how the female body, indeed pregnancy and birth, has been captured by medical technology was when I saw a card in a Brussels office announcing a forthcoming birth, which featured a sonogramme of a few-months-old foetus. This shadowy technical reproduction of the inside of a pregnant woman has the significance once reserved for the actual birth. The mother is not only reduced to a body but in this picture the receptacle that the medical gaze penetrates and interprets through technology.

14. Having recently had a baby (January 1995) in modern Italy, the difficulty of exercising choice was brought home to me. I just managed to avoid a caesarean. Luckily, I had a doctor with whom I had made a 'pact' beforehand, and who therefore gave me 20 more minutes 'to push' in order to avoid an emergency C-section. Caterina was born naturally, with great cheers, in less than the 20 minutes allowed (the cord had been wrapped twice around her neck and body). But of the ten friends who had babies around the same time, all had caesareans and they, like me, had attended natural birth classes and had had healthy pregnancies. Italy has one of the highest rates of caesareans in the world, though also one of the lowest infant mortality rates, which reflects just where the control and emphasis lie – with the baby and medical intervention, not the mother's choice or life experience. This personal experience is confirmed by statistics. Figures published by ISTAT show that, from 1981 to 1991, the number of caesarians per live births increased from 11 per cent to 22 per cent, and in some regions up to 30 per cent. According to Dr Gaetano Marie Fara, Director of the Institute of Hygiene at La Sapienza, University of Rome, 15 per cent of the 112,500 caesarians performed in Italy each year are unnecessary (*Vivere Sani e Belli*, 1996: 7).

15. This medicalized environment is not just confined to technology but also psychology. Diane Eyer (1992), in her fascinating study of the myth of mother–child bonding, traces the different schools of thought on the roles of mothers in relation to women's changing status and the impact it has on doctor–patient relations as well as mother–child. See also Oakley (1994).

16. Ester Boserup, in 1970, was the first to draw attention to what we now call gender blindness. Since then the United Nations agencies UNIFEM and INSTRAW have produced many important reports and studies that statistically verify women's contribution to development. For recent studies, see *Development Journal of SID*: 'Alternative Economics from a Gender Perspective' 1995.1; UNDP *Human Development Report 1995*; *The World's Women 1995*.

17. It would be interesting to compare the different amount of money spent

on primary health in the South and on medical intervention in cases of infertility in the North.

18. Duden (1993), in her history of the experience of the female body, makes the illuminating point that the lived experience of the pregnancy and health was quite different in other ages. In earlier times, women's experience of their body was listened to by a medical practitioner within their psychological and social *milieu*. The medical gaze had not yet become the authoritative vision, which treated people as patients or bodies removed from their individuality and social context, to be interpreted only by medical expertise (see also Harcourt, 1987 and Foucault, 1986).

19. In preparation for ICPD, SID, together with the Sustainable Development Policy Institute (SDPI) and the International Development Research Centre (IDRC), held a meeting in Pakistan in November 1993. The results are published in 'People, politics and power', *Development* 1994.1.

20. UNCED is an example of how it was attempted to graft gender issues on to mainstream issues. The main tenet of that conference was the need to combine environmental concerns and population issues within a holistic view of development, the primary goals of which include the alleviation of poverty; secure livelihoods; good health; quality of life; improvement of the status and income of women and their access to schooling and professional training, as well as fulfilment of their personal aspirations; and empowerment of individuals and communities (Agenda 21, Chapter 5, paragraph 16). At the same time, it underscored the fundamental linkage between improving the status of women and demographic dynamics, and their effective, equitable participation in all levels of decision-making (Agenda 21, Chapter 5, paragraph 12).

21. An example of this type of alliance has been the work of the Women's Alliance for Alternatives to Development, made up of Southern and Northern women's networks, which looked at issues of trade and economics regionally, and then pooled their knowledge in strategic interventions at the World Summit for Social Development and WCW (Antrobus, 1996; Harcourt, 1994b).

22. The term 'sustainable livelihoods', I first heard at the Miami Women's Congress for a Healthy Planet in 1991, at the session led by Rosina Wiltshire of DAWN (Wiltshire, 1992). SID has also been working on the concept of sustainable livelihoods and currently has a three-year programme in 20 countries (SID, 1996).

23. Throughout the book, power relations, particularly in relation to patriarchal structures, are discussed where in fact power domination is probably the most useful way of understanding power. The concept of empowerment, however, is embedded in our approach, where it refers to the means through which people, men and women, are enabled to take charge of their own lives. This means that power is not so much handed down to people by those in authority, but that people use their own abilities and create their own opportunities to be in charge of their life choices. Throughout the book, we avoided the temptation to go into deep academic philosophical debates about power, as we felt comfortable with the broad understanding of power and the current use of the term empowerment.

24. The book is based on a pilot phase funded by the Swiss National Science Foundation. The research project, 'Sustainability for Future Generations: the Relevance of Inter-Generational Transfer of Knowledge for Health and Population Programmes', is an attempt to discover the patterns of women's reproductive decision-making with reference to their life-stages; and to review current population policies within the sustainable development framework. The hypothesis being that a) policies have failed because of the non-acknowledgement of the fact that women's reproductive decision-making is determined by their social and family status, as mediated by their life-cycle stage; and b) that current population policies have not been conceived in the sustainable development framework. Additionally, the research seeks to develop an appropriate methodology that is gender-sensitive, is conceptualized for and with women rather than about them, and enables insights into women's perceptions and their decision-making about health and reproduction. (Comment contributed by Khawar Mumtaz and Fauzia Rauf.) The study was conducted in five countries, and each of its components is self-contained, designed specifically for each country but with a common framework and objective. It has now been selected for further funding for the next four years.

## References

Amalric, F. and T. Banuri (1994) 'Population: malady or symptom?', *Third World Quarterly*, Vol. 15, No. 4.

Antrobus, P. (1996) 'Bringing grass roots needs to the international arena', *Development: journal of SID*, 1996.3.

Apffel-Marglin, F. and S. A. Marglin (1990) *Dominating Knowledge: development, culture and resistance*, Oxford, Clarendon Press.

Aslanbeigui, N., S. Pressman and G. Summerfield (eds) (1994) *Women in the Age of Economic Transformation*, London, Routledge.

Bakker, I. (ed.) (1994) *The Strategic Silence: gender and economic policy*, London, Zed Books.

Boserup, E. (1989) *Women's Role in Economic Development*, London, Earthscan.

Braidotti, R., E. Charkiewicz, S. Hausler, S. Wieringa (1994) *Women, the Environment and Sustainable Development*, London, Zed Books.

Carnoy, M., M. Catells, S. Cohen, F. H. Cardoso (1993) *The New Global Economy: the information age*, University Park, Penn., Pennsylvania State University Press.

Correa, S. (1994) *Population and Reproductive Rights: feminist perspectives from the South*, London, Zed Books.

Davis, S. (1996) 'Making Waves: advocacy by Women NGOs at UN Conferences', *Development: journal of SID*, 1996.3.

DAWN, (1994), *Dawn Informs 1995/4*.

de Barbieri, T. (1993) 'Gender and population policies: some reflections', *Reproductive Health*, No. 1.

Duden, B. (1992) 'Population', in W. Sachs (ed.) *The Development Dictionary: a guide to knowledge as power*, London, Zed Books.

Duden, B. (1993) *Disembodying Women: perspectives on pregnancy and the unborn*, Cambridge, Mass., Harvard University Press.

Eyer, D. (1992) *Mother–Infant Bonding*, New Haven, Yale University Press.

Feather, J. (1994) *The Information Society: a study of continuity and change*, London, Library Association Publishing Ltd.

Foucault, M. (1986) *History of Sexuality*, vol. 1, Harmondsworth, Penguin.

GVU Surveying Team (1996) *GVU's 4th WWW Use Survey Home Page*, March.

Haraway, D. (1990) 'A Manifesto for Cyborgs: Science, Technology, and Socialist Feminism in the 1980s', in L. Nicholson (ed.) *Feminism/Postmodernism*, New York and London, Routledge.

Harcourt, W. (1987) 'Medical Discourse relating to the female body', unpublished thesis, Australian National University.

Harcourt, W. (1992) 'Sex, Lies and Population: a view from the North', paper in Phillips (ed.) *Power, Population and the Environment: women speak*, Canada, WEED.

Harcourt, W. (ed.) (1994a) *Feminist Perspectives on Sustainable Development*, London, Zed Books.

Harcourt, W. (1994b) 'Globalization from a Gender Perspective', CREW, Brussels.

Harcourt, W. , L. Woestman and L. Grogan (1995) *Towards Alternative Economics from a European Perspective*, Brussels, WIDE.

Harcourt, W. (ed.) (1995) *Cultural Changes in Women's Life Stages*, Paris, SID-Unesco.

Harcourt, W. (1996a) 'Gender and Economic Dimensions of the Information Society', CREW, Brussels.

Harcourt, W. (1996b) 'Women networking for sustainable development', unpublished paper given to Institute of Social Studies, The Hague.

Harding, S. (ed.) (1993) *Feminism and Methodology*, Bloomington and Indianapolis, Indiana University Press.

Hartmann B. (1995) *Reproductive Rights and Wrongs* (revised edition), Boston, South End Press.

Huws, U. (1994) 'Teleworking and training for women', *Reflections on women's training: a wider vision*, IRIS Publication.

Hynes, H. P. (1991), 'The Race to Save the Planet: will women lose?', *Women's Studies International Forum*, Vol. 14, No. 5.

*In Context*, (1992), 'Birth, sex and death: human family planning', Spring, No. 31.

International Forum on Globalization (1995) *Pamphlet*, San Francisco.

ISIS (1995) 'Asian Women On-Line', *Women Envision*, No. 29, September.

Jacobus, M. (1990) *Body/Politics: women and the discourse of science*, New York and London, Routledge.

Kabeer, N. (1994) *Reversed Realities: gender hierarchies in development thought*, London, Verso.

Katz, C. and J. Monz (eds) (1993) *Full Circles: geographies of women over the life courses*, London, Routledge.

Klein, R. (1989) *Women Speak Out about their Infertility*, London: Pandora Press.

Lykke, N. and R. Braidotti (eds) (1996) *Between Goddesses, Monsters and Cyborgs: feminist confrontations with science, medicine and cyberspace*, London, Zed Books.

Mitter, S. (1995) 'Women in the New World Order: voices of workers from the Third World', *Oxfam Discussion Paper 6*, Oxford, Oxfam.

Mouffe, C. (1993) *The Return of the Political*, London and New York, Verso.

Nakano, G., E. Change, G. and L. Rennie Forcey (eds) (1994) *Mothering, Ideology, Experience, and Agency*, New York and London, Routledge.

Nussbaum, M. and J. Glover (eds) (1995) *Women, Culture and Development: a study of human capabilities*, Oxford: Oxford University Press.

Oakley, A. (1994) *Essays on Women, Medicine and Health*, Edinburgh, Edinburgh University Press.

Panos (1995) 'The Internet and the South: superhighway or dirt-track?', *Panos Homepage*.

Phillips, G. (ed.) (1992) *Power, Population and the Environment: women speak*, Canada, WEED.

Rose, H. (1987) 'Victorian Values in the Test-Tube: the politics of reproductive science and technology', in M. Stanworth (ed.) *Reproductive Technologies: gender, motherhood and medicine*, Cambridge, Polity Press.

Rubin Suleiman, S. (ed.) (1986) *The Female Body in Western Culture*, Cambridge, Mass., Harvard University Press.

Sachs, W. (ed.) (1992). *The Development Dictionary: a guide to knowledge as power*, London, Zed Books.

Sayers, J. (1982) *Biological Politics*, London and New York, Tavistock Publications.

Schmeiser, L. (1995) 'Women on the Web', *Computer-Mediated Communication Magazine*, Vol. 2, No. 3, March.

Sen, G. and R. Snow (eds) (1994) *Power and Decision: the social control of reproduction*, Cambridge, Mass., Harvard Centre for Population and Development Studies.

Sen, G., A. Germain and L. C. Chen (1994) *Population Policies Reconsidered: health, empowerment and rights*, Cambridge, Mass., Harvard Centre for Population and Development Studies.

Shiva, V. (1989) *Staying Alive*, London, Zed Books.

Society for International Development (1996) *Towards Sustainable Livelihoods*, Rome, SID/Centre for Respect of Life and Environment.

Spallone, P. (1989) *Beyond Conception: the new politics of reproduction*, London, Macmillan Education.

Sparr, P. (1994) *Mortgaging Women's Lives: feminist critiques of structural adjustment*, London, Zed Books.

Speth, G. (1994) *UNDP Memorandum*, New York, UNDP.

Spybey, T. (1992) *Social Change, Development and Dependency*, Cambridge, Polity Press.

Stanworth, M. (ed.) (1987) *Reproductive Technologies, Gender Motherhood and Medicine*, Cambridge, Polity Press.

Swantz, M-L. (1995) 'Women Entrepreneurs in Tanzania: a path to sustainable livelihoods', *Development: journal of SID* 1995.1.

United Nations (1995) *The World's Women 1995 Trends and Statistics*, New York, United Nations.

UNDP (1996) *Human Development Report 1995*, New York, Oxford University Press.

Vickers, J. (1991) *Women and the World Economic Crisis*, London, NGLS/Zed Books.

*Vivere Sani e Belli* (1996) Anno 5. no. 15, 12 April.

Webster, J. (1995) 'Gender and Information Technology', *The European Journal of Women's Studies*, Vol. 2, No. 3, August.

WIDE (1996) 'Defying Marginalization: on the road to Beijing', *WIDE Bulletin*, March 1996, Brussels.

Wiltshire, R. (1992) *Environment and Development: grassroots women's perspectives*, Barbados, DAWN.

Woliver, L. R. (1991) 'The influence of technology and the politics of motherhood: an overview of the United States', *Women's Studies International Forum*, Vol. 14, No. 5.

# 2

## Competing ideologies: adolescence, knowledge and silences in Dar es Salaam

BRIGIT OBRIST VAN EEUWIJK AND
SUSAN MLANGWA

In the past decade adolescent sexual activity and teenage pregnancy have become a highly controversial issue in many transitional societies, including Tanzania. Various institutions, organizations, activists and professionals express concern, conduct studies, develop and perhaps implement projects and programmes. A number of distinctive yet overlapping ideologies contend for hegemony. This study looks at how adolescent sexual activity and teenage pregnancy are perceived and handled on various levels of contemporary Tanzanian society. How do researchers, policy-makers, health planners and women activists view the problem? What do they contribute to solve it? How do those concerned, namely the teenagers and their families, experience the situation? What could be done to negotiate an improvement of reproductive health that respects adolescents' choice and meets their different environmental, cultural, political and economic needs?

### Tanzania: a brief background

The United Republic of Tanzania is the largest country in East Africa, covering 940,000 square kilometres. It lies south of the Equator and shares borders with eight countries: Kenya and Uganda to the north; Rwanda, Burundi, Zaire and Zambia to the west; and Malawi and Mozambique to the south. The legal entity called Tanzania is a union between the mainland country of Tanganyika, which became a nation independent from British rule in 1961, and the island of Zanzibar, which joined the union in 1964. From 1961 until 1985, when he voluntarily stepped down, Julius Nyerere was head of state. His Tanzanian socialism became known across the world under the name of *Ujamaa*.

In the 1980s, the economic crises in Africa deepened. Tanzania was one of those states where *per capita* income was declining, owing to both internal and external factors. A National Economic Survival Programme (NESP) was followed by a Structural Adjustment Programme (SAP) and, in 1986, Tanzania, which for a decade had stood as a symbol of opposition to these policies, signed an accord with the International Monetary Fund (IMF).

The economic and political liberalization has brought about and still causes many fundamental changes in the daily life of Tanzanian people. The stores are now better stocked and many commodities are available, but people had to create many 'sideline jobs' in the unregistered private sector to generate the income needed for daily survival. Vuorela (1992: 112) points out that these jobs should more correctly be called 'survival activities', because they are responses to the material necessity of meeting the widening gap between official incomes and excessively high prices for commodities.

## Methodology

This study employs a gender-sensitive, qualitative and participatory approach. Four research activities have been carried out: a review of selected literature; key-informant interviews in institutions and organizations; community-based research in a ward of Dar es Salaam; and a workshop with resource people.

For the literature review we designed a checklist of topics, which we refined as we went along. In the key informant interviews we followed a rough guideline of lead questions. The community-based research employed a combination of focus-group discussions, and key-informant interviews. Since inter- and intra-generational transfer of knowledge was at the centre of our interest, we decided to select participants representing different gender and generation categories, i.e. grandmothers, grandfathers, mothers, fathers, adolescent girls and adolescent boys.

Table 2.1 Composition of the sample

| Social category | Focus groups | Key informants | Total |
| --- | --- | --- | --- |
| Mothers | 28 | 5 | 33 |
| Fathers | 25 | 4 | 29 |
| Grandmothers | 29 | 2 | 31 |
| Grandfathers | 18 | 2 | 20 |
| Adolescent girls | 26 | 2 | 28 |
| Adolescent boys | 29 | 3 | 32 |
| Total | | | 173 |

With each of these social categories we conducted three focus-group discussions and several key-informant interviews. In the focus-group discussions, participants talked to each other following a guideline prepared by the field researcher. This method can provide insights into how a group thinks about an issue, about the range of opinions and ideas, and about the inconsistencies and variation that exist in a particular community in terms of beliefs, experiences and reported practices. It cannot be used to build up a detailed picture of specific beliefs or real behaviour. The former can best be obtained by key-informant interviews, the latter by participant observation. For obvious reasons, participant observation was rather limited by the topic itself.

## Competing ideologies

Mbunda (1991: 61) introduces the concept of 'sexual ideology' to refer to a special system of ideas, beliefs and values, held by each ethnic group in Tanzania, that told people that there is only one appropriate way to deal with sexuality, including teenage sexuality. Today, Mbunda adds (1991: 71–2), modern Tanzania, with its diversity of ethnic groups, has no single sexual ideology and no national equivalent of the traditional elders, who exerted powerful control to ensure that the ideology was followed. Especially in an urban environment such as Dar es Salaam, ethnic diversity combines with new ideas and values, spread via mass media, schools and clinics, and the various, often competing and even conflicting, religious beliefs imported from the East and the West.

We suggest that the term 'sexual ideology' can be used to refer to any special system of ideas, beliefs and values regarding sexuality, whether it is held by an ethnic group, a religious group, a professional group or a political group, if it is linked with an authoritarian claim to be the only appropriate way for individuals to think, feel and act. If we use the term in this broader sense, we can discern a number of distinctive yet overlapping sexual ideologies in contemporary Tanzanian society, namely a traditionalist-moral, a medical, and a feminist sexual ideology. Particularly the first two, the traditionalist-moral and the medical, compete for hegemony, and this struggle has shaped the family planning agenda, particularly with regard to teenagers.

Family planning in Dar es Salaam dates back to 1959, when the Family Planning Association of Dar es Salaam was founded (Rwebangira, 1994: 193–5). In 1967, this became a national organization and changed its name to Family Planning Association of Tanzania (*Uzazi na Malezi Bora Tanzania*, UMATI). Since the early 1970s, family planning has been provided as a component of comprehensive maternal and child health services throughout Tanzania. Rwebangira points out that although UMATI's constitution gives directives on guidance to adolescents in preparation for their future role as parents, in practice it excludes most of them from contraceptive services. The registration card for UMATI requires particulars about 'the husband', thus making it clear that these services are meant for married women.

In Tanzania, as in many other countries, public opinion has long been marked by hypersensitivity and virtual hostility towards family planning initiatives. Efforts to introduce family life education in schools – the term for sex education – have met with sustained resistance from the majority of Tanzanians. At a seminar in 1984, for instance, members of parliament categorically rejected the government's plan to introduce family life education in schools (Rwebangira, 1994: 194)

*The medical sexual ideology*  In the late 1980s and the early 1990s, a growing number of researchers began to investigate the medical and educational implications of teenage sexuality (Mpangile and Mbunda, 1992), and the *Demographic and Health Survey 1991/1992* (Bureau of Statistics, 1993) for the first time provides segregated data on adolescents. These data document that, at the age of 15, 23 per cent of girls have had sexual intercourse; by the age of 18, the legal age of marriage, it was 65 per cent (Bureau of Statistics, 1993: 56)

While many of these girls become sexually active at a tender age, only 2.9 per cent of them said they ever used a modern family planning method.[1] This rate is very low, even compared to the low overall acceptor rate of 14.1 per cent (Bureau of Statistics, 1993: 34). The percentage of all women currently using modern contraceptive methods is still lower, namely 2 per cent for the 15–19-year-old girls and 5.9 per cent for all age groups (Bureau of Statistics, 1993: 35). As in all other age groups, many more teenage girls said they knew modern methods (68.7 per cent) and sources for information and services (58.4 per cent) than actually used them (Bureau of Statistics, 1993: 33). It is thus hardly surprising that by age of 19, almost 60 per cent of the young women have had a child or are pregnant (Bureau of Statistics, 1993: 29). Not all young women feel ready to become mothers. A study of four government hospitals in Dar es Salaam revealed that out of 455 women, 33 per cent treated for induced abortion were 14–19 years old (Mpangile, Leshabari and Kihwele, 1993)

These efforts on the part of health planners and researchers illustrate that only in the past decade have Tanzanian adolescents become recognized as a distinctive group in terms of reproduction-related health risks, a trend long established in industrialized countries (Kulin, 1988).

During a workshop organized by the United Nations Population Fund (UNFPA) and the National Family Planning Programme (NFPP) in Dar es Salaam, concerned experts argued that there were neither clear policies nor laws that dealt directly with adolescent health (*Daily News*, 1993a, 1993b).

This was amended in the revised edition of the National Policy Guidelines and Standards for Family Planning Services Delivery and Training, issued by the Ministry of Health (1994). In these new guidelines, adolescents are one of the target groups for priority recruitment and they are explicitly mentioned in many important statements. The guidelines say, for instance, that '[a]ll males and females of reproductive age, including adolescents irrespective of their parity and marital status, shall have the right of access to family planning information, education and services'. They further promise that '[s]exually active adolescents who seek family planning services shall be counselled and provided with family planning methods that are appropriate to them'. In the new five-year plan of the NFPP, health planners also put an emphasis on reaching the youth (*Daily News*, 1995). Since these Ministry of Health policy guidelines and the new five-year plan of the NFPP serve as instruments to guide the implementation of ideas about appropriate ways to think, feel and act with regard to reproductive health, it seems that the medical sexual ideology has recently gained ground. However, it is a long way from policy-making to implementation.

The NFPP is located in the Ministry of Health. It trains family planning service providers and conducts free workshops and seminars for adolescents and parents, to educate them on family planning. The NFPP approach is first to counsel the adolescent to say no; if the adolescent persists in sexual activity, the counsellor may introduce contraceptives.

UMATI has a large library and resource centre, and sensitizes the public through seminars, workshops, publications and the media, but its major programme focus now is on actual service delivery. The UMATI staff believes that Tanzanian society has gone beyond the need of information campaigns and awareness raising on contraception and family planning. People know about these issues, but there is a lack of basic community-based health and family planning services. UMATI operates two clinics in Dar es Salaam, namely Muhimbili Medical Center and Mnazi Mmoja. In Muhimbili Medical Center they offer all types of family planning, including surgery.

Most of UMATI's family planning services are delivered by community-based volunteer distributing agents. There is a training programme of youth peer counsellors in Dar es Salaam. Young men and women are selected by UMATI to participate in their two-week training programme, including organizational and leadership training. These young counsellors receive condoms and spermicides for distribution in their neighbourhoods. The programme is not administered through schools; past experience has shown that many parents react with hostility towards such efforts. Currently, UMATI has a network of 22 trained peer counsellors, eleven men and eleven women, with eleven stations in Tanzania. In Dar es Salaam there are two stations, one in Mtoni and one in Miburani, both in Temeke District.

Like any other ideology, sexual ideologies should be critically assessed. The medical sexual ideology has been contested by social scientists who warn against the 'medicalization' of human procreation. As Tumbo-Masabo (1994b: 213) puts it:

> Teenage girls are now on the international agenda and given priority as an issue. For years they have been viewed through the neutral lens of 'reproductive health' – an umbrella term not only signifying the absence of sexually transmitted diseases, HIV/AIDS, high-risk pregnancies, abortions, low birth weight, etc., but also implying additional goals such as 'safe motherhood' and reproductive well-being. In this manner, the regeneration of life was subsumed under a medical concept, health. What once occurred in the West was repeated in Africa; a moral order was replaced by a scientific biomedical system; the priest and the shamans gave way to the doctors.

One of the main points of critique is, in other words, that medical sexual ideology de-contextualizes adolescent sexuality and teenage pregnancy and reduces them to a mere health problem, which can be solved with technical know-how. It neglects the issue of power in gender relations. It renders local cultural concepts of 'fertility', 'motherhood', 'fatherhood', the transition from 'girl' to 'woman' and from 'boy' to 'man' meaningless. There is also the danger that women become viewed and dealt with by authorities as objects whose fertility has to be controlled.

*The traditionalist-moral sexual ideology* Tanzanians adhering to a traditionalist-moral sexual ideology raise similar points of critique, but they are most concerned with moral standards. They fear that the new technical know-how of contraception leads to a breakdown of local beliefs and values. This ideology is still dominant in many spheres of life, particularly in the field of education. We have already mentioned that in 1984 members of parliament categorically rejected the government's plan to introduce family life education in schools. Since then, representatives of religions, and other non-governmental and governmental representatives have continued to meet in a number of seminars, and jointly prepared a syllabus on Family Life Education (FLE).

In a number of pilot schools, family life issues were gradually introduced at Standard 6 and 7 of the primary and Form I to IV of the secondary level. Emphasis is on life in totality, but sub-topics such as teenage pregnancy and abortion are introduced. So far, teaching 'safe sex' has remained a stumbling-block, not only in schools and among parents, but also in government. The first phase ended in 1993 and was evaluated by internal and external advisers. The second phase should start soon. It is planned to cover 10 per cent of primary schools in the country, 20 per cent of secondary schools, all teachers' colleges and the Department of Education at the University of Dar es Salaam. In other words, FLE will now become part of the national curriculum.

The FLE approach is conceptually rooted in what has become known as 'traditional sex education'. According to Mbunda (1991), who carried out a study of traditional sex education among twelve ethnic groups of Tanzania, learning about sex was a lifelong process intimately integrated into daily life, perpetuated at developmental turning points, for instance puberty and marriage, by intensive, narrowly focused training. Sex education was a responsibility, in one way or another, at one stage or another, of the whole society. It involved everyone – family, clan, neighbourhood, territorial authority – because everyone was affected. Sex education, in the form of parental education in social roles, began at home and continued until children formed their own households. The role of the parents was the key. When Mbunda carried out this study, he was working for the Tanzania Parents' Organization (WAZAZI). The WAZAZI (meaning 'parents' in Kiswahili) is affiliated to the ruling CCM party. It has a mandate to be the 'spokesperson' of parents and to ensure the provision of secondary and technical education to the children of Tanzania. From 1984 to 1993, WAZAZI was involved in a project sponsored by UNFPA on 'Responsible Parenthood and Family Welfare'. The focus of this project was to educate parents, because WAZAZI was concerned about a lack of responsibility on the part of the parents, and especially about men's attitude to family planning. A manual was written, people trained and films shown to sensitize the public all over Tanzania. One of the problems faced by this project was the lack of variety in family planning methods that it could offer. Public awareness was increased, but for service provision the project had to collaborate with other organizations, for instance UMATI, and this collaboration was not without problems.

A third organization with a similar approach is called Elimu ya Malezi ya Ujana (EMAU). This NGO was founded by the Christian Council of Tanzania and UMATI in 1976. The aim of EMAU was, and still is, to produce responsible adults. It started, very small, in response to problems facing youth. The initial strategy was to give seminars on puberty and its consequences to youth leaders of churches to create a multiplication effect. However, the multiplication effect was poor, partly because of a high turnover of youth leaders. They came up with a new strategy aimed at training teachers in youth counselling.

Since EMAU did not succeed in winning the collaboration of the government and could not offer financial and material support to the trained teachers, these often failed to start counselling centres in their schools. Still, EMAU is widely known throughout Dar es Salaam through distribution of publications and public lectures in school. EMAU later changed its strategy again to youth counselling at a central place. In 1995, after long preparation, they have started youth counselling services at their headquarters in Dar es Salaam. Two individual counselling sessions and one group counselling session are offered per week. Experience has shown that group counselling is more highly favoured, especially by girls. Adolescents learn about this programme through schools, at bus stops and in churches.

The traditional-moral ideology has been criticized by both medical professionals and feminists. Medical professionals keep warning about the health risks of adolescent sexuality, and argue that sound physiological and contraceptive knowledge should form part of FLE in primary and secondary school. Many medical practitioners agree with feminists who claim that the traditionalist-moral ideology is hypocritical because it pretends that adolescents do not have sex even though everyone knows that many of them do.

*The feminist sexual ideology* This leads us to the third ideology identified above, the feminist sexual ideology. In Tanzania, several feminist groups have expressed concern about teenage sexual activity and pregnancy. They have initiated a variety of activities to raise public awareness and to help those in need. Here we can report on only a few of these activities. In Dar es Salaam there are two organizations that provide assistance to teenage mothers. One of them is UMATI. Since 1986, UMATI has run a youth centre in the Temeke District of Dar es Salaam. This youth centre provides vocational training in tailoring, and community-based health education and services. UMATI also assists these young girls to continue their education in private schools. In Tanzania, pregnant girls are expelled from government schools. The second group is called Baby Care Women Association (BACAWA).

This NGO, founded in 1989, offers vocational training for 12–18-year-old girls. These girls came from different parts of Tanzania and have different backgrounds. Some of them were prostitutes, others adolescent mothers, and some came from broken homes. They live together for a period of nine months to learn different skills that will improve their life options, for instance sewing, book-keeping, opening a bank account, AIDS and family planning awareness and counselling. The aim of BACAWA is to educate the girls so that when they return to their homes they will be able to pass their skills on to others in so-called 'women's clubs', of which ten have been initiated so far in rural Tanzania.

Another feminist initiative is the Teenage Girls and Reproductive Health Study Group, begun in 1989–90. This is a group of researchers drawn from the Women Research and Documentation Project and the Institute of Development Studies Women's Study Group, both of them located at the University of Dar es Salaam. They were joined by a senior researcher from the Swedish Council for Research in the Humanities and Social Sciences and were awarded funding by the Swedish Agency for Research Co-operation with Developing Countries (SAREC). The first results of their project have been disseminated through a publication (Tumbo-Masabo and Liljestr, 1994) and a series of gender seminars. It is through these channels that the researchers intend to sensitize resource persons from EMAU, UMATI, the relevant government ministries and other organizations. The Teenage Girls and Reproductive Health Study Group is currently in the second phase of its work, which includes some studies of teenage boys.

In their publication they examine a wide spectrum of issues, of which we selected one that we consider most crucial, namely the social construction of early motherhood. Chambua and his colleagues (1994: 30) write:

> In this contemporary social construction of the 'teenage girl', the population issue and the medical risks associated with early pregnancies are the main elements that define her as a problem. Therefore, all pregnancies below the age of eighteen are not considered desirable. In societies where marriage at the outset of menarche has been practised for centuries, this must sound incongruous.

In Tanzania, early marriages were common in most communities as a means of forestalling premarital sex and pregnancy (Kassimoto, 1985). It was only in 1971 that the Tanzanian government passed a new Law and Marriage Act. Academics and legal experts hailed this as a milestone and as pioneering legislation in Commonwealth Africa, because it grants women legal equality with men (Rwebangira, 1994: 187–8); but it also means that the legal age of marriage has been increased. The new law sets the minimum age at marriage at 18, although this can be reduced to 15 for girls, with parental approval (Rwebangira,1994: 188).

In other words, we have to ask ourselves whether Tanzanians regard early marriage and pregnancy as a problem? More precisely, we should ask which segments of contemporary, pluralist Tanzanian society regard early motherhood as a problem? Is 'the teenage girl problem' not a Western construct that has recently been exported to countries like Tanzania? Neither we nor Chambua and his colleagues (1994: 32) argue that teenage pregnancies are desirable and should be the norm. The point is, as Phoenix (1991) has shown, that the negative social construction of early motherhood provides the conceptual frame within which teenage pregnancies are investigated and discussed. If we, as researchers, start with the assumption that early motherhood is a social problem, we end up reinforcing popular beliefs instead of providing evidence of all those teenage mothers who succeed as well as women over 20. Perhaps, even more importantly, we help to avoid addressing other highly sensitive issues. As Chambua and his colleagues (1994: 32) put it:

> What would happen if we instead constructed 'the old men's problem' and brought it into the limelight? Maybe it would throw more light on the teenage girls' difficulties than further studies on them would do. What would be the outcome if we approached the population problem and the medical risks of reproduction by focusing similar long-term attention on 'men's' uncontrolled desire?

Adherents of the traditionalist-moral sexual ideology criticize feminist sexual ideology for uprooting the existing social order, for example gender relations, and making men look bad. By depicting the teenage girl as a victim, oppressed, exploited, seduced and silenced, feminist sexual ideology describes only one side of the coin. What about all the girls who trap men by becoming pregnant? What about the girls' insatiable desires for entertainment, luxury and a comfortable life? Many health professionals, on the other hand, seem to have incorporated a gender perspective. They agree that socio–political changes are necessary if the situation of adolescents is to improve. At the same time, however, they regard the health-risks as the most urgent problem, and believe in technical solutions.

Our own stance is closest to feminist sexual ideology. Doing research on adolescent sexuality and writing this paper, however, shows that we are not completely free from the image of 'the teenage girl problem'.

What we try to do is to critically reflect our own stance and to listen to the adolescents and their families in order to capture some aspects of how they view adolescent sexual activity.

## Views of adolescents and their families

In order to capture the views of those directly concerned with adolescent sexuality and teenage pregnancy, we carried out community-based field research from October 1994 to February 1995. The following key questions guided us: whom do adolescents turn to in search for advice and support in sexual matters? Where do they get their knowledge on sexuality, conception and contraception?

*The setting* An area called Malapa in the Buguruni Ward of Ilala District in Dar es Salaam was selected as the study site. It is located near the city centre and shares many characteristics with other neighbourhoods in Dar es Salaam.

Half of the area is taken up by a densely populated unplanned settlement, where houses are built close to one another in varying styles and materials. The other half is owned by the Anglican Mission, and still has open spaces with meadows and majestic mango trees. Judging by the type of houses, people in this part of Malapa have a slightly higher standard of living. However, both parts of Malapa have a similar infrastructure. The city garbage collection system does not reach here; garbage is piled up and later dug into the earth. There is electricity, but its availability depends on the rationing system of the city government. Water is in short supply; even though many households are connected to a pipe system, most people have to buy water from street sellers.

Like all other urban neighbourhoods in Dar es Salaam, Malapa is inhabited by diverse ethnic groups. The participants in our study represent this diversity. They referred to themselves as WaZaramo, Wa-Ndengereko, WaBondei, WaNyamwesi, WaYao, WaLuguru, WaPogoro, WaChagga, WaHa, WaZigua, WaPangwa, WaNyakyusa, WaSambaa, WaJita, WaSukuma, and WaHaya. One family came from Burundi, and one man was half African and half Arab. In terms of regions, these people said they originated from Dar es Salaam, Tanga, Tabora, Morogoro, Lindi, Kigoma, Kilimanjaro, Coast, Iringa, Mbeya, Mara, Kagera, Mwanza and other regions of Tanzania.

Residents differ not only in terms of ethnic origin but also in terms of professional and educational background. Our sample of 173 people included businessmen, petty traders, priests, office clerks, policemen, housewives, peasants, guards, secretaries, teachers, nurses, retired officers, a doctor and a lawyer. While some had no formal education, others had graduated from university; most had left school after standard 7.

*Types of knowledge and channels of communication* We first analysed the discussions and interviews in each gender and generation group in terms of statements about the 'real' situation in the past and in the present, that is, the situation as people report it. For our next step, we compared these statements about the 'real situation' with statements about the 'ideal' situation, i.e. how people would prefer things to be. In the course of this analysis of people's statements, a clear distinction emerged between different 'types' of knowledge, namely knowledge of behavioural norms and knowledge of physiology and contraception.

In the three focus-group discussions with 28 mothers, the participants agreed that in the old days, mothers passed knowledge in the form of behavioural norms on to their daughters. They said, for instance: *'usitembee ovyo'* ('do not walk around aimlessly'); *'tulizana'* ('be calm and patient with life'); *'kutokuzurura usiku'* ('do not wander about at night').

These teachings were part of general life education and became more specified during *unyago* (initiation rites). Today, some mothers still hold on to their traditional role of imparting only behavioural norms, while others teach their daughters physiological and contraceptive knowledge, for instance the specifics of ovulation and conception. Other sources of sex education in contemporary life mentioned by the mothers are the school, peers, boyfriends and elder siblings. It is notable that only one mother mentioned the clinic as a source. This points to the fact that mothers do not seem to see an association between family planning services and adolescents. Most mothers in our sample agreed that forces beyond their control, particularly the changing social and cultural environment, economic hardship, and new life styles and temptations, reconcile them to the idea that adolescents do need physiological and contraceptive knowledge. With a few exceptions, mothers feel that their daughters should know about and use modern contraceptives, but that somebody else, preferably the school, should teach them.

In former times, fathers used to teach both girls and boys behavioural standards regarding adolescent sexuality. Their role was to instil fear and exert control. Today, men feel that they depend on women for information from the family planning services, and they tend to hold mothers responsible for bringing up their children. Other sources of contemporary sex education mentioned by the fathers are the media (videos and drama), the school and peers. Fathers further emphasized changing values as a factor influencing adolescent sexuality. Like the mothers, they face the dilemma that according to their convictions adolescents should not receive physiological and contraceptive knowledge, but owing to current circumstances some of them might need it. Most fathers agreed that the school, not the parents, should teach adolescents about sexuality and the use of contraception.

All generation and gender groups agreed that in former days it was the grandparents who were responsible for transmitting sexual knowledge between generations. The grandmothers, in fact, expressed a strong disappointment that adolescent girls today no longer want to listen to them but rather receive their knowledge from the media and the school. Many grandmothers think they still have an important role to play. As one of them put it, the mother should ask the grandmother to talk to her daughter, because these two generations are in a joking relationship with each other. Others felt that adolescents should receive physiological and contraceptive teaching in school, not in primary but in secondary school. Still others argued that young people should not be exposed to sex education until they finish school and are free to marry. Then the parents and UMATI could join hands in the task.

The grandfathers stressed the role of the elders in mediating sexual knowledge during the traditional initiation rites for *jando* (boys) and *unyago* (girls). Today, they feel, the rites are no longer performed properly, yet no viable alternatives are available. While some grandfathers reported that they had a good relationship with adolescents and were able to impart behavioural knowledge to them, others said that the youngsters no longer listened to them. Most grandfathers agreed that adolescents usually turn to their peers for advice and support in sexual matters. Other sources of information they mentioned were the radio, and direct observation of the family environment and adult conduct. With regard to the ideal situation, some grandfathers suggested prayer to God. Most of them, though, agreed that the school should be the main transmitter of knowledge. As one of them put it: 'Parents should warn, schools should teach, and adolescents should decide.'

The adolescent girls in our study knew that in former days sex education was in the hands of the grandparents, while the parents imparted and watched over behavioural norms. Since the teenagers did not bring up the topic spontaneously, it does not seem of much importance to them. What they eagerly volunteered was that they receive their knowledge regarding sexual matters from various persons, such as grandmothers, fathers' sisters and sisters. This indicates that adolescent girls today get advice and support from female relatives belonging to different generations. One taboo, however, seems to be retained by most adolescents: '*Kuongea na mama mambo haya ni mwiko!*' ('To discuss these issues with the mother is taboo!'). Other sources of sex education mentioned by the girls were radio, books, the school, peers and the boyfriend. When asked about the ideal situation, many girls said they wished to discuss these matters with their mother. The girls mentioned that they needed not only more knowledge, but personal counselling, and, especially, access to contraceptives at the clinics. As one of the girls put it: 'Even if we have knowledge of contraception, we do not know whether we can receive contraceptive services in clinics.'

Adolescent boys, like girls, did not mention initiation rites. They received their information on sexual matters from friends, brothers and the radio. Although the boys in our sample seemed to know more about modern contraceptives than the girls, they were also very eager to obtain more precise information. In fact, they did not really know whom to turn to for advice and support in sexual matters. They were uncertain whether their parents could help them, but if it were their choice, the boys would prefer them. Apart from parents, a few boys mentioned the school.

## Silences versus ignorance

In a recent community-based study of teenage mothers, Tumbo-Masabo (1994a) found that the women in her sample had learnt about sex through discussion with peers. Parents and relatives were not willing to tell them openly what they needed to know. Questions from girls are commonly interpreted as a sign of rudeness or knowing too much. Most girls thus learnt about menarche when they had it, that is to say their mothers, grandmothers or maternal aunts explained it to them only after seeing their first menstrual blood. The fact that some mothers transferred sexual knowledge mirrors changing conditions, because in the past the role of imparting knowledge about sexuality and conception was played by persons other than the parents. Commonly, relationships between adjacent generations were restricted, and excluded discussions about sexual matters, while relations between alternate generations, i.e. between grandparents and grandchildren, were close, easy and involved intimate issues. Though mothers and other female relatives are willing to tell a girl about menarche, conception and procreation, they do not elaborate on the whole reproductive process. Consequently, teenage girls often find themselves confused by the misinformation that they gather from unreliable sources of knowledge, including relatives, peers, print and electronic media.

Moreover, it seems that many women of the older generations are also not properly informed. Focus-group discussions in three wards of Temeke District in Dar es Salaam (Mdungi, 1995) revealed that, especially among the non-users of family planning methods, there is a misconception about modern contraceptives, backed up by widespread rumours about side effects and complications. Although at the beginning of the discussions the majority of the participants claimed to know a lot about family planning, it became evident later that their knowledge of modern contraceptives was very limited and distorted. Most of what they claimed to know was untrue.

Our study confirms, and perhaps refines, these findings. If we compare the answers of all gender and generation groups, we find that the knowledge transmitted from parents to adolescents on how to deal with sexuality and contraception is basically that of behavioural standards, that is rules and warnings. A culturally defined zone of silence exists between parents and their children, especially between mothers and daughters. For a daughter, it is *mwiko* (taboo) to discuss sexual matters with her mother.

Grandparents, uncles and aunts may impart knowledge about menarche, traditional contraceptives and birth, but physiological knowledge of the body, reproduction and contraception is rarely conveyed. This is due to ignorance in the literal sense; there is no culturally defined zone of silence between these social categories, neither in the old days nor today. Elder siblings and peers have become at least as important as elder family members as sources of advice and support. In other words, the trend is from inter- to intra-generational transfer of reproductive knowledge.

New and often fragmented knowledge passes through various non-familial channels, for instance the media and the schools. What is surprising is that all gender and generational groups except the adolescents themselves mentioned schools as preferred transmitters of reproductive knowledge, whereas when reading the literature and interviewing experts, we had gained the impression that most parents reacted rather hostilely towards sex education at school. Several explanations come to mind. The massive FLE campaign may have achieved its aim in reaching the parents, or the parents may be glad to delegate responsibility to the school. What is taught at school is perhaps not considered immoral.

Another surprising finding is that adolescent boys and girls would like to obtain advice and support from their parents. This view is shared by few parents; it would necessitate a fundamental change in parent–child relations. We found it particularly striking that adolescent girls expressed a need for access to family planning services. They feel they need not only more knowledge but also personal counselling and, especially, safe contraceptives. Based on these findings we drew up the following preliminary recommendations:

- family planning service providers should implement the new policy and make sure that the adolescents who ask them for support and advice receive information, education, counselling and contraceptive methods that are appropriate to them;
- adolescents should be informed about their right of access to family planning services;
- parents should be encouraged to take their role in sex education seriously;
- adolescents, particularly teenage mothers, should be supported.

### Reactions of service providers

As a fourth research activity, we organized a one-day workshop in Dar es Salaam on 13 March 1995 (Dar es Salaam Urban Health Project, 1995). This workshop aimed to bring together a group of resource people to discuss the preliminary results of this field study, to review current actions in the field of family planning, particularly for adolescents, and to generate ideas that could be incorporated into the study and lead to future interventions. The workshop was attended by 28 people from governmental and non-governmental organizations, such as the National Family Planning Programme of the Ministry of Health, the Muhimbili University College of Health Sciences of the University of Dar es Salaam, religious organizations, the government health services, and the Project Assistance Unit of the Dar es Salaam Urban Health Project.

We first presented the key findings of our field study, and then put up the conclusions and recommendations for discussion. The participants of the workshop decided to work in groups on each of the four recommendations and to present the results of the group work to the plenary. We received the following feedback to our recommendations.

- Family planning service providers should implement the new policy and make sure that the adolescents who ask them for support and advice receive information, education, counselling and contraceptive methods that are appropriate to them. Parents should be involved in the process of improving family planning services for adolescents. It should be clarified whom we mean by adolescents, whether only those aged 13–19? Separate sections for family planning for adolescents should be set up in clinics, dispensaries, schools and community outlets. Different methods of counselling should be tested. Networking with other institutions and organizations should be improved.
- Adolescents should be informed about their right of access to family

planning services. This information could be coupled with information on AIDS prevention. A 'sex education syllabus' or, better, 'health education syllabus' should be developed. It should be discussed with different bodies including parents, religious groups and other organizations, so as to reach an acceptable compromise. 'Sex education' teachers should be trained. Adolescents might be asked directly to find out the best ways of contacting them.

- Parents should be encouraged to take their role in sex education seriously. A step-by-step procedure should be followed to inform and educate the parents, engaging all available media. Sex education should start early and be gradual so that a comprehensive knowledge can be attained by the end of standard 7.

- Adolescents, and particularly teenage mothers, should be encouraged to build up positive life options. To allow pregnant girls to continue school might encourage parents to marry off their daughters early, as they will not be expelled from school; this would not be helpful in terms of women's emancipation. Special schools for 'drop outs' should be created. The work should be done at the grass-roots level involving communities in problem solving, for instance in women's clubs. Existing family planning videos directed at adolescents should be used, or new ones developed. Information on modern family planning methods and economic skills should be integrated in traditional *unyago/jando* training.

The original recommendations were revised to include some of these suggestions and were then submitted to the Dar es Salaam Urban Health Project as a background paper for the operational plans of 1 July 1995 to 30 June 1996.

## Discussion and conclusion

Earlier in this study we raised the question of whether the 'teenage girl problem' was not a Western construct that has recently been exported to countries like Tanzania? Friedman and Edstr (1983: 7) characterize the 'teenage problem' as follows: a number of factors operating in developing countries have contributed to a change in reproduction-related risks for adolescents. They include an apparent trend to a lowering of the age at menarche, an increase in age at marriage, changes in values brought about by increasing urbanization, exposure to foreign cultures through migration, tourism and mass media, and a decline in the prevalence of the extended family. These factors in turn heighten the chances of unwanted adolescent pregnancies, abortion and childbirth.

In Tanzania we also observe the changes described by Friedman and Edstr. We can interpret them as facets of the impact of modernity on economic, political, social and cultural institutions. During our focus-group discussions and key-informant interviews, parents and grandparents constructed links between changed living conditions and the sexual behaviour of their children.

By the age of 19, almost 60 per cent of young women have had a child or a pregnancy. The sad fact that 33 per cent of the women treated for induced abortion at four government hospitals in Dar es Salaam were from 14 to 19 years old shows that pregnancy is considered a problem, if not by the adolescents themselves, then by the people who advise them to induce an abortion. Last but not least, the girls in our focus-group discussions clearly expressed a need not only for more knowledge about sexuality and contraception, but also for personal counselling and, especially, access to contraceptives at the clinics. We could thus conclude that not only health professionals but also parents, grandparents and the adolescents themselves consider teenage pregnancy to be a problem. But a closer look reveals an important difference. While health professionals and adolescents regard teenage pregnancy as a problem, parents and grandparents speak mainly of adolescent sexual activity as a problem. It is true that teenage pregnancy is a result of adolescent sexual activity, and one is tempted to say that both groups, therefore, speak of the same phenomenon. But the two views differ in their implications. If so many adolescents are sexually active, it does not help much and, in fact, is hypocritical to withhold knowledge about safe sex. Adolescents obviously have practical knowledge about sex, but they lack precise information about preventing pregnancies.

This brings us to the second issue, the different 'types' of knowledge regarding sexuality, conception and contraception. We might assume that in traditional sex education the emphasis was on imparting ritual, social and normative knowledge, while modern sex education stresses the technical and practical knowledge. The distinction between 'traditional' and 'modern' sex education is not as clear as it may seem. In former times, parents were expected to impart behavioural standards aimed at controlling adolescent sexual behaviour, while grandparents, other relatives and initiators introduced the young people to the more practical aspects of menarche, intercourse, conception and local forms of contraception. Today, there are many adults of all walks of life in Tanzania who want to build on the tradition of imparting behavioural standards. This attitude is mirrored in the FLE approach, which teaches primary and secondary school children biological facts as part of general life education, but no knowledge about safe sex. The promoters of the

FLE approach also seem to regard teenage sexual activity, not teenage pregnancy, as the main problem. But who is supposed to carry on and improve the more practical teachings formerly given by grandparents and initiators? There appears to be a vacuum, which institutions and organizations are reluctant to fill.

Another important distinction is that between correct and incorrect knowledge, in reference to both traditional and modern sex education. Many guardians of traditional knowledge feel that the rites are no longer performed properly; teenagers' knowledge of the modern type, on the other hand, is generated by observation and hearsay, and thus tends to be distorted and incomplete. In other words, there is not only too little information coming too late, as Tumbo-Masabo (1994a: 169) suggests, but the information that reaches adolescents is often of poor quality.

There is clearly a need for an improvement in the quality of social and normative as well as technical and practical knowledge. The quality of information is closely linked to the 'who' and 'how' of communication. In former times, these channels of communication were defined by social structure and cultural norms. The sexual ideology of the ethnic group clearly defined when and what kind of information should be passed on, from whom to whom. Girls were usually taught by their grandmothers or aunts, boys by initiators. Today, some of these channels have become obstructed: grandmothers and aunts do not always live in the vicinity, and school does not allow adolescents to spend prolonged periods of time in the villages. At the same time, considerable pressure is now put on the parents, who were formerly exempted from the transmission of 'technical' or 'practical' knowledge about sex. Since most family planning programmes address mothers in child-bearing age, these mothers have become regarded as new channels of information, not only by professionals but also by husbands and by the adolescents themselves. This collides with the culturally accepted silence that used to exclude them from assuming responsibility for the consequences of adolescent sex and, at least partly, explains why many mothers are reluctant to break this silence. The new demands on parents, particularly mothers, call for professional assistance. Fathers should be reminded of their responsibility and, together with the mothers, should be offered guidance and counselling in learning their new role. Today, most Tanzanian adolescents and their parents are exposed to competing sexual ideologies which reach them through various channels, but mainly through schools, the media and peers. The school has in fact become a widely accepted channel of sex education, both among parents and among service providers; but let us stress once more that safe sex is not taught in detail. The radio, videos and drama have also been mentioned by many respondents in our study, but not in a particularly favourable way. Some people felt offended that such intimate issues should be discussed in public. Others mentioned that videos and TV drama frequently generated immoral thoughts and behaviour in their children. Print media, i.e. books, leaflets and brochures, were mentioned, mainly by the adolescents themselves. However, we gained the impression that none of these texts served the purpose of providing medically correct and easily understandable information. This is a pity, because the great advantage of print media is that people can refer to them whenever they want to refresh their memory.

Apart from schools and media, most emphasis was given to peers as sources of information. Peers now form a strong communication system. However, the problem is the content of peer information and communication: it is often inadequate and fragmented. At least two organizations, namely EMAU and UMATI, build on peer influence and try to improve peer communication by special training. Until now, however, the effect of peer counselling in Dar es Salaam has not been very big in terms of geographical coverage.

The possibilities of combining the media and peer culture as main channels have, to the best of our knowledge, not yet been fully explored in Tanzania. There is, for example, no youth magazine that serves as a platform for youth to ask questions and to exchange experiences. Another possibility might be the production of carefully designed comics to impart medically correct and ethically sound knowledge in an attractive form.

Another potential channel of communication is family planning clinics. If the new MOH guidelines are going to be implemented, an important step towards filling the above-mentioned vacuum has been made. The right of access to family planning information, education and services will be granted, an expressed need of adolescent girls in our study. How does it help to have some knowledge of modern contraceptives if one does not receive good counselling and access to them? The new MOH guidelines, however, are prone to differing interpretations. What exactly are 'family planning methods that are appropriate to' teenagers? It will depend on the meaning given to these words whether or not adolescents will be given the right to practise safe sex. Another danger is that adolescents become easily stigmatized as 'loose girls', if they are seen at family planning clinics. Special precaution should be taken to ensure the confidentiality and privacy of service provision.

Other initiatives, for instance BACAWA and the UMATI Youth Centre in Temeke, are directed not at adolescents but at teenage mothers as target groups. This is certainly an important contribution to building up positive life options; but it can be argued that such training is important for all adolescents, not just for teenage mothers. Many parents and grandparents in our sample have pointed out that teenage pregnancies are often a consequence of economic hardship and of temptations of 'the lovers' gifts' (Komba-Malekela and Liljestr, 1994: 139). To help adolescents to find meaning in life and to develop skills that generate a reasonable income may make an indirect, but nevertheless considerable, contribution to solving the problem.

It is obvious that a variety of interventions are called for in order to tackle such complex problems as adolescent sexuality and teenage pregnancy. Much is already being done in Dar es Salaam and other parts of Tanzania. Many decision-makers and implementers are aware and concerned to do their best. The main contribution of our study, as we see it, is to raise the question of whether adolescent sexuality is, in fact, a problem of the adult generation, whereas the young generation considers pregnancy their main problem. This important difference might serve as a guide for future policy-making, as well as programme-planning and implementation. If we agree that pregnancy, not sexuality, is the public health problem to be addressed in Dar es Salaam and in Tanzania, our main task is to assist adolescents and their families to make informed choices about and responsible use of modern contraceptives.

## Acknowledgement

No study of this sort can be made without the time and aid of many busy, well-informed people. In Tanzania, the Dar es Salaam Urban Health Project (DUHP), particularly Dr Peter Kilima and Ms Zuhura N. Mdungi, gave us invaluable assistance and advice. Prof Marcel Tanner and Dr Nick Lorenz, of the Swiss Tropical Institute in Basel, Switzerland, showed a keen interest and gave generous support throughout our study. From the members of our international research team we received continuous encouragement, inputs and critical comments. Funding was granted by the Swiss National Science Foundation and the Swiss Development Corporation. Many others have been most helpful, particularly the adolescents, their parents and grandparents, and the resource persons of various organizations and institutions who kindly shared their experiences with us. We wish to thank them all.

## Note

1. In the Tanzania National Demographic and Health Survey, modern methods were defined as the pill, IUD, injection, vaginal methods (foaming tablets/diaphragm/foam/jelly), condom, female sterilization and male sterilization. Not all of them are defined as 'appropriate' for adolescents.

## References

Bureau of Statistics (1993) Tanzania Demographic and Health Survey 1991/1992, Bureau of Statistics, Planning Commission, Dar es Salaam.

Chambua, S. E., M. K. Rwebangira, R. Liljestr and E. J. N. Urassa (1994) 'Facts about and images of teenage girls in Tanzania', in Z. Tumbo-Masabo and R. Liljestr (eds), *Chelewa, chelewa. The dilemma of teenage girls*, Uppsala, Nordiska Afrikainstitütet.

*Daily News* (Tanzania) (1993a) 29 January.

*Daily News* (Tanzania) (1993b) 1 February.

*Daily News* (Tanzania) (1995) 6 March.

Dar es Salaam Urban Health Project (1995) 'Maintaining and promoting reproductive health in adolescence', unpublished report of a workshop held on 13 March 1994 in Maelezo Hall, Urban Health Project, Dar es Salaam.

Friedman, H. L. and K. G. Edstr (1983) *Adolescent reproductive health. An approach to planning health service research*, Geneva, WHO Offset Publication No. 77.

Kassimoto, T. J. (1985) 'Attitudes of parents, students, ex-pregnant schoolgirls and administrators on the expulsion of pregnant girls from schools: a case study of Dar es Salaam and Mbeya Region', unpublished MA dissertation, University of Dar es Salaam.

Komba-Malekela, B. and R. Liljestr (1994) 'Looking for men', in Z. Tumbo-Masabo and R. Liljestr (eds), *Chelewa, chelewa. The dilemma of teenage girls*, Uppsala, Nordiska Afrikainstitütet.

Kulin, H. E. (1988) 'Adolescent pregnancy in Africa: a programmatic focus', *Social Science and Medicine*, Vol. 26, No. 7.

Mbunda, D. (1991) 'Traditional sex education in Tanzania. A study of 12 ethnic groups', Margaret Sanger Center, New York, Planned Parenthood of New York City.

Mdungi, Z. N. (1995) 'Perception of family planning among women of childbearing age: focus group discussions with women from 3 wards of Temeke District in the city of Dar es Salaam', unpublished report, Urban Health Project, Dar es Salaam.

Ministry of Health Tanzania (1994) 'National policy guidelines and standards for family planning service delivery and training', Revised Edition, Ministry of Health Tanzania, Dar es Salaam.

Mpangile, G. S. and W. M. Mbunda (1992) 'Information on adolescent sexuality in Dar es Salaam. An annotated bibliography', unpublished manuscript, Dar es Salaam, UMATI.

Mpangile, G. S., M. T. Leshabari and D. J. Kihwele (1993) 'Factors associated with induced abortion in public hospitals in Dar es Salaam, Tanzania', *Reproductive Health Matters*, Vol. 2.

Phoenix, A. (1991) *Young Mothers?*, Cambridge, Polity Press.

Rwebangira, M. K. (1994) 'What has the law got to do with it?' in Z. Tumbo-Masabo and R. Liljestr (eds) *Chelewa, chelewa. The dilemma of teenage girls*, Uppsala, Nordiska Afrikainstitütet.

Tumbo-Masabo, Z. (1994a) 'Too little too late', in Z. Tumbo-Masabo and R. Liljestr (eds), *Chelewa, chelewa. The dilemma of teenage girls*, Uppsala, Nordiska Afrikainstitütet.

Tumbo-Masabo, Z. (1994b) 'Conclusions', in Z. Tumbo-Masabo and R. Liljestr (eds), *Chelewa, chelewa. The dilemma of teenage girls*, Uppsala, Nordiska Afrikainstitütet.

Tumbo-Masabo, Z. and R. Liljestr (eds) (1994) *Chelewa, chelewa. The dilemma of teenage girls*, Uppsala, Nordiska Afrikainstitütet.

Vuorela, U. (1992) 'The informal sector, reproduction and the economic crisis', in H. Campbell and H. Stein (eds), *Tanzania and the IMF. The dynamics of liberalization*, Boulder, Colorado, Westview Press.

# 3
# Cross-generational knowledge transfer on reproductive health among women in Ghana

MIRANDA N. GREENSTREET AND
R. A. BANIBENSU

This chapter is based on part of the findings of a large demographic study of 529 women over the age of 15 in five regions of Ghana, and looks at the transfer of knowledge and communication between grandmother, mother and daughter. The chapter focuses on the findings related to knowledge transfer on reproductive health practices and knowledge, gender relationships and women's status in Ghanaian society. The main issues which the chapter seeks to cover are: the status of girls' education; the incidence of and attitudes towards teenage pregnancy; the changes in the choices of marriage and childbirth patterns, according to women's age, and the decision-making of parents and daughter, wife and husband, families and communities; and the interruption by modernity of the traditional inter-generational transfer of knowledge on sexuality and reproductive health.

The opinions of Ghanaian women on these issues are gathered from an extensive survey, that covers many more areas of women's lives. The findings of the survey are supplemented by the researchers' observations and peer-group discussions, in order to present examples of the types of mores and gaps in knowledge surrounding these issues, including, in particular, a monitoring of the women's dissatisfaction with current gender relations in Ghanaian society, which is still strongly patriarchal. The case study aims to sketch some of the shifts in knowledge transfer of reproductive health among the generations, and to gauge the main problems Ghanaian women face, in this historical transition between traditional and modern life, when making reproductive choices that fulfil their own needs.

## Demographic profile of Ghana

Ghana, a country on the west coast of Africa, covers an area of 238,537 square kilometres and has a fast-growing population estimated in 1995 at 17.2 million. Women make up a little over half, with a male–female ratio of 1:1.02. The population is growing rapidly at the rate of 3.1 per cent per annum, with children under 15 making up approximately 45 per cent of the population (children under 5 constitute 19 per cent). The high number of children results in a high dependency ratio, which has serious implications for women. Women are expected to devote their time and energy to maintaining the dependent population by carrying the burden of housekeeping, child care, and the general nurture and upkeep of the family and community.

Infant mortality stands at 82 per 1,000 live births, and the mortality rate for children under 5 stands at 132 per 1,000 live births. Despite attempts to improve health conditions, maternal mortality is 214 per 100,000 live births. The total fertility rate is 5.5, and life expectancy for women is 57.5 years (for men it is 53.9 years). Safe motherhood services are provided by the Ministry of Health, the Christian Health Association of Ghana (CHAG), the Ghana Social Marketing Foundation and the Planned Parenthood Association of Ghana (PPAG) through community-based distributors and clinics.

Malaria remains the most serious disease, followed by upper respiratory tract infections, diarrhoeal diseases and skin diseases. A vigorous immunization programme is in place, particularly for young children, but the population is not yet adequately covered.

The educational system, modelled on the British system, is made up of nine years' basic education, a further three to five years at secondary level, and a tertiary level of three to four years at various training institutions, polytechnics and universities. Few women attain tertiary-level education. In the last national census of Ghanaians over 15 enrolled in education, 13 per cent of the total number enrolled were boys and 7 per cent were girls. The enrolment of girls in the educational system drops consistently the higher the level.

Ghana has a large number of ethnic groups, among whom the Akan are the most prominent. Loyalty to one's ethnic group is very strong, giving rise to a mosaic of customs and traditions that influence people's decisions and attitudes. Each ethnic group has its distinct language, and within the major languages there are dialects. Attempts to develop a common local language as the lingua franca have been unsuccessful, therefore English is used as the official language.

*Religious affiliations* Religious and secular life are closely interlinked in Africa. Christian women make up 80 per cent of the women surveyed; 18 per cent are Muslim or profess traditional religious affiliations, and 2 per cent are Buddhist or other non-traditional Ghanaian religions.

However, although most Ghanaians call themselves Christians, many openly or secretly observe traditional religions. For example, many women state that they would take their sick children to a traditional healer, whose methods are based on strong doses of traditional religious practices. Couples worried about barrenness or impotence are just as likely to follow the advice of the traditional priest or healer as that of the local medical doctor.

There is a strong faith in the power of ancestors to control the individual and the community. Libation, a style of prayer to the gods and ancestors, is taken very seriously during such ceremonies as weddings, 'outdooring' of children, puberty rites and other transitional points in the life cycle.

Islam, like Christianity, was externally imposed and is largely found in the Upper West and Brong Ahafo regions of Ghana. With the numbers of Islamic schools being established, this situation is likely to change.

*Occupation* Ghanaian women are extremely industrious, and responsible for the sustenance of their family. The most common occupation is trading, followed by farming. Rural areas and urban centres abound with women traders operating at varying levels. Rural Ghanaian women traders rise as early as four o'clock in the morning in order to reach the farm gate for a lift, and arrive at the market by seven in the morning. Others make uncomfortable trips sitting with their produce (such as yams, maize, vegetables, cassava, plantain and similar farm products) on the back of trucks along bad roads. Even those trading manufactured products in more urban areas have to be up extremely early, in order to prepare the family's food before they leave at six to reach their selling points, or to collect their wares. Sometimes the small scale of the stock makes outsiders wonder if it is worth the effort, the profit appearing so small. However, as the women can combine small-scale trading with housework, caring for children, their husbands and members of their extended family, productive and social-reproductive work complement each other.

Farming is also usually on a small scale. The large farms are about a hectare in size, and others are smaller than an acre. Most married women own the farms jointly with their husbands, with whom they collaborate, but some women choose to develop their own small farms to supplement the income from the family farm.

Other common occupations among the women in the study are: teacher, nurse, seamstress, clerk, beautician, artisan and student.

## Methodology and findings

The study is a cross-sectional survey of 529 women undertaken in five regions in the country: north-western corner (Upper West region); middle-west (Brong Ahafo region); south-central portion (Central region); the south around the capital city zone (Greater Accra region); and the eastern flank of the country (Volta region).

The cross-section encompasses most of the sub-cultural groupings in Ghana, representing Ghanaian women over 15 from urban, semi-urban and rural areas of the country. The responses gathered by the survey, therefore, reflect both modern and traditional views.

With such a wide coverage it was necessary to have a tight sampling. Accordingly, sampling followed a multi-stage design. After selecting the regions, three districts from each region were sampled and a random list of towns drawn up. In the City of Accra, suburbs were demarcated. In each selected town, streets and lanes were mapped out and a systematic sample made. Depending on the size of the town and the number of women to be selected, each interviewer was to enter the $n$th house on the street and interview a woman. Where possible, for every three successive houses entered, one each of the three generations was to be interviewed. The generations were defined for the interviewers as: teenagers (15–19); women (24–49) and old women (50 or over). Where the right generation was not represented in the household selected, they were to interview a woman in the house. If no women were available, interviewers moved to the next household where a woman was available for interview.

The main tool used by interviewers was an interview schedule drawn up in English by a team of adult educators and researchers. The main schedule was then given to independent linguists to translate into the main language used in each of the regions sampled. A converse translation was later carried out by another set of language experts in order to ensure that the various concepts in the schedule were translated appropriately. After translation, both the English version and the local language versions of each schedule were discussed and the necessary amendments made. The local language schedules were then pre-tested on women in each of the regions, in towns not falling within the sample. The schedule was then adjusted according to the pre-test before preparing the final version for the field.

Interviewers from each region were given two days' intensive training to ensure that they were well prepared for the interviews. The interviewers were then sent (under supervision) to carry out the interviews. The returns were edited and cleaned for coding, data entry and computer analysis. In addition, a series of Focus Group Interviews (FGI) were conducted among the three generational groups.[1]

*Education* It is difficult to ascertain how many women have received basic-level education. Of the women surveyed, three out of every ten never attended school and two out of ten had only primary school education. Primary school covers only the first six years of Basic Education, which does not take them to a level of functional literacy. Most lose all or most of the skills acquired at school by the time they become teenagers. Two out of ten had completed Basic Education (six years primary and three years junior secondary school); graduates from junior secondary school would best be described as semi-literate. Out of the 529 women surveyed, only 27 per cent had attained a level of education that gives them some sense of autonomy and a reasonable level of literacy. About a quarter of these have acquired only vocational education, in many cases equivalent to the junior secondary school level but with the addition of an acquired, marketable skill. This leaves only about 20 per cent of the women with enough education to enable them to be autonomous from their husbands.

From the attitudes the survey records, it appears that despite education being theoretically open to both girls and boys, the system does not favour the girl child. There is a customary prejudice about sending girls to school. The earlier a daughter is married, the higher the family prestige. An additional reality of educational life in Ghana is teenage pregnancy, which impacts mostly upon girls. Girls find it hard to return to the classroom, as they are out of step with their peer group and are not easily accepted back. Sometimes this leads to psychological problems, especially when, as is not uncommon, parents do not support their daughter's return.

Among some Ghanaian ethnic groups, pre-marital pregnancy leaves a serious social stigma not only on the girl but on the entire family. The girl can lose the right ever to step into her parental home, and she may be completely ostracized by the community. Families that have gone through such an experience once are reluctant to allow the girls to go to school lest they fall into the trap a second time. In some cases, girls are sent away from the community in order to continue their education.

*Family planning* There is a general awareness, among the women interviewed, of family planning, irrespective of the fact that the concept may not always be fully understood. Most associate it with child spacing, maternal health and responsible sex life and parenthood. A few, however, see family planning as an attempt to prevent women from having the number of children they would like to have.

Despite the widespread awareness of family planning, it is not widely practised. Slightly fewer than three out of every ten women in the five regions practise family planning. Reasons for not using family planning are given as: husbands' objection because they suspect wives of wishing to have extra-marital affairs; fear of community ridicule; taboos surrounding sex-related issues; lack of privacy in family-planning centres; and rumours that the methods are dangerous and unhealthy (for example: the loop – IUD – is lost in the body, leads to cancer of the uterus and cervix and chronic waist pain, and the oral pill makes a woman fat).

With the women who practise modern family planning, the oral pill seems to be the most popular device. More popular, though, is 'natural family planning' as promoted by the Catholic Church and the Christian Council, or abstinence. Many women abstain completely from sexual relations with their husbands or partners for well over two years after childbirth. Another phenomenon is the length of time of ovulation after the birth, particularly in the Brong Ahafo and the Central regions, where it is commonly three years. These women state that they do not need modern family planning.

The survey found that the knowledge of traditional methods to regulate births is being lost as women turn to modern methods. Some of the traditional methods are concoctions prepared from herbs, roots and tree bark, as well as an extended period of lactation – up to two years. Another popular method is for the woman to move out of the marital home and stay with her parents until the child is 2 to 3 years old, when she returns (this is discussed in more detail below).

*Marriage and childbearing patterns*  Ghanaian women have children early. One explanation for this is that girls mature very early. Girl children begin to engage in housework between the ages of 7 and 9 years. By the time girls reach 13–15, they are established housekeepers, able to care for their younger siblings. By puberty they are physically and socially marriageable. Puberty rites are traditionally carried out by this age, where a woman's chastity and virginity are proven and honour is bestowed on the whole family. Once these rites have been carried out, the girl is betrothed and married.

Of the women interviewed, 30.4 per cent were married by the time they were 19. Two-and-a-quarter per cent were married between 11 and 14, though it is not always possible to determine age accurately. The peak age of marriage stands at 20. The introduction of modern education, however, is changing this traditional rhythm, as girls are spending longer in school. The result is a prevalence of teenage pregnancy out of wedlock (see above).

When asked if they chose to marry when they did, two-fifths of those surveyed said yes. A little more than one-third stated that they had not planned to be married, but had been compelled by circumstance. Some women married men they did not know, and the decision had been taken wholly by their parents and husbands. When asked if they should have the right to make the choice themselves, 55 per cent said yes. In relation to teenage girls marrying, however, 40 per cent said that parents should take the decision.

The high percentage opting for parents' choice for teenage girls is significant. Most Ghanaian women agree that teenagers have very little experience in life, and cannot adequately assess the qualities of a future husband who is attracted to a young teenage bride. They explained that the danger is that when a woman loses her youthfulness and looks, her husband will look elsewhere. In these cases, parents are more capable of making choices for their daughters. Others, on the contrary, argued that parents have their own welfare, not their daughters', at heart; they have an eye on the wealth of the man's family, hence their decision may not always be to the girl's benefit.

As the woman grows older and more mature, parental authority is less highly regarded. Of women between the ages of 20 and 35, more than 60 per cent replied that the women alone should decide whom they should marry. Only one in six suggested that the parents should have a say. Of women who are 40 or more, and of those who have established themselves in business, or who work as professionals, 80 per cent said women should take their own decision.

*Number and spacing of children* A clear majority of Ghanaian women take the decision on the number of children they should have, together with their husbands or partners, or by themselves. Only one out of ten women would let their husbands take such a decision alone. Parents play a minimal role in this, but many mothers-in-law are known to put pressure on their daughters-in-law to have a large number of children. In the Ashanti region in particular, a woman who gives birth mainly to girls is actively encouraged by her family to produce more. Many women cannot resist this pressure, and they continue to have children until they reach menopause.

This tendency is strengthened by the traditional rites performed when a woman produces her tenth child. At this point there is a grand celebration, and a *badu guan* (tenth-child-sheep) is offered for her fertility. The celebration is bigger when a majority of the ten children are boys. This tradition, though still observed, is losing its significance for those living in the cities; it can no longer be afforded, and there is a growing lack of respect for tradition among urban communities, as women, particularly from other ethnic groups, tease friends who appear to be caught in a dilemma between traditional and modern urban values.

Generally, there is dissatisfaction with births that happen too frequently. When the children are born close to each other, adequate care becomes a problem for the couple, and infant mortality increases. In the Volta region, the entire society frowns on births occurring too frequently. In the past, the woman stayed with her parents until the child was at least 2 (sometimes more), before she was allowed to go back to her marital home. If she became pregnant before that, her husband was often accused by her family of attempting to 'kill' their sister or daughter.

## Shifts in the inter-generational transfer of knowledge

Strong lines of communication exist between the three generations. Grandmothers play an important role in keeping communication lines open between their children and grandchildren. Knowledge transfer tends to be on the level of moralizing and socializing rather than explicit instruction on family planning and reproductive choice. The grandmother is often used as a conduit of information between parents and children. For example, if a mother wishes her daughter to marry a particular man, the grandmother is assigned the task of talking to the young woman.

Grandmothers are chosen because the relationship between grandmother and granddaughter is close, often closer than the relationship between mother and daughter. Also, Ghanaian tradition values age and experience. Therefore a granddaughter is expected to respect, even revere, her grandmother. It is widely believed that if you disobey or displease a grandmother, she can leave a curse on you which follows you all your life; this myth adds to the grandmothers' power to influence.

Modernity, however, is tending to subvert this established rapport between the first and third generations. Young girls in the 1990s are liable to question, even scorn and ignore, their grandmothers. Instead they rely on the information gathered from schools and peers. As one woman commented: 'The girls of today are very disrespectful. When you call them for such discussions, as we used to do in the past, they simply snub you. One of my granddaughters told me once: "Mama, but you are talking of things of yesterday; today we don't do things that way!"'

Grandmothers, however, are still able to discuss sexual and reproductive issues openly, in contrast to their daughters and granddaughters.

Hence mothers continue to encourage their daughters to ask their grand-mothers for intimate information. Mothers tend to be uncommunicative and avoid discussions with their daughters. For example, one of the researchers observed a family scene when the 'protector condom' was being advertised on TV. A 9-year-old child asked her father when he was going to buy 'some of that' for them, so that they also could 'be happy' (the advertisement's slogan). The man became confused and avoided the issue, telling the child to ask its mother. She too was unable to answer. The researcher, an experienced lecturer in nursing, was able to intervene, telling the child that she is too young now but when she grows up to be a mother she can choose to use 'protector condom' or 'be happy' with her husband. The example illustrates how sex is a taboo topic in the home.

The inability of parents to discuss sexuality with children in modern times contrasts with traditional sex education. Sex education took place at critical periods in a girl's life cycle, beginning with the menarche. The women kept a close eye on girls during this period. At first menstruation, the girl was taken out of the family home and given special instruction on how to observe bodily hygiene, and told that menstruation was part of her natural development. A maternal aunt would hold the girl's hand, keep her company and talk to her about how to care for herself.

Girl children observing their first menstruation were expected not to touch any food in the house. Food was brought to her, or cooked at her 'isolation camp'. She was considered 'unclean' for those five days or so, and men thought that if they came into contact with menstrual blood, it would defile them.

The puberty rite followed the period of isolation. Normally, several young women went together through the initiation, which could range between one week and two years. Among the Krobo, and in some parts of the Volta region, there was an elaborate preparation lasting between six months and two years. Several girls from different families were brought together and taken through intensive education. This included housekeeping, bodily hygiene, dancing, and intensive sex education, including bedroom ethics. All young women in the community were expected to undergo this training completely removed from their own homes, under the guidance of a revered old woman assisted by some other women elders.

This practice was critical in defining women's coming-of-age. It was considered a disgrace for the whole family if a girl fell pregnant before going through this ritual. Not only did it leave a lasting stigma on the family, but custom demanded that such a girl did not set foot again in her father's home. The idea behind this was to encourage and enforce chastity, and to prepare girls for an honourable marriage.

Similarly, sex education used to be introduced during the marriage preparations. When a suitor approached the family for the hand of a young woman, the mother, grandmother, aunts, and in some cases the father instructed her in the do's and dont's of married life, and at the final ceremony community members offered advice. With the influence of Christianity and formal education, these practices have died out. Women also rebelled against them, as they felt they were practices through which men instilled into women a sense of inferiority.

Another important ritual, among a section of the Ewes almost extinct now in Ghana, is *Funyinyi*. When a young married woman had her first pregnancy and was nearing the birth of her child, she underwent a special ritual involving the whole family, who together went through a series of mini-rituals. These were intended to ensure that nobody within the family had anything against the pregnant woman, and that there was no misunderstanding between her and any family member. If such an issue was identified, the ritual was held up and the matter thrashed out; a 'peace ritual' followed to ensure safe delivery. With ritual performed and the whole family seated, a series of educational episodes was enacted. These taught handling and care of the new baby, etiquette and similar things that would ensure the baby's survival. The woman was then confined until she delivered the baby.

Today this tradition has almost died out, but it does not seem to have been replaced by any similar ceremony that could educate young mothers on such matters. The traditional extended family is losing its cohesion, the younger women are becoming more independent, and many of them travel alone to towns and cites unable to receive this instruction. The strong bond between the three generations seems to have become weakened, thereby creating some social distance between grandmothers and their granddaughters, but it is not completely shattered. Thirty-five per cent of our respondents receive some education from their mothers, and another 15 per cent from their grandmothers and other relatives. A large majority, however, suggested that parents and, to a lesser extent, other relatives, should be entrusted with the responsibility of educating their daughters about reproductive health.

Despite this general consensus, only a third of all the women interviewed discussed such issues with their daughters. As mentioned elsewhere, a large majority of women regarded matters relating to sex and reproduction as taboo topics, and they are too shy to discuss it with their daughters. Some held that discussing issues of this nature will encourage promiscuity: 'You will ruin them and they will go in for the boys,' one woman explained. Girls interviewed said that they are able to acquire more information on sexuality during their biology classes, and sometimes at church. Added to this they have ample opportunity to interact with their peers, where much information, accurate or not, is exchanged. Since most of the schools in the country are mixed, they also have the opportunity to start relating to boys early.

Unhappy communication between mothers and daughters was illustrated during the field research. We encountered one situation in which a mother, in talking to her daughter about sexuality, raised her voice angrily, shouting: 'You stubborn girl, I am warning you! Boys are dangerous and will fool you and as soon as you get pregnant they will ignore you, leaving you to suffer! I do not want to see you walking with any boy from today onwards.' The daughter walked away mumbling. Other women stated they would like to talk to their daughters about sexuality but confessed that they themselves were ignorant. Three women from different towns said during our interviews: 'I do not think one should worry very much about what we tell our daughters. The important thing is to provide for their needs adequately. If you fail to do this, whatever education or talking takes place between her and yourself is useless. The result is, she will fall an easy prey to a boy who proves to be able to satisfy these needs.'

## Changing gender relations

Parental control of when and whom a daughter should marry has been very strong in Ghanaian tradition. Such control seems to be weakening today, but a majority of the women interviewed would still allow their parents to have a say in when and whom they should marry. On the other hand, we discovered that a majority of these would not want their fathers to have a hand in the choice. So whereas parental control is still evident, the influence of the father, especially in selecting a fiancé for his daughter, is not welcome.

With regard to the number of children they should have, an overwhelming number of women would rather keep parents completely out of the matter. But whereas a majority would not allow their husbands alone to determine the number, they are equally of the opinion that they themselves should not have the sole prerogative in the decision. They prefer the couple to decide together. The women complained that when they think they have enough children, their husbands tend to press for more. Many submit to this pressure for the sake of peace in the house. As one woman stated: 'Ah, you know men; even when you object, they will press on till they have their own way.'

This feeling of helplessness before their husbands' demands is more pronounced in the rural than in the urban areas. In the urban centres there is more pressure from husbands in families engaged in basic primary production, such as fishing and farming. For women employed in the modern sector, there appears to be greater opportunity to resist such pressure from 'troublesome' husbands. The more educated the woman, the greater the independence she enjoys and the greater the respect the husband has for her.

Most women do not regard themselves as being at all powerless when it comes to the spacing of children, especially if this should have an effect on their health. Indeed, Ghanaian traditional norms demand that there should be some minimum distance between siblings. A few women cannot stop their husbands, as they are afraid that they will take a mistress or another wife.

There is a common view that a woman should quietly submit to her husband any time he demands sexual relations. However, three-quarters of the women interviewed felt that they had the right to refuse: 'Submitting quietly to your husband, each time he says he needs you, is like selling yourself out. Oh, no! No woman should ever do that,' said one respondent. Of the one-quarter who stated that they would submit when their husbands demand sexual relations, one woman said: 'Whenever men are in the mood there is nothing you can ever do to stop them; much as you would like. In view of this, one enters into an unpleasant confrontation which is sometimes more difficult to handle than simply giving the man his way. After all, he is your husband!' Asked whether they protect themselves from unwanted pregnancies in these circumstances, we discovered that very few do so, as some of these men object to their wives using family planning.

One cannot interpret this lack of contraceptive use simply as powerlessness on the part of the woman. It is a far more complex issue. For the Ghanaian woman, the cohesion of the family as a unit is highly valued. Women are careful not to damage relations or to break the marriage, as many feel that they do not have the right to initiate a divorce. Those who do, experience difficulties. One woman became 'fed up' with her husband's misbehaviour with other women, and so she took the initiative, and bought the required drinks and other items in order to inform the elders that she wished to have a divorce. Although the elders tried to stifle her efforts, she insisted and pushed the divorce through. She threatened the elders not 'to drag their feet' or she would remove the drinks and other items, telling them 'to go and be his wife', as she 'had had enough'.

Interestingly, half of the women interviewed said that they would allow a husband to marry a second wife if the husband insisted; so long as they were respected as the senior wife. They stated this in connection with cases in which the man wants more children, and they, as wives, realize that they are not prepared to have any more, on health and economic grounds. Indeed, in some of the northern regions, a rightful heir to a 'skin' may not be granted that right if he does not have many children. A woman in this situation often has little say. In traditional Ghanaian society, the social norms permit polygamy, and these norms are still prevalent, though they are diminishing slowly.

## Conclusion

Although inter-generational communication on reproductive health still exists, it is greatly reduced. Modernity has interfered with the interaction of the three generations; young girls tend to ignore once-revered grandmothers; and relations between mothers and daughters are difficult. The disruption of the transfer of traditional knowledge, caused by modern education, external religions and new life styles, leaves silences and gaps at important transition points of a woman's life cycle, which do not seem likely to be filled under present educational, health and population policies. Women and young girls are handicapped by a continuing gender discrimination that prevents them from achieving sufficient levels of education to shrug off social and cultural prejudice. In addition, traditions no longer offer support and necessary information, leaving many women unsatisfied and yet without access to knowledge and services that could enable them to become fulfilled. It seems ironic that even though Ghanaian women are so hard-working and often economically independent, owing to their trade and farming activities, their decision-making power is eroded by their low level of education combined with the continuing strength of patriarchal authority.

Given the complexity of the issues that the study covers, this chapter only skims the different attitudes and environmental factors that lead to Ghanaian women's reproductive decisions. The conclusion that women in Ghana continue to be vulnerable to traditional pressures, often complicated rather than helped by modern interventions, suggests that much more needs to be known about the impact of modern life on these women's lives, which are in social, economic and cultural transition. The apparent tendency to sweep aside traditional practices with the promise of what modern society has to offer, in such a poverty-stricken country as Ghana, leads only to increasing service deficiencies and further economic and cultural erosion. The gaps and silences have to be filled not only with relevant modern knowledge and technology, but also by paying attention to the useful elements of traditional knowledge before they become completely lost. Respect for traditional Ghanaian generational interaction needs to be reinstated in order not to disrupt social cohesion completely in the face of continuing economic difficulties. Most of all, men have to take up their responsibilities to support and enhance their wives' and daughters' reproductive choices, by recognizing the role they have to play as fathers and husbands in maintaining family reproductive health. Educational support, medical and technical assistance are clearly needed, but only if introduced in a culturally sensitive way, based on women's (of all ages) own realities of sexuality and reproduction. Men need to be educated to understand the need to choose safely (in the social and the medical sense) when to have sexual relations, how to space and limit numbers of children, again with programmes that are sensitive to the changes in men's roles during the social transition currently being experienced in Ghanaian society. Strategies cannot be introduced from outside. Rather, they have to be developed together with Ghanaian women – the teenagers, the mothers and the grandmothers – and their men, with time and money devoted to building lost confidence among generations and restoring healthy gender relations.

## Note

1. The most interesting group was women who had experienced teenage pregnancy. Because of their shared history and the support they could offer each other, they were able to discuss their views frankly.

## References

Adepoju, A. and C. Oppong (eds) (1994) *Gender, Work and Population in Sub-Saharan Africa*, Geneva, ILO.

EZE (1994) 'Gender and Development in Ghana, Preliminary Assessment of Approaches to Women and Development of Selected NGOs and Churches', Report to the Protestant Association for Co-operation in Development, EZE–Germany, on a visit to Ghana, 30 April–22 May.

Greenstreet, M. (1994) 'Population Policies in Africa and the Extended Family', paper delivered at SID regional conference on 'Building Global Human Security', Harare, Zimbabwe.

Greenstreet, M. and R. A. Banibensu (1995) 'Sustainability for Future Generations: The Relevance of Intergenerational Transfer of Knowledge for Health and Population Programmes', University of Ghana, Legon, Institute of Adult Education.

Sai, F. (1994) *Adam and Eve and the Serpent. Breaking the Bonds to Free African Women*, Legon, Ghana Universities Press.

# 4
# Codes of honour: reproductive life histories of domestic workers in Rio de Janeiro

JACQUELINE PITANGUY AND
CECILIA DE MELLO E SOUZA

This chapter analyses the social, cultural and economic context of women's reproductive careers for a specific occupational group: domestic workers of Rio de Janeiro, Brazil. It is based on ethnographic research conducted for a larger project, the International Reproductive Rights Research Action Group (IRRRAG) research project.[1] The organization Citizenship, Studies, Information and Action (CEPIA) was responsible for the local project in Rio de Janeiro with domestic workers, which included a particular interest in women's reproductive experiences and decisions throughout the life cycle, and in the inter-generational transfer of knowledge regarding such experiences.

A brief overview of Brazil's socio-economic and political context in the past 30 years, of the work and social conditions of domestics, and the research methodology used, forms a general background for our findings and analysis. A life cycle approach has been central to our analysis, in which we demonstrate how family roles and socialization, geared toward family subsistence, direct women for social reproduction throughout their lives, whether it be paid or unpaid work. Beginning at adolescence, social reproduction overlaps with production. For these women, work is central to the reproductive choices they can or cannot make. Reproductive choice is then examined in light of the climate of social change over recent decades in Brazil, which introduced new values regarding gender relations, sexuality and reproduction, with medical culture playing a large role in the definition and homogenization of reproductive culture. Although traditions that silence women in conversations with their younger counterparts on sexual and reproductive matters still exist, women believe this silence has been a disservice to them. While informal networks of personal relations are important sources of information once women marry, the significance of the media in Brazil as sources of information and in the introduction of new images of modernity cannot be overestimated.

## Brazil's socio-economic and political context

Brazil, the fifth-largest country in the world, is a multi-racial, multi-cultural society. Slightly more than half the population, basically of European descent, is white, while Blacks of African descent make up the majority of the remainder. An ideology of racial democracy disguises strong racial discrimination. Portuguese is the common language, bridging the various regions of the territory. Politically, the country is organized as a federal republic, with state and municipal governments. As in most Latin American countries, women, non-whites and the lower-income population have been traditionally excluded from power. From 1964 until 1985, most of civil society was excluded under the military dictatorship, which exercised varying degrees of coercion and state control over individual freedom and political liberty.

As the world's ninth-largest economy in terms of gross income, Brazil is a country of contrasts. The wealth produced by its sophisticated, complex industrial and commercial sectors, and by the modern, export-oriented agriculture, is unequally distributed among its 150 million inhabitants and among its regions: 53 per cent of the GNP goes to the richest 10 per cent of the population. The South-East is the richest and most heavily populated region, and the North-East the poorest.

The modernization of the Brazilian economy was accompanied by a systematic deterioration in the value of the minimum monthly wage. This value, determined by the federal government, is insufficient to live on. In December 1995, it corresponded to US$110, while the ideal minimum wage to meet the survival needs of a family of four is estimated at approximately US$800 (DIEESE, 1995).

The impoverishment of the worker has resulted in an increase in the number of family members contributing to its subsistence, leading, along with other factors, to a dramatic expansion in female participation in the labour force since 1970. From seven million women then active in the labour market, this number jumped to 25 million in the early 1990s. Today, women make up approximately 40 per cent of the economically active population (EAP), one of the highest rates in Latin America. However, their position in the labour market points to the still prevailing gender inequality in Brazilian society. Women constitute the majority of workers receiving the minimum wage or less, and their presence decreases as the income scale rises. Women's average wage is 54 per cent of that received by men, even taking into consideration similar levels of education (CEPIA/FLACSO, 1993). Afro-Brazilian women suffer the lowest level of education and income, working in occupations demanding the least qualification, such as domestic service. They earn an average of two minimum wages, while average earnings of white men and women are, respectively, 7.6 and 2.4 minimum wages (Arilha *et al.*, 1995). Other factors accounting for women's increasing participation in the EAP include changes in consumption patterns, the expansion of the labour market, and rural exodus, changes in behavioural and cultural values regarding gender roles, and the introduction and dissemination of new birth-control methods since the 1960s.

Although 18 per cent of the population is still illiterate, women have significantly increased their participation in education. They spend as long in education, on average, as men (4.7 years), and maintain parity at all levels. This is a result of cultural changes regarding the role of women in society, and also of the requirements of a growing labour market over the last 20 years. These economic, educational, and cultural changes have taken place in the general political context of struggle against the authoritarian government. It is in this period that Brazil also began the process of demographic transition. Until the 1970s, the Brazilian government believed that a sizeable population would contribute favourably to economic development, besides being crucial for the occupation of such a huge territory. The code of medical ethics even prohibited propaganda for contraception and abortion. Despite this governmental pro-natalist position, family planning was unofficially introduced on a large scale by private international organizations in the 1960s. By the 1980s, the rate of sexually active women in reproductive age using contraception was 71 per cent, similar to that of Europe and the US, leading to a significant decrease in fertility rates. Yet, while women in the North have access to a wide range of contraceptives, this is not the case in Brazil, where the absence of the state has allowed manufacturers complete control of supply. The pill and sterilization, regardless of the women's physical or social conditions, were practically the only contraception available (Pitanguy, 1994).

One of the main reasons for the absence of the state in this area has been, and still is, the pressure of the Catholic Church, a major interlocutor of government, civilian or military, in matters concerning reproduction. In daily life, most Brazilian women, needing to regulate their fertility, do not follow the strict Catholic principles such as the exclusive use of natural methods of family planning. However, the Church hierarchy influences public policy and legislation regarding this issue, creating pressure to impede the use of contraception, especially the IUD, considered equivalent to abortion, and sterilization, seen as a mutilation; to prevent public hospitals from providing legal abortions in cases of rape and of risk to life; and even to impede educational campaigns on the use of condoms in the context of the AIDS epidemic.

Structural changes, such as the massive female entry into the labour market, the increasing impoverishment of the rural and urban labour force, urbanization, and growing access to contraception or to voluntary, clandestine abortion,[2] coupled with the government's *laissez-faire* policy toward private foreign anti-natalist organizations, explain the demographic transition. Faria's (1989) meticulous analysis of government policies under military rule, however, points to some overlooked factors, such as the building of a modern telecommunications infrastructure throughout Brazil. Despite wage deterioration, direct consumer credit made the acquisition of durable goods, mainly household appliances such as television and radio, possible. Exposure to the media encouraged consumption, introduced and reinforced positive images of medical, technical, and scientific developments and new values, attitudes, and models related to sexuality, family, and social status. Modernity and a capitalist rationale, both favouring small families, were promoted in this decade as dominant cultural values. The legitimation of medical authority and intervention in health care sanctioned conscious intervention in biological processes. However, while the new demand for contraception came from all segments of the population, but the state failed to provide a programme on family planning, the supply was left to the market, and consequently poorer people have faced tremendous difficulties in attempting to regulate their fertility.

Brazil's official position towards family planning changed during the 1970s and 1980s, when the economic model based on the premise that 'the cake should grow first, to be shared later' showed symptoms of decline. Decreases in the growth rate of the GNP, the burden of an increasing external debt, and the perverse social effects of this model, including even an increase in child mortality in certain parts of the country, reinforced by the prevailing values of modernity and the advancement of neo-malthusian population theories, account for this change.

Internationally, Brazil has taken different positions in the UN Conferences on Population, according to its internal policies and international alliances. At the Bucharest Conference in 1974, the government, along with the rest of the Group of 77,[3] countered Northern countries' pledge for contraception as a key instrument of development with the argument that development in itself was the best contraceptive. At the 1984 Mexico Conference, the G-77 did not reach such a consensual position; Brazil had already embraced a more neo-malthusian outlook (Germaine and Pitanguy, 1994). At Cairo's 1994 Conference, the international women's health movement had gained maturity and visibility. One of the main achievements of that meeting was to place the debates on population within a new paradigm, that of reproductive health and rights. Brazil, now under a democratic system, had, in spite of the Church's pressures, adopted a reproductive health programme that included the constitutional right of couples to choose the number of children they have. It therefore supported these changes, for which women's movements had fought for decades. Beijing's 1995 Women's Conference confirmed Cairo's achievements and moved beyond them, recommending, for example, the review of punishments of women who had had an abortion, already seen in Cairo as a public health issue.

Political mobilization during the 1960s consisted of a general opposition to the government, demanding civic rights and economic reforms. During the 1970s, the political scene became more complex, with the appearance of new actors on the stage: women's movements emerged in Brazil along with other social movements. In the late 1970s and early 1980s, in a context of a political opening,[4] labour unions revived and social movements were strengthened, addressing issues of social inequality other than class, such as gender, race, and ethnicity, in the formulation of a new concept of democracy (Pitanguy, 1994).

The feminist agenda, encompassing issues such as domestic violence, gender equality in the labour market and in family law, the right to choose when and if to have children, and the decriminalization of abortion, gained visibility throughout the late 1970s and 1980s, bringing new themes to the political discourse of Brazilian society, and playing a crucial role in the political process of the affirmation and expansion of reproductive rights.

Organized in groups all over the country, and also working within other organizations such as political parties, labour unions, the bar and other professional and civic entities, women's rights activists gained some influence in politics as the feminist movement was among the first to gain access to government. When the democratic opposition won the elections for governors in the more important states of the country, feminists pushed for the creation of institutional machinery within these governments. The first State Councils for Women's Rights were created in São Paulo and Minas Gerais in 1983. Today, there are approximately 15 of these councils working at municipal and state level. In 1985, also in São Paulo, the first specialized women's police station (DEAM), serving victims of domestic violence, was created. This experience of providing a space within the police apparatus where domestic violence was seen and dealt with as a crime has been spreading throughout the country, and today there are approximately 200 DEAMs in operation, five of which are in the state of Rio de Janeiro. Also in 1985, a very important step was taken in the direction of governmental commitment towards women, with the creation of the National Council for Women's Rights (CNDM), an organ advising the Presidency and ministries on federal policies regarding women. This organ had a mandate to propose new laws, to suppress discriminatory ones, and to develop its own programmes in the areas of violence, health, labour, education, and culture. When the new constitution was written and voted on at the national congress (1986–88), CNDM worked jointly with domestic workers' organizations, among others, to propose constitutional provision of their social rights.

## Domestic service in Brazil

Whereas in the 1970s, during the period of economic growth, there was a significant increase in the number of jobs in the industrial sector, this was not the case in the 1980s, when the decline of the economy, including the steady decay of the agricultural sector, led to a significant increase in the relative weight of the tertiary sector. This general trend is especially noticeable in regard to women's whereabouts in the labour force: in 1977, 59.4 per cent of working women worked in the service sector, rising to 72.6 per cent in 1988 (CEPIA/FLACSO, 1993).

Paid domestic service is the activity that absorbs most of the female urban labour force. There are an estimated eleven million domestics in Brazil, about 350,000 in the State of Rio de Janeiro (including those with formal and informal work relations). This is one of the few options open to unqualified women. Domestic workers are predominantly women of colour, migrants from rural areas, Catholic, earning between one and two minimum wages (US$110–220 per month) and who have not completed the first five years of basic education; there is a high incidence of illiteracy. Thus, our sample, on which the case study is based, is taken from one of the poorest social groups in Brazil.

Until 1888, when slavery was finally abolished in the country, domestic service was carried out by slaves of African descent. Capitalism maintains, sometimes re-creates, pre-capitalist activities which coexist with it (Saffiotti, 1978; Souza, 1980). Redefined in Brazil by the introduction of wages, domestic service nevertheless continued to be loaded with slavish symbolism. Because it takes place in private, domestic work was not subject to any legislation until 1972. In 1988, under the new constitution, domestic workers gained additional social and labour rights. But they still constitute the only sector of the urban workforce not entitled to the full range of rights to which other occupations are entitled. This is a general trend that permeates other Latin American countries (Chaney and Castro, 1989).

The attainment, even if only partial, of legislation has been a critical factor in the improvement of conditions for domestics, as well as for a change in their expectations and social representation. Underlying and supporting these changes is the increasingly prevalent notion of *cidadania* (citizenship), which emerged with the transition to democracy in the early 1980s. This concept is incompatible with older socio-cultural patterns, and gradually contributed to their breakdown. The labour legislation reinforces the notions of rights, and establishes a new model of interaction between employer and employee. Although rights and obligations are frequently infringed, the judicial system is quite effective in enforcing the legislation, much more so than in other areas.

Working conditions vary according to the type of employment sought. Domestics can choose to live in or not. Live-in domestics face longer work hours, greater emotional, economic and social dependency on employers, and more isolation. Those who return home every day face arduous journeys. The latter group has the choice of working in one or more homes every week. Those who work at least three times a week in the same household are protected under the legislation mentioned above. Domestics who work on a daily basis in different homes earn more money, but the work is heavier and they have no legal rights. Despite the variation in work conditions, they all share the hardships of this type of employment.

Far from being a means of social improvement (Souza, 1980; Rubbo and Taussig, 1983), domestic work is a survival strategy for those most disadvantaged in terms of income, gender and race. They suffer not only from low wages, but also from the sparse allocation of social benefits: they are poorly served by housing, sanitation, transport, health and education.

Besides the legal and work conditions that distinguish the domestic worker from other workers, the nature of her work is also distinct. It is one of the few employment relationships involving two women (Rillins, 1985), determined by conditions of class and race. They share the domestic universe with unequal power, with the complementary roles of supervision and performance, making the relationship tense and conflicting. The relationship between employer and domestic is critical for the reproduction of social inequality within the family, where the tasks of giving and receiving orders are socialized. This socialization process involves socio-economic as well as psychological and symbolic factors that reinforce dependency (de Mello e Souza, 1990). Racial and class tensions are reproduced in the employer–employee relationship. At the same time, by performing the housework, the domestic eliminates from marital relationships possible tensions resulting from the sexual division of labour.

Job satisfaction for the domestic worker is determined first and foremost by her relationship with her employer and with the family.[5] There
is an expectation of friendship with the employer, where friendship is
frequently defined as a mother–daughter relationship,[6] reinforced by the
perpetual infantilism with which women employers treat them.[7] Some
domestic workers seem to try to satisfy their emotional needs through
their relationship with the employer's children, who take the place of
the children they never had or could not bring up (LENIRA, 1982).
The emotional need to personalize work relationships comes from social
and affective privations in childhood,[8] as well as from work conditions,
which limit horizontal social contact and the formation of family ties.
Consequently, when appraising her job, conditions of work become
important to the domestic only when there is no emotional bond with
the family.

The psycho–social dynamic of the employer–domestic relationship
reinforces patronage and consequently the mystification of exploitation.
Identification with the employer is common, particularly for the live-in
domestic worker who has no other models, and frequently acquires the
style of dress, the intonation and expressions of her employer (Kofes,
1982; LENIRA, 1982). This identification increases the competition
between both women, and also the distance between the domestic worker
and her family of origin. The idealization and sense of identification
with the employer overrides the sense of exploitation and dependence,
thus hindering the development of class consciousness (Jelin, 1977: 138).
This lack of perception of exploitation is aggravated by the aspiration
to become a 'member of the family', and the isolated nature of their
work. Due to the social devaluation of their work, and the lack of
perception of themselves as a political and economic force, domestic
workers present one of the lowest levels of union membership, lower
than that of other female workers.

The Association of Domestic Workers, like other social movements
in the 1960s and 1970s, had its beginnings in Catholic groups. According
to union leader Aparecida, 'the Association began in JOC, Young
Catholic Workers, as a group of domestic workers who became conscious
of the importance of having an organization to defend their interests'.
JOC integrated many different categories of workers, and the domestic
workers realized that others had unions to defend their rights, and they
'were the only ones who did not'. In the words of a union leader:

> It happened in Copacabana [a district in Southern Rio]. I was passing and I
> saw a group of people surrounding a woman on the steps of a church. During
> the conversation, I found out that she had worked seventeen years as a maid,

had a stroke and ended up in a hospital. When she left, she was unable to work. Now she was there, in the street with her things, crying, homeless, without a family, begging. This happened in 1960. I foresaw my own future there, and vowed things would not stay that way. I spoke to one colleague, then to another, and we got a group together. We met in the streets, in the squares. The group grew. I learned that other domestic workers like me were becoming aware of their situation. New groups were formed.

The Association of Domestic Workers of Rio de Janeiro was established on 28 January 1961, by 18 women. Domestic workers in other states were also beginning to organize, and they held their first national meeting in São Paulo in 1968.

The association, which gained union status only in 1989, currently has over 2,000 members. In the city of Rio, there are about 90,000 domestic workers, according to the union's directors' estimates. Members pay a monthly fee of 1 per cent of a minimum wage, but, during our fieldwork, only about 400 members had fully paid their dues.

Domestic workers face particular difficulties in participating, such as an undefined work schedule for those who live in, and long journeys and family responsibilities for those who don't. As a result, activists present a profile also seen in other social movements: post-menopausal women with no children or grown children. In addition, union participation is often seen, by both employers and domestic workers, as a breach of a supposed pact of loyalty; union leaders tell of the fear of some members that their employers might find out that they are affiliated or attend union activities. The domestic worker who is a member of a union and conscious of her rights appears to some employers as a threat.

Nevertheless, particularly in large urban centres, domestic workers are organizing so as to obtain rights already achieved by other workers, such as the delimitation of work hours. They have also established national and continental networks to strengthen the domestic workers' movement. The Union of Domestic Workers of the City of Rio de Janeiro actively participates in this struggle, by trying to increase the number of members, linking up with other groups in other municipalities of the State, and by integrating in the Confederación Latino-americana y del Caribe de Trabajadoras del Hogar (CONLACTRAHO).

## Research methodology

Our research was carried out in Rio de Janeiro, Brazil's second largest city. Rio has been a major economic and cultural centre, attracting migrants from all parts of the country. Until 1960, Rio was the national capital, with its economy largely supported by the service sector. After the transfer of the political centre to Brasilia, Rio has been suffering a systematic process of impoverishment. Besides the six million inhabitants of the city proper, there are another six million in the surrounding districts, which make up the metropolitan area of Greater Rio. A large part of the low-income population lives in these suburbs, including domestic workers, who daily face long, expensive journeys to work.

Our sample consisted of female domestic workers, most of whom were active members of their union. This choice was based on the fact that domestic work accounts for most female urban employment, and domestics are thus representative of one of the largest occupational groups in Brazil.

Our sample gradually increased with the use of various reseach instruments, and the need to diversify demographically, so that variations in age, marital status, union membership and working conditions could be considered. We worked initially with the board of directors of the Union of Domestic Workers – mainly single, post-menopausal women not involved in a relationship – in group interviews. Then a focal group on reproductive health was organized with 21 members of the union, followed by the application of a questionnaire to a larger and more diverse group: 45 domestic workers, of which eight were directors of the union, 18 members of the union, and 19 domestics who were selected in the union's waiting room. The latter group had distinct characteristics: unemployed, with an average age of 39 (the other groups' average age was 48), and half of them married. Finally, in-depth interviews were conducted with 14 workers: nine directors over 50, and five non-members between 25 and 35. Eighty-two per cent of research participants were women of colour, which reflects national statistics on race, ethnicity and domestic service. Most of them were Catholic, and had not completed elementary school. Most union directors and members were single and lived in, while non-members were married or separated and commuted to work. The union was central in arranging contacts with all the women who participated in the project. Some women participated in all phases of the data collection, and the total number of participating domestics was 48.

## Reproduction and poverty: family roles and subsistence

Domestic workers devote themselves to the tasks involved in social reproduction throughout their lives, owing to the socio-economic conditions of their families of origin. As children they find little stability in family life. They are passed around the homes of relatives or friends and neighbours. This circulation of children is common as a subsistence strategy in different regions of Brazil.[9] Girls start doing housework very early. At the age of 4 or 5 they start helping with child care so that their mothers can work in the plantations. They complain of being driven as slaves by their own mothers, as well as by other female relatives who take them in. Thus work dominates their lives, and their life histories overlap almost completely with their work histories.

At the age of about 6, they also start accompanying their mothers to the fields. Family life is dominated by collective effort geared to family subsistence, though there is a large gap between the quality and quantity of the workload of sons and daughters. Daughters have a significantly greater workload and are expected to handle any kind of work. Sons do very little housework (mainly chopping wood and fetching water) because most domestic chores are thought of as feminine. While boys are paid for their work, and can usually keep part of their money, girls are rarely allowed to keep theirs. Thus, within the family, the sexual division of labour socializes girls for the double shift and a certain readiness to take on whatever needs to be done for the family's subsistence and not for their own gain. Girls are socialized to obey orders and to be responsible for social reproduction. When they start looking for work outside the home, they are qualified only for agricultural or domestic work (and even so they need additional training to work in the homes of urban middle- and upper-class families, since the demands of these households are so different from their own). In an attempt to make more money than the meagre and unstable wages of rural workers, they migrate to cities where domestic work is the only job for which they are qualified.

The migration process starts with a relative or friend in the city who finds a job for the young woman. Domestic work at this point is quite convenient, because it combines employment with room and board, but the drawback is that it does not offer the migrant a new community of peers, and it places her in a work relationship where she is extremely dependent. Employment is found through connections, of which she has very few. In addition, she is undergoing a process of adjustment to urban life, which involves learning the tasks of social reproduction in middle- and upper-class families.

As domestic workers they re-engage in the tasks of social reproduction, disconnected from biological reproduction. These women are thus filling in for another woman who is mother and housewife: first their own mother (or other relative) and then their employer. Within their family of origin, one daughter frequently postpones or gives up the chance of marriage because of her responsibilities in her parents' household. As domestic workers, they cannot adequately assume the social reproduction of two families nor economically support one of their own. Knowing that marriage and child-bearing will jeopardize their employment, and that they will not be able to provide for and mother their children, many of them bypass the option of having families of their own. As Honória, one of the directors of the union, told us, 'It is forbidden for a domestic worker to have kids. How will you raise a child in a "madam's" house? You have to have your own place and raise them like you were raised.' In addition, the isolated nature of their work and the lack of community and contact with men from their own background make it difficult for domestic workers to find a partner. If, however, they do marry and have children, many of them will not be the primary carers.

In a life marked by lack of choice, social reproduction is imposed while biological reproduction is prohibited. Such conditions are central in women's reproductive decision-making, as discussed below. Social reproduction becomes the equivalent to production, acting as the structuring factor of these women's lives.

Domestic work is the only means of subsistence in urban areas for women who are at the bottom of the social pyramid owning to their socio-economic class, gender, and race. Social mobility or occupational change are very remote. Education and marriage are possible channels for mobility, but these must surmount the obstacles of long hours or long journeys, and the isolation which is part of the nature of the job. These hardships also interfere with women's sense of autonomy and self-determination. The entrapment of domestic work is summed up in their own words: 'I am a domestic because I do not know how to do anything else. I do not know how to do anything else because I am a domestic.'

## Sexuality and reproduction: cultural norms, values, and beliefs

From childhood to old age, life is marked by transitions and ruptures which introduce different 'classes of age'.[10] The elements that define these classes, although ultimately related to chronological age, are in fact related to the way this chronology is translated into social and cultural terms. It is possible, therefore, to say that throughout their lives, people are always related to one of these classes of age, whose values and codes mark their most intimate experiences. One's sense of uniqueness can only be understood within these broader collective parameters. In many societies, these classes of age also represent specific constituencies with demands for particular rights. Many countries have special laws and norms for the children and the elderly, for instance.

These classes of age are also surrounded by behavioural norms, taboos, and rituals, which usually vary significantly between men and women according to the patterns of gender relations prevailing in that society. Although the relations of men and women to their classes of age are mediated by a complex network of variables, gender seems to play a key role, cutting across social class and race, introducing strong differences for men and women in the way they symbolically and concretely experience their life cycles.

The concept of different classes of age is particularly important for the analysis of our findings, for certain values regarding sexuality and reproduction will entail normative behaviour according to age group. The domestics in our sample come from a rural background, which means having been raised within a traditional value system. These traditional values are frequently transformed or replaced after exposure to urban life. Nevertheless, they constitute a frame of reference for these women regarding their childhood and adolescence on the one hand, and how they raise their daughters on the other. Our description of this value system by no means implies its survival intact, nor a rigidity, but rather a reconstitution of an ethos whose traits often emerged throughout our research.

Central to this value system is a belief in the natural differentiation between men and women, and a notion of female honour that justifies attitudes, norms, and representations regarding gender, sexuality, and reproduction. These women's first images of femininity were deeply marked by ideas of purity regarding their body and their sexuality.

The meaning of purity and virginity is extensive, encompassing sexual knowledge, desire and experience in very general terms. This includes avoidance of anything with a sexual connotation, such as images, words and conversations. The female mind and body must be preserved from the pollution of sexuality: no bodily contact between the opposite sexes, no exposure of the body to the masculine gaze, and no verbal stimulation of sexual desire, knowledge or curiosity. In short, the preservation of female honour instils an inter-generational silence on all sexual and reproductive matters between sexually active women and virgins, and it confines women to the domestic sphere, completely immersed in family life under the protection of their father (in their family of origin) and later of their husband (in their own family), whom they must obey.

> My mother was not the kind to talk with us and we were very private. 'Don't hang around with other girls, because they can be a bad influence on you; friends will only take advantage of you.' So she preserved us, pushed us to church all the time. If we wanted to go to a party, she would not let us go with friends in case we picked up bad habits. (Maria do Carmo)

Sexual experience, through its embedded meanings of purity and pollution, separates women into two different classes.

Since female honour is a requirement for marriage in rural settings, it is assumed (unless there is explicit evidence to the contrary) that unmarried women are innocent virgins who cannot be contaminated with sexual matters lest they compromise their value in the marriage market. Underlying the value of honour and virginity is the conception of the female body as an object, whose value increases or decreases according to purity, contamination, and pollution (Grupo CERES, 1981).[11] This product, like others in the market, loses value with use.

Silence about sexuality is a strategy for preserving female honour and enhancing her worth, but it entails control by women themselves and learned behaviour. Since marriage and motherhood are the goals of women's lives, it becomes clear why extensive efforts are made to preserve a daughter or sister in a sexually pure state. Within marriage, sexuality is a wife's duty toward her husband and is limited to her husband. For women, the alternative to the virgin turned wife and mother is the negative image of the whore. A woman's body is dangerous territory which must not be managed by the woman herself but by others. Confinement to the domestic space and devotion to familial tasks maintains her honourable state throughout life. Women's role as mothers outweighs any other, and is therefore central to their social identity. Deviations from this normative trajectory are frequent in urban areas, especially as women adapt to new life styles and become independent of their family of origin. Today, in urban settings, there is a rupture in this pattern of evaluation of femininity, since some would become even more acceptable and desirable if they combined domestic tasks and work outside the home. The 1981 research findings of *Espelho de Venus* reveal a greater commitment to traditional values, especially that of female honour. Fifteen years later, our research with domestics points to significant differences, mainly due to the increasing role of the mass media in the diffusion of the values of modernity, but also to similarities regarding attitudes to sexuality, mainly in regard to the role of silence between classes of age.

These traditional values, images and messages become confused and ambiguous within urban culture, where people are quick to catch on to the dubious and often contradictory traits associated with the ideal woman, who is increasingly more aggressive and androgynous. It is also necessary to take into account our research group being composed mainly of women over 40, who refer to a childhood lived prior to the spread of urban culture in rural settings, especially regarding sexuality and the role of women in society. These are arriving more and more in rural areas through TV soap operas and radio programmes. Yet a double moral standard still encourages male sexual initiative and aggressive performance as the basis of a man's identity, even after marriage. Masculinity is affirmed through these traits, while a certain restraint is expected in female sexual behaviour.

## Inter-group silence and information from informal networks

Van Gennep (1960) points out how rites of passage are crucial in the shaping of individual identities and in giving a sense of order to the ambiguity of social life. Two events, menstruation and sexual initiation, which function as rites of passage, with different impact according to the social context, separate women into three distinct groups. With a girl's first period she passes from the status of *menina* (girl) to that of *moça* (virgin young lady). Through sexual intercourse (supposedly at marriage), she becomes a *mulher* (woman). Among domestic workers, our findings point to each of these three stages in the life cycle being connected to corresponding information concerning the body that should not be shared with the younger groups. One must have experienced puberty and sex to be able to speak about it or to hear others do so. To mention such topics in the presence of a *menina* (pre-menstruating female) would be disrespectful.

Adolescence is a relatively recent classification, resulting from economic, demographic and cultural changes that took place basically in affluent Western societies. The time span in which individuals can remain adolescents depends largely on socio-economic criteria and cultural values. In situations of poverty, childhood is but a brief period before the burdens of adulthood. Girls menstruate between the ages of 9 and 12 in Brazil, and with this rite of passage usually begin dating. Early pregnancy or marriage also abruptly shortens adolescence for these women, who frequently pass from childhood to adulthood with adolescence a brief transitional period. In Brazil, the age group 15–19 is the only one in which fertility rates are increasing. Sexual maturation and initiation are determining markers in the female life course.

Inter-group silence is most evident in our data concerning menstruation. Approximately half of the women knew nothing about the onset of menstruation and were completely taken by surprise and frightened by their first period. Only after the event would a female relative or friend take them aside and explain that the bleeding would be a normal, monthly occurrence from then on. Although they felt a change in status – as *moças* (virgins, young ladies) they could date and participate in the conversations of other *moças* – they were not informed of their new physiological ability to reproduce. The other half of the women interviewed knew something about it through a friend, aunt or sister, or overhearing conversations, though this knowledge was fragmentary and incomplete. What they all had in common, however, was that their mothers appeared the most silent of all. 'She was too shy to talk about such things with me,' they said.

Although experienced at different ages, the first sexual relation is also perceived as a rite of passage toward womanhood, her introduction into a new class of age. This is also a moment of ambiguity, where mixed messages of purity and correct behaviour are in conflict with the idea of being attractive and seductive. 'So I wanted to do a lot of things with him, but with the education I received I shouldn't. A woman should know how to behave.'[12]

Even after they are married, women do not learn anything about sexuality or reproduction from their mothers. Usually, friends or neighbours are the chief source of information about contraception, and the people with whom they share their experiences. For two of the women, with a higher educational level and socio–economic background, the medical system was their main source of information. Perhaps the gynaecologist did not appear more often in our data because most of the women in our sample were post-menopausal, sexually inactive women. In addition, access to public health care is difficult, expensive and time-consuming, while the medical appointment itself is so brief that there is no time to inform and educate the patient.

Television, however, is a very important source of information. It reaches Brazilian homes like no other appliance, in all classes and regions of the country, showing a way of life and a worldview dominated by consumption. In Brazil, there are approximately 35 million TV sets, which serve an average of three people, suggesting that well over 100 million Brazilians are exposed to television. Although the media have been very important in changing mores and customs, TV has been basically silent in terms of factual information about family planning. Only recently, due to the AIDS epidemic, has television been used by the government for educational campaigns promoting the use of condoms. AIDS has also brought new issues to the mass media. Casual sex, homosexuality, and the call for a more active female role in protecting women from STDs are themes of TV and radio programmes, and even of prime-time soap operas.

The widespread influence of the media is confirmed by our sample of domestics, who reported television and radio as their chief leisure activity. For many domestics, who have minimal social contact during a day of work, the radio keeps them company while they cook and clean homes, and television entertains them during evenings and at weekends, and in turn informs and educates them about local, national and international events. They refer to television as a source of information, much more than other media, especially with regard to the public sphere. In the realm of sexuality and reproduction, they report having learned from the media more about AIDS than any other reproductive health and rights issue.

## Gender relations, work, and sexuality: inter-generational changes

Although normative culture values women's devotion to family and household, and delimits her space to the domestic, women are increasingly working outside the home. Work brings about significant changes in gender roles and relations. First, work allows a woman to enter and become mobile in the public sphere. Rather than confined to her home, she gains the freedom of 'coming and going' as the women themselves put it. Second, she gains economic independence, which means not depending on a man for her subsistence, and being in a position to negotiate the family budget and the sexual division of labour. As a consequence, she becomes more autonomous, self-assured, conscious of her rights. Through the experience of work, women start making demands within the home and perceiving themselves to be equal to their partners, although they still struggle to handle the double shift.

'My husband was always against me working. But when I had to, he had no choice. Then I think he liked it. When I worked, everything I earned went towards covering what we needed at home. ... And now I make demands too. He accepted it and will have to do so in the future' (Selma, 27-year-old domestic worker). This perception of equality is gradually extended to more areas of their lives and relationships. It becomes a standard to evaluate different aspects of their marriage: the division of labour, family decisions and sexuality.

The value of work in shaping women's identity was highlighted in the research (Arilha et al., 1995 and Grupo CERES, 1981). 'I think the world would be better if all women had an occupation and a responsibility. I am here, ironing, with a lot of responsibility.'[13]

The importance of perceiving herself as someone capable of mobility and autonomy resulting from her participation in the labour force is particularly relevant if we consider that throughout their childhood and adolescence, unlike their brothers, girls are restricted in their spatial mobility. Although this was a major complaint in our interviews, most women who have children believe that differential socialization is necessary for sons and daughters, though they do not wish to confine their daughters to the extent that they themselves were confined.

Adolescence, which coincides, for most of our informants, with their entry into the labour force, is also a time of sexual discovery and exploration. Several women secretly engaged in sexual intercourse with their boyfriends. The boyfriends were key figures in their sexual socialization, for they frequently provided information unavailable elsewhere. In two cases, they also arranged for a gynaecological consultation for the prescription of birth control. This is the time in a woman's life cycle when the man is most involved in contraception, perhaps because the stakes are so high: impregnating an unmarried woman will bring serious trouble from her family.

> Well, I was going to have sex with my fiancé and we were afraid I could get pregnant. My mother was very strict, but I was also very young, and afraid of her. ... So he said: 'let's go to the doctor', and I said 'no way'. 'We have to go because if you get pregnant your mother will kill both of us.' And my father! He would strangle him! He was afraid of my father. I was kind of irresponsible. I didn't care about these things. (Cila, 31-year-old domestic worker)

Man's relevance at this moment is related to his role as her initiator in sexual life, the person from whom a woman learns what sexuality is. The emphasis on the male figure as the provider of information and experience is accentuated, as the values of purity and honour for women and performance and expertise for men are deeply introjected.

For those domestic workers who lived where they worked during this period, dating was more difficult. They complained that their job situation, in middle-class neighbourhoods, limited their contact with working-class men. For some of these women, employers directly sabotaged romantic relationships. In any case, if they did fall pregnant, our data indicate that the perceived impossibility of having children as a domestic leads some of them to seek an abortion, although they would have preferred to have a child. The social representation and cultural value of men changes throughout the life cycle. Men are appreciated most during adolescence, during dating and courting. Many married women said that alcoholic and physically abusive husbands were responsible for much of their suffering. Nevertheless, married women in their twenties and thirties with 'nothing really to complain about', who described their husbands as 'good men, good companions', perceive their spouses as first and foremost people who control them and interfere in their freedom. All in all, although there are great differences in degree, women perceive their husbands as a burden.

When my husband is at home, he seems to be watching me all the time. He asks for something to eat, 'oh, come here', and then he wants to chat about something. But when I am alone, I feel different, I feel free and light-hearted, able to sing, to yell, to put the radio on really loud, to listen to whatever music I feel like listening to. Sometimes there is a song I like to listen to because I like the lyrics. And then he thinks I like it and listen to it because I have another man on my mind. (Selma, 27-year-old domestic worker)

In their discourse, these women did not appreciate their husbands as providers, as sexual partners, nor for the marital status they confer, nor the symbolic value of 'having a man', as is commonly the case among women from middle and upper segments of the population. Marriage and motherhood, the central elements of female identity, are experienced by these women as oppressive. Among domestic workers who commute, perhaps as a consequence of the experience of freedom that comes from work outside the home, many perceive the traditional role of housewife as imprisoning. Husbands and children are often felt as limitations to their freedom, and they agree in pointing to late adolescence as the happiest time of their lives.

When I was single, I had no worries. What I most want is that my kids turn out OK, but you are always worrying about something, from the moment you know you're pregnant. You worry about birth. Then after the baby is born, you worry about a cough, illness, and then school, and then jobs. So in the end you can no longer be happy after you have children. Mothers can no longer be happy; when I was single, there was nothing of this. There was just me and that was it. (Lenice, 46-year-old house cleaner)

As a result, with the experience generated from work and parenting, women have become increasingly motivated to control their fertility throughout their life cycle. The most significant inter-generational change in reproductive choice is the reduction of the ideal number of children, revealing a transition in the Brazilian family in different regions and socio-economic classes.[14] The tradition of having many children, in which children are said to 'raise themselves', is supplanted by the modern conception of the family with one, two, or three children, justified by the hardships of everyday life. Such hardships include women working outside the home, low wages, and single parenthood. This new model is shared by old and young, who refer to the past as 'different times'. Motivated by an aspiration to social mobility, these mothers want to have fewer children so that they can provide and care for them better. 'I want them to be more educated than I was and to be able to be somebody, have more choices than I had,' they all say. Thus, we perceive that smaller families entail rearing children differently and having different aspirations for them as well.

Along with menarche and sexual initiation, menopause also introduces women into a new class of age. While menopause clearly marked the end of female fertility for these women's mothers, many women today actively interfere in their physiology by choosing tubal ligation as a method of birth control. While some report a more relaxed sexuality after surgery, most women believe sterilization brings about frigidity. Such belief often spares them from the perceived marital obligation to be sexually available to their husbands, who seek sex daily. Others, separated from their husbands, choose sexual abstinence. In any case, the class of age encompassing menopausal and post-menopausal women is associated with sexual inactivity. The live-in domestics we worked with in this age group consider sexuality 'something of the past'.[15]

Menopause is a process surrounded by contradictory feelings, related on the one hand to an increase in freedom and autonomy (children are grown up and autonomous domestic workers are usually active in the labour market long past menopause), and on the other hand to a perception of loss in such social values as sexual attraction and fertility.

## Reproduction, medical culture and women's choices

The inter-group silence discussed above, and women's lack of access to adequate information concerning reproductive health, reinforce the notion that there is a reproductive career inherent to women's condition and lives. The concept of 'reproductive career' is useful here, for it allows us to see certain patterns of behaviour and attitudes throughout the life cycle. The predominant trajectory in our data is as follows. The young woman is sexually initiated during adolescence with a more experienced and/or knowledgeable boyfriend (or husband). She is not concerned with contraception, though he (the boyfriend) is. She falls pregnant and marries. With recurring pregnancies, she gradually becomes more concerned and active in her contraceptive attempts. Nevertheless, negative experiences with the pill, lack of knowledge of alternatives and male prejudice against condoms lead her to give up on contraceptive aids at least temporarily, substituting for it withdrawal, the rhythm method, or nothing at all. When she is past her ideal family size (which varies between one and three children), she becomes quite desperate and will seek sterilization at all costs. Thus, it is women's own reproductive experience and career, linked to their model of ideal family size and their accumulated knowledge about contraception and reproduction, that will provoke this gradual change from a passive to an active attitude.

Structural factors limit the reproductive choices that poor urban women make. Besides socio-economic conditions and job constraints, the health-care system to which they have access will determine their chances of adequate care and the information they receive. In Brazil, the public health-care system is precarious and often inaccessible. Furthermore, economic constraints, such as the extra expense of the bus fare or a day of work that must be missed to see a doctor, interfere directly in domestics' ability to seek care. Poverty interferes indirectly too, through illiteracy or limited education and the inaccessibility of written information. In short, access to medical information is scarce and limited to infrequent and short medical appointments.

Such limited medical information cannot be checked or expanded except through an informal network of personal relations. Since the doctor does not have the time nor the proper conditions to allow him/her to inform the patient adequately for the patient herself to make an informed decision, this process is abbreviated, according to his/her own perceptions of the lower-class patient, values regarding gender and sexuality, and scant medical education on contraception. Efficacy and efficiency are valued by medical professionals, who justify their preference for the pill and female sterilization for poor patients by considering their burdened life styles, their economic limitations and the hardships of child rearing. Within this dominant medical view, women cannot or should not have the necessary control over their sexual relationship to guarantee the efficient use of barrier methods, for example. Contraception should not interfere in the sexual encounter, and birth control methods that disconnect the two are preferred. Thus, contraceptive choice privileges male convenience. Cultural conceptions of gender also shape medical recommendations.

Our data indicate that women who seek medical guidance about contraception are not informed of all their options and what each one entails, though medical discourse is constructed in such a way as to convey the feeling that there is choice. For example, in one woman's account of seeking medical guidance for contraception:

> *Cila*: We [my boyfriend and I] went to the doctor, his family's doctor. He requested all those exams and then he said: you have three to choose from. I will prescribe you three and you choose whichever one you want. So I chose *Microvolar* and I stuck to it.
> *Cecilia*: But did he mention any other option? The IUD? Anything else?
> *Cila*: No, because he is against the IUD.

The contraceptive pill is regarded by doctors and their patients to be *the* birth control method, and is recommended professionally as such.

Both doctors and patients consider various brands of the pill as constituting the alternatives, as in the example above. Thus, medical assistance discards all other possibilities, apart from an occasional attempt to use the IUD. The doctor–patient relationship is based on patronage in which the doctor is the powerful authority who cares for the needy patient.[16] This kind of relationship leaves no room for critical evaluation of the medical care received by the patient.

Although the impact of medical culture may not be direct (if women do not seek medical care frequently throughout the life cycle), it is none the less present and influential in indirect ways, such as via the media. The hegemonic influence of the medical system has contributed to the legitimation and standardization of a specific reproductive trajectory, with overuse of the contraceptive pill, sterilization, and caesarean sections as routine procedures for everyone.[17]

## Conclusion

The life cycle approach is central in our analysis of how women's social and family status changes according to sexual and reproductive norms appropriate to their class of age. Menstruation, sexual initiation, motherhood and menopause have traditionally been significant moments of passage for women. More recently, competing values have introduced significant changes in women's lives, such as work and a smaller family. This has been achieved at the cost of an overburdened reproductive and productive body, which has suffered from clandestine abortions, pregnancy and birth under precarious health-care conditions, and the difficult side-effects of the pill and early sterilization. The need and desire to limit fertility is experienced in the context of the historical failure of Brazilian governments to provide a wide range of reversible contraception to low-income women and men. Female sterilization is so widespread that it is even possible to recognize the existence of a normative cultural construction of sterilization, in both rural and urban areas. Medical technology has thus introduced a new marker in women's lives: sterilization as the end of fertility and biological reproduction. This marker is more explicit in their discourse than menopause – a subject also treated as taboo.

Our research reveals that work and activism have been key elements for empowering these women. The nature of their work, domestic service, is subjecting and imprisoning, and they have, throughout the years, managed to resist and negotiate many times, though at others they have acquiesced to unfavourable working conditions. But work, for married women especially, has introduced mobility, autonomy, economic independence, and notions of equality into their lives and relationships. Overall, the balance seems to have been positive. The elaboration of formal rights in legislation, as is the case with labour rights, has also enabled women to think of themselves within the new framework of *cidadania* (citizenship) and to have access to citizens' rights. On the darker side, women's silence towards younger women regarding sexuality and reproduction, and the overall inaccessibility of information eliminate possibilities of choice and control over their bodies, relationships and lives. The limitations in reproductive choice contribute to the burden of marriage and motherhood, where they do not report finding much happiness.

Our findings thus draw attention to the urgent need for policies addressing the dissemination of information through the educational curriculum, medical services, and the media, especially television and radio. Given the importance of the medical system in providing guidance and information, medical training should be attentive to the relations of power, dependency and contempt toward dominated social groups, which pretend to justify retaining information from the patient. Without such emancipation, it is difficult for women to perceive themselves and act as agents of their own health.

Governmental use of the media in education should be expanded beyond AIDS. Television and radio should include in their programming education on family planning and reproductive choice, on male responsibility towards reproduction and sexual behaviour, and women's rights.

Besides the much-demanded implementation of the governmental programme on sexual and reproductive health (PAISM), women must have the necessary means of seeking health care, such as secure transport and the right to seek medical care without losing wages for missed work. Although we have witnessed the emergence of public policies in the area of biological reproduction, very little has been done in terms of social reproduction, to relieve women from the heavy load of combining work and child care.

Domestics in Brazil and in other countries must be granted the full range of labour rights extended to all other workers. This includes, but is not limited to, established work hours and tasks, paid overtime, and the right to labour benefits independent of the number of days worked per week in the same household. In addition, specific policies geared towards their particular working conditions could ameliorate those that hinder the formation and care of their own families.

We also need to learn more about men's roles in reproductive choice, and how they are coping with such drastic changes in gender roles and family values. If the media are to be important instruments of education, we must investigate how they have been actively informing women and reinforcing certain cultural values regarding reproduction, and how these dominant values have been appropriated by poor women and integrated with their own values and beliefs.

## Notes

1. The IRRRAG (International Reproductive Rights Research Action Group) Project was carried out in seven countries under the co-ordination of Dr Rosalind Petchesky from Hunter College, University of New York. In Brazil, the project was co-ordinated by Ana Paula Portella and involved ten researchers from women's groups in three different states. CEPIA's research in Rio was co-ordinated by Helena Bocayuva and conducted by anthropologists Carmen Dora Guimarces and Cecilia de Mello e Souza. The IRRRAG project aimed at investigating urban women's sense of entitlement and the conception of reproductive rights of poor rural and urban women; how they make reproductive decisions; to what extent they resist and accommodate to cultural norms and behaviour; and how their socio-economic, legal and political contexts impact on their reproductive lives.

2. Although abortions are illegal in Brazil (except in cases of rape or when the woman's life is at risk), there are an estimated 1.4 million abortions performed every year (Alan Guttmacher Institute, 1994).

3. The G-77 is a block of developing countries from different regions, which tends to take consensual positions in UN Conferences.

4. Brazil has gone through a gradual process of democratization, starting in the mid-1970s. Only in 1985 was a civilian president elected.

5. Other studies (de Mello e Souza, 1990; Rubbo and Taussig, 1983; Souza, 1980) have said the same.

6. Salem (1980) notes the frequent construction of the employer–domestic relationship as a mother–daughter relationship, and de Mello e Souza (1990) examines the social and psychological roots of this projection in her life histories of domestics.

7. See Kofes (1982) and LENIRA (1982).

8. As girls, these women were frequently passed around the homes of better-off relatives, friends, or neighbours. Even for those who grew up in their family of origin's household, it is very common to hear from them that a sister raised them or that they in turn raised their younger siblings. In any case, they mothered early in life more than they were mothered and as adults they still long for someone to take care of them. See de Mello e Souza (1990) for a lengthier discussion of how a good employer is frequently defined as 'a good mother'.

9. See Claudia Fonseca's (1986) study of the circulation of children in Porto Alegre, Brazil.

10. Classes of age is a concept used in anthropology to classify age groups within society that share certain attributes, values, norms of behaviour (see citation).

11. The book *Espelho de Vênus, Identidade Social e Sexual da Mulher* (1981) is the result of research conducted by Alves, Barsted, Boschi, Pitanguy and Ribeiro, who formed a feminist group called Grupo CERES. Fifty-three women of different ages and social strata were interviewed, on issues of sexuality throughout their life cycles.

12. Vanda, 23-year-old domestic worker, in *Espelho de Vênus*.

13. Elisa, 47-year-old domestic worker, in *Espelho de Vênus* (p. 382).

14. While the average number of children in the 1960s was 6.0, in the 1980s it dropped to 2.7 (CEPIA/FLACSO, 1993).

15. This conception of menopause also appeared in Quintas's (1987) sample of poor women living in slums in north-eastern Brazil, and in Grupo CERES (1981).

16. Our findings confirm those of Boltanski's (1989) research in France, in which he found that the greater the socio-economic and educational distance between the doctor and the patient, the more submissive the patient.

17. FIBGE's (1987) national household survey (PNAD) found that 70 per cent of Brazilian women between 15 and 54 used some form of contraception. Among these women, 40 per cent were on the pill, 44 per cent were sterilized, and 16 per cent relied on other methods. In some states, approximately 70 per cent of the women in this group were sterilized. C-section rates vary between 35 per cent and 100 per cent, according to the type of clinic or hospital. See Berquó (1993) on the overuse of sterilizations and de Mello e Souza (1994) on the abuse of c-sections.

## References

Alan Guttmacher Institute (1994) *Clandestine Abortion in Latin America*, New York, Alan Guttmacher Institute.

Arilha, M., H. Bocayuva, S. Diniz *et al.*, (1995) 'Brazil', IRRRAG National Research Report, manuscript.

BEMFAM (Sociedade Civil Bem-Estar Familiar no Brasil) and DHS (Programa de Pesquisas de Demografia e Sazde) (1996) Pesquisa Nacional sobre Demografia e Sazde. Relatorio Preliminar. Rio de Janeiro, Brazil/Calverton, MD, USA, September.

Berquó, E. (1993) 'Brasil, um caso exemplar: anticoncepção e partos cirúrgicos à espera de uma ação exemplar', *Revista Estudos Feministas*, Rio de Janeiro, Vol. 1, No. 2.

Boltanski, L. (1979) *As Classes Sociais e o Corpo*, Rio de Janeiro, Graal.

CEPIA/FLACSO (1993) *Mulher em Dados: Brasil*, Santiago, Chile, FLACSO.

Chaney, E. and M. García Castro (eds) (1989) *Muchachas No More: Household Workers in Latin America and the Caribbean*, Philadelphia, Temple University Press.

Douglas, M. (1976) *Purity and Pollution: An Analysis of the Concepts of Pollution and Taboo*, London, Routledge and Kegan Paul.

Faria, V. E. (1989) 'Políticas de governo e regulação da fecundidade: consequências não antecipadas e efeitos perversos', *Ciências Sociais Hoje*, São Paulo, ANPOCS, Vertice.

FIBGE (Fundacão Instituto Brasileiro de Geografia e Estatística) (1987) Pesquisa Nacional de Amostra de Domicilo (PNAD) 1986, Rio de Janeiro.

— (1992a) *Síntese de Indicadores 1989–1990*, Rio de Janeiro.

— (1992b) PNAD 1991, Rio de Janeiro.

Fonseca, C. (1986) 'Orphanages, foundlings and foster mothers: The system of child circulation in a Brazilian squatter settlement', *Anthropological Quarterly*, 59(1).

Germaine, A. and J. Pitanguy (1993) 'Population policies and the women's movement', in *Women and Population Policies*, Santiago, Chile, ISIS International.

Grupo CERES (1981) *Espelho de Vênus: Identidade Social e Sexual da Mulher*, São Paulo, Brasiliense.

Jelin, E. (1977) 'Migration and labour force in Latin America: the domestic servants in the cities', *Signs*, Vol. 3, No. 1.

Kofes, M. S. (1982) 'Entre nós mulheres, elas as patroas e elas as empregadas', *Colcha de Retalhos: Estudos sobre a Família no Brasil*, São Paulo, Brasiliense.

LENIRA (1982) *Só a Gente que Vive É que Sabe: Depoimento de uma Doméstica*, Petrópolis, Vozes.

Mello e Souza, C. de (1990) 'Gender, class, and domestic work: the servant employer relationship in Brazil', paper presented at the Beatrice Bain Conference, University of California, Berkeley.

— (1994) 'C-Sections as ideal births: the social construction of beneficence and patient's rights in Brazil', *Cambridge Quarterly of Healthcare Ethics*, Vol. 3.

Pitanguy, J. (1994) 'Feminist politics and reproductive rights: the case of Brazil', in G. Sen and R. Snow, *Power and Decision: The Social Control of Reproduction*, Boston, Harvard School of Public Health.

Quintas, F. (1987) *Sexo e Marginalidade: Um Estudo sobre a Sexualidade Feminina em Camadas de Baixa Renda*, Petrópolis, Vozes.

Rillins, J. (1985) *Between Women: Domestics and their Employers*, Philadelphia, Temple University Press.

Rubbo, A. and M. Taussig (1983) 'Up off their knees: servanthood in southwest Colombia', *Latin American Perspectives*, Vol. 10, No. 4: 5–23.

Saffioti, H. (1978) *Emprego Doméstico e Capitalismo*, Petrópolis, Vozes.

Salem, T. (1980) 'Mulheres faveladas: Com a venda nos olhos', in *Perspectivas Antropológicas da Mulher*, Rio de Janeiro, Zahar.

Santos, Ely S. (1983) *As Domésticas: Um Estudo Interdisciplinar de Realidade Social, Política, Econômica e Jurídica*, Porto Alegre, Ed. da Universidade.

Souza, J. Filet Abreu de (1980) 'Paid domestic service in Brazil', *Latin American Perspectives*, Vol. 7, No. 1.

Van Gennep, A. (1960) *The Rites of Passage*, Chicago, University of Chicago Press.

Vila, M. B. (1993) 'Modernidade e cidadania reprodutiva', in *Revista Estudos Feministas*, Rio de Janeiro, Vol. 1, No. 2.

# 5

# Inter- and intra-generational knowledge transfer and zones of silence around reproductive health in Sunnakhi

KHAWAR MUMTAZ AND FAUZIA RAUF

This chapter seeks to explore how women's reproductive knowledge and decision-making are determined by their social and family status, as mediated by their life cycle, in a remote Punjabi village, Sunnakhi. The case study examines the perceptions of women living in a very traditional culture, in particular the changes due to NGOs working in the area, and to the village's participation in the national economy. The study seeks to probe the depth of patriarchal culture in such intimate areas as sexuality and reproductive health, by looking not only at the knowledge of reproductive health but also at the silences. The highly complex nature of social relations prevailing in Sunnakhi is examined by looking at the inter-generational and intra-generational transfer of knowledge about reproductive health, and the major gaps in information about sexuality and reproductive rights. In addition, the study enquires whether any of these women are beginning, even if quietly, to challenge patriarchal authority and control.

## The Pakistani context

Pakistan has an area of 88.2 million hectares (the same area as Norway, Sweden and Denmark combined). The country is made up of four provinces (Punjab, Sindh, North-West Frontier province [NWFP] and Baluchistan) and a special-status northern area. It contains wide geographical diversity, from snow-capped mountains to one of the world's largest riverine basins (the Indus plains), an extensive coastline, arid highlands and desert. This diversity is matched by that of its people. The majority, the Punjabis and Sindhis, live on the riverine plains; the Pathan tribes live in the north-western region (NWFP) and the Baluch along with some Pathans in the mountainous plateau of Baluchistan. Almost 95 per cent of the population is Muslim. Pakistan is primarily an agricultural country, and an estimated 70 per cent of its population lives in the rural areas. The total population is about 128 million and growing at the annual rate of 3 per cent. Women make up 47.5 per cent of the population. Ranking 132 in the world in terms of human development (UNDP, *Human Development Index*, 1994), the indicators for women are particularly poor. Only 18 per cent are literate, in rural areas 9 per cent; the maternal mortality rate stands at 5 per 1,000 live births; and the average fertility rate at 5.6 children. Only 12 per cent of currently married women aged 15–49 use contraceptives (NIPS, 1992).

Despite regional diversity all women in Pakistan find themselves bound by age-old customs and practices and the common perception that they are dependants. But there is evidence of change. The marriage age for women has gone up to nearly 22; there is a demand for girls' schools, even in rural areas; there is greater awareness regarding nutrition, hygiene, family planning, immunization of children and tetanus coverage of pregnant women (UNICEF, *Situation Analysis of Children and Women in Pakistan*, 1992). At the policy level, sustainable development as a framework for planning has been adopted by the government (Government of Pakistan, 1992).

In the run-up to the ICPD in Cairo in 1994, population policies in Pakistan came under critical review. Efforts are under way in the post-ICPD period to reorient policies to meet the challenge that rapidly growing population poses. With the issue of population high on the official agenda, the present study is timely, not only for providing a better understanding of women's health and reproductive needs and choices, but also for identifying directions for action.

## Methodology

The methodology used was essentially participatory. The objective was to elicit qualitative information on women's perceptions of different aspects of their lives. Women were therefore provided with the maximum opportunity to speak, separately and in groups. Given the sensitive nature of the information being sought, a number of factors were taken into consideration prior to going into the field. One was that the study should be focused on a single community; another was that it should be carried out with the collaboration of an organization that has a good rapport with the community. This was necessary to secure the acceptance of the villagers and facilitate smooth interaction, and also to enable collaborative intervention in the future. Sunnakhi village was thus selected, because a community development organization (referred to henceforth as 'the Organization') was already working in the village.

The Organization was helpful in introducing the three-member Shirkat Gah team[1] to the villagers and building up a rapport with the community. It was formed in 1992 in response to the devastating floods that displaced hundreds of villages in Pakistan, and undertook to provide relief and rehabilitation work in 14 villages in southern Punjab, including Sunnakhi. The Organization's approach is broad-based and focuses equally on health, legal awareness and education. The research team collected as much information as possible on the geographical situation, social set-up and way of life of the community beforehand. The staff of the Organization was very helpful in providing an overview of its intervention and sharing information about the area. Personal observations were also shared.

The project and the methodology were discussed in detail with the Organization before going into the field, and its views and opinions about the project solicited prior to finalization of the research plan. The village was visited long before the actual research began. This was done to break the ice and to develop an understanding with the community. The field team also attended a camp, arranged by the Organization, on domestic violence, and used the opportunity to interact with the women, discuss the project and plan the interviews with them. As the village is very small and homogeneous, with not much difference in people's economic conditions and their way of life, the selection of women to be interviewed was made according to caste and religious sect (given below).

The basis for these criteria was the apparent variance between these groups in behaviour and attitudes towards women. Women from eight families belonging to the four castes living in the village were selected, and interviews with three women at different life stages from each family were attempted. However, not all women in each selected family could be interviewed, for a variety of reasons, while some individual women volunteered themselves for interview. A total of 23 women were interviewed, some of whom gave opinions on selected (by them) questions only and did not respond to all queries. Their responses are included wherever they are relevant. At least two families from each caste were covered, except the Shidi caste, where only one family was interviewed, as there are proportionately fewer Shidi families in the village. In the case of three families, only one woman from each could be interviewed, as other women were not available or did not agree to take part. The open-ended interviews were conducted through questions that ranged from general ones about their homes, surroundings, children, relationships, etc. to specific ones related to reproductive and sexual health at different life stages.

A checklist was developed to facilitate the investigation, and was used mainly as a point of reference. Women were free to talk about any other issue in addition to the questions asked. Interviews were recorded in two to three sittings, according to the women's convenience. The team stayed in the village during the research period. This enabled greater insight into the villagers' way of life and helped in building a closer relationship with the women. The different life stages being investigated were: i) puberty/pre-marriage: girls ranging from 11 to 18; ii) active reproductive: married, divorced or widowed, between 20 and 40; iii) menopausal: women ranging from 45 to 60.

Despite extensive preparation, there were some problems during the research. Firstly, the women, who were quite comfortable interacting with outsiders, owing to the Organization's work in the village, had not been exposed to the kind of sensitive questions that this study posed, particularly those related to the body and reproduction. Secondly, the research team's staying with a Sunni family caused some resentment among the Shia families. In addition, tension between one of the families interviewed and the Organization necessitated extra time and effort on the part of the research team, in order to remove scepticism.

The most serious obstacle, however, was the ideological one of maintaining silence on issues of sexuality, which are considered very personal and therefore not appropriate for open discussion. This particular obstacle was partly overcome by discussing sensitive matters on a one-to-one basis rather than in a group situation. While married women were more amenable to this method, younger unmarried women were forbidden to speak on these issues altogether. There were also a few cases of unforeseen work or other need to leave the village making somebody unavailable. Despite problems, the research team, through its interactive approach, managed to gather rich and incisive information.

## The setting

Sunnakhi, a small somewhat isolated village consisting of approximately 100 households, is situated in the riverine plain of Punjab at the western side of the River Chanab. There is no paved road to the village, and it has neither hospital nor health centre. There is a middle school (grade 8) for boys, and a primary school for girls, but without a proper building or teacher. The government-appointed teacher comes in once a week and holds classes in a villager's house. The Organization has set up an informal school, where attendance is low owing to lack of confidence in the teacher's abilities. There is electricity in the village, and three houses have television sets, where women and children gather to watch programmes, especially soap operas. Each compound has its own hand-pump, used by all the households in that compound. Some houses have fixed electric motors with their water pumps. Wood is the commonly used fuel. Those who have orchards or their own trees meet some of their fuelwood needs from these, the majority purchases it from the market.

Sunnakhi has a strong caste system. There are four main castes in the village: Chichra, Hinjara, Sheikh and Shidi. People of Chichra caste belong to the Muslim Shia sect and the rest to the dominant Sunni sect. Each caste consists of five to eight households, which are inter-related and clustered next to each other. The Chichras used to be big landowners, but over time most of them have sold off their land and are now either working in the nearby factories or as casual labour on other people's land. Marriages usually take place within the same caste, the exceptions being the Hinjara and Sheikhs, who inter-marry as they belong to the same religious sect (Sunni). The Chichras, being the only Shia, never marry outside their caste. Exchange marriages (a man and a woman from one family marrying to a man and woman from another family) are very common in the village. This is seen as a way of ensuring security for the daughter/sister concerned, and is a form of arranged marriage common all over the country. It is also a mechanism for keeping property within the family. In situations where *watta satta* (exchange) is not possible, special security in the form of property and maintenance is demanded by the bride's family. There are instances where exchange marriages are not possible owing to the unavailability of a girl/woman, and the deal arrived at is to pledge a yet-to-be-born-daughter in exchange.

All four castes follow *purdah* (seclusion and segregation) norms for women, with the Shias being stricter than the others in not allowing women to move around by themselves even inside the village. Physical violence against women is more frequent and widespread among the Chichras. As in the rest of Pakistan, preference for male offspring is a deep-rooted cultural norm in Sunnakhi. The village has an extended family system, where various members of the family live in the same courtyard but maintain separate kitchens. This enables them to provide support for each other in difficult situations, but to retain independence in their daily routine. The joint family in its traditional form is thus non-existent in this village.

The village's biggest problem is recurrent floods. Throughout the year people fear that they might have to face them again. There have been two heavy floods in recent years. One struck in 1993, depriving the whole village of their homes, belongings and livestock. People of the village adopt different strategies to combat flood, for example, as soon as the rainy season begins they start building huge, tower-like structures with stones, wood and bricks, and place all their household items and valuables on these to save them from the water. Some people who have relatives outside the village move out and return after the floods. The government also provides some relief by distributing food, medicine and cash. However, the villagers consider that the cash given by the government is very little and covers only health expenses. The effects of the flood are long-lasting. Standing water causes a number of diseases, such as colds, fevers, acute stomach problems and eye diseases, and plants and crops are destroyed. Substantial numbers of trees and small plants were ruined during the last flood, with standing water rotting fruit trees and destroying the wheat crop.

Sunnakhi is a semi-agricultural village. The majority of the people are engaged in menial skilled casual labour outside the village, in factories and other sectors. Most of the land in the village is owned by absentee landlords who live in the nearby cities of Multan or Muzzafargarh. Among the residents of the village a small number own land, not more than one to two acres in size, which they do not necessarily cultivate because of the small size of the holdings. Instead, they give out land on contract and work in nearby towns in the services or production sectors. A number of the landless in the village contract other people's land for cultivation. Largely, families belonging to the Chichra caste cultivate contracted land. Livestock ownership is common as a supplementary means of income.

There is no sharp class differentiation among the people in the village, and economically their status is more or less the same. Women in the village contribute to the family income and most of them are engaged in piece-work, such as stitching soles, embroidery, sewing clothes, making *parandas* (cotton thread and tinsel ribbons for the hair) and weaving mats. The raw material is delivered to the women by middlemen, either from outside the village or from within. The work is laborious and time-consuming, while the wages are nominal. Most of the income is spent in the household or used to build up household savings.

## The households

Each extended family covered in this study shared a courtyard, but their constituent parts did not necessarily share a kitchen or pot. Their sizes varied betwen five and 17 members. While being at broadly the same economic level, there was some variation in their incomes, as there was in the complexity of relationships within each family. This section briefly gives each family's composition.

*Family one* This was an unusual Shia family of Chichra caste, with the male head of the family having married three times. His first wife had died, leaving three children. He subsequently married two women, and both the wives were living with him in the main house, sharing the same kitchen. There were altogether eleven family members, spanning three generations – the male household head and his wives, mother and children. The family used to own cultivable land and fruit trees, but as men migrated away in pursuit of better earning opportunities, the land was gradually sold off. The male head of the family, a high school graduate, searched unsuccessfully for an office job, and is now tilling other people's land. They have a two-roomed house with a big courtyard and their own hand-pump. The family's earnings are not sufficient to meet their needs. To supplement the household income, the eldest daughter (18) and the third wife stitch shoe soles for a contractor. The second wife belongs to a slightly better-off family from another village and has inherited some land from her parents, which she had to sell because the family needed cash. Since she also has three sons, she is the favourite daughter-in-law and step-mother. Wife number three, on the other hand, is not from the same caste and her family background is not too well known; she therefore does not receive similar treatment and has to work hard to gain favour. The two wives and the eldest daughter were interviewed. The mother-in-law was not available.

*Family two* This too is a Shia family of the Chichra caste. Here both the male and female household heads, who are cousins, had been widowed before their marriage to each other. She had 13 children (eight of whom died) from her first marriage, and he eight from his first. All her surviving children are married and live in the nearby town of Muzaffargarh. They have no children in this marriage. Altogether twelve persons, including children, shared the courtyard. The father and mother with his two unmarried daughters have a room and kitchen, and his son and daughter-in-law with their three children have a separate room and kitchen. All members of the family are illiterate. One of the two daughters had been engaged, but the engagement was broken off when the boy's family objected to his sister's exchange marriage with the father. The male head of the family is too old to work, therefore the main source of income for the family is the son's earnings from his job in a factory, and the small piece of land that they cultivate. Only the mother gave an interview. Initially, the family had agreed to interviews

with one of the daughters and the daughter-in-law, but then declined
(see reasons in section above). The extreme shyness of the younger
women and their reluctance to speak in front of the males, who were
constantly present, was an added reason.

*Family three* The third is a Chichra family, where again only the
unmarried eldest daughter (aged 15) could be interviewed as the mother
refused. This family consists of a mother and father, five daughters and
a son. All are illiterate. In this family the father was too ill to work and
the brother too young. The main earners therefore were the mother and
the two eldest daughters, who stitched shoe soles. Their land, which is
contracted out, is the other source of income.

*Family four* A Sunni family of the Hinjara caste, with ten members.
Besides the male and female household heads, there is a married son
with a wife and four children (three sons go to school, the daughter is
only three years old), who maintain a separate kitchen, and two
daughters, one of whom is divorced. The household had been cultivating
contracted land, but, because of the father's ill-health, the burden of
work has fallen on his wife and daughters, who also stitch soles, weave
*chatais* (mats) to order, and tend the buffalo, whose milk is an important
source of income for the family. The son is a casual labourer and his
wife supplements the household income working on piece-rate stitching
soles, like a large number of other women of the village. Three women
were interviewed here: the mother, the unmarried daughter and the
daughter-in-law.

*Family five* The family belongs to the Hinjara caste, with very complicated relationships. It consists of two brothers married to two sisters
from outside the village. One of the couples had no children, but
adopted another brother's son, who they educated up to class 8. The
other couple has a daughter and a son. The son goes to school and the
daughter, who is uneducated, on growing up was married to her uncle
and aunt's adopted son. Thus after marriage she continues to live in her
maternal home, but her status is now that of a daughter-in-law. This
family is small by village standards, with only one child. The three
adult males in the family are employed, two in government service (one
works in a family planning unit) and one as a casual labourer. They also
cultivate the land they own and have a buffalo, whose milk is sold. This
was a relatively better-off household, and the women were not involved
in any contractual or piece-rate work for additional income. The family
has a less strict attitude towards women, none of whom wear the *burqa*

(veil), and the married ones are allowed to go out of the village un-escorted. The older of the married sisters even goes to the fields to cut and collect fodder.

*Family six*   A Sunni Sheikh family was the only female-headed house-hold. The woman, a widow whose husband had died in 1993 during the floods, lives with her two daughters and three sons. Her mother-in-law lives nearby with one of her other sons. The eldest child is a daughter of about 13. There was immense pressure on the mother to remarry, but she preferred to remain single. Her husband had been a government servant, therefore she received a provident fund on his death, to which she added money from the sale of the cattle they had owned, and started a small business. On alternate days she purchases utility items and groceries from Muzaffargah and sells them from her house. On the days that she goes to Muzaffargah, her mother-in-law comes to look after the children. She also receives a monthly pension on her husband's behalf. This was one of the two households in the sample where the daughters were going to school. The elder daughter was sent to Muzaffargarh up to class 8, and the younger one is attending the village school. The mother wants the daughter to become a school teacher. In the interviews conducted in this family, besides the mother and the older daughter, the mother-in-law was also included, as she spends a substantial amount of time in this house.

*Family seven*   This is one of the few Shidi families in the village. This is a typical household, consisting of elderly mother and father living with their one married and five unmarried sons, two unmarried daughters and five grandchildren. The married son maintains a separate kitchen and living space for his family in the same compound. This large household is sustained by the earnings of the father and the married son, who are casual labourers, and by those of the mother and the daughters, who stitch shoes The eldest daughter in this house is studying in the home school run with the support of the Organization. She, her mother and her sister-in-law were the ones interviewed.

*Family eight*   This is a Sheikh family with a mother and father, two sons and one daughter. The daughter, only 18 years old, is divorced, and so is one brother. The daughter's marriage was a *watta satta* (exchange) marriage, where her brother was married to her husband's sister. Soon after the marriage, she discovered that her husband was interested in some other girl and had been forced to marry her. Within days of her marriage she was sent back. The brother reciprocated by sending back his wife, and both the marriages ended in divorce. The father is a postman and the brother a causal labourer. This is one of the rare households in the village that grows vegetables in their yard, largely for home consumption. The surplus, if any, is sold. The mother and daughter work in the fields and the latter also stitches shoes. Only the daughter could be interviewed, as the mother had to go away for a few days when the interviews were being conducted.

## Women's lives, continuity and change

Women's lives in Sunnakhi are governed largely by tradition and custom, which throughout Pakistan, in varying degrees, value a woman for her power of reproduction and as an object of sexual satisfaction. As such, women are denied their identity and are viewed as 'visitors' in their parental homes, kept in trust until married and sent to their 'own homes', that is to say their husbands'.

Women's chastity and family honour are closely linked, and even the slightest misdemeanour (always related to sexual behaviour) by a woman results in dishonour for the family. Consequently daughters are kept secluded and well guarded, and married off as early as possible to prevent any possibility of misbehaviour. But women are not unaffected by change, which even this village, remote as it is, has experienced. Most women's lives follow the age-old pattern of early marriage, child-bearing at a young age, household chores and child care.

In the households investigated, all married women had children except one divorcee, whose marriage lasted only a few days (family eight), a recently married young woman (family five) and one woman who was infertile (family five). Almost all had been married very young, some soon after attaining puberty, i.e. between 13 and 15 years of age (women's estimation of their ages was not exact, as no birth records are maintained; since 12 was considered to be the age of menstruation, it was assumed that when a girl menstruated she was 12 years old), and had children within the first few years of marriage.

In accordance with custom, women's mobility in Sunnakhi is very restricted. Women, especially the young and unmarried, are generally not expected to go anywhere outside their courtyards and caste clusters unescorted, not even to the fields. Going outside the village is absolutely out of the question, the exception being a visit to the *pir* (holy man) or a *mazaar* (shrine), but that too is only for married women. Restrictions were found to be stronger in the Shia families, where the wearing of the *burqa* was essential. In the case of one family, the grandmother wore a *burqa* when she went to the fields to cut fodder, but she could take it off, while the daughter, if she accompanied her, had to keep hers on (family eight).

The educational level of both men and women is minimal among the families interviewed, but whereas that of the men improved in successive generations, that of the women indicated a shift (marginal at that) only in the third generation. Given the seclusion practices, it is not surprising that there is a reluctance to send girls to schools. Almost all the male children in these families were going to school, while only few girls were being sent. The exceptions were the two daughters of the widow who had defied local norms, had not remarried and was asserting her independence (family six). Hers was also the only case where a daughter was sent to the secondary school in Muzaffargarh. Most other girls were sent just to the local primary school.

Women's main activities are seen as revolving around the home. Besides the usual household chores of cooking, cleaning and child care, like other rural women in the country they also look after the livestock. In addition to cooking daily meals, women seasonally prepare pickles and fruit preserves. These are usually just for home consumption and can be stored and used through the year. Most of the women's time during the day, in some instances up to six hours, was spent in cash-income generation.

All women, except in one relatively well-off household (family five), where there were three male earners and only one child, were found stitching soles for shoes, weaving *chatais* to order, doing embroidery or other sewing – all for remuneration not commensurate with the time and effort spent (see Table 5.1). The money earned was a welcome addition to the household finances and was spent almost entirely in the household. Very little was saved.

**Table 5.1** Women's income-generating activities

| Activity | Rate | Time |
| --- | --- | --- |
| Stitching shoe soles | Rs.2.50 per piece | 1 hr. per piece |
| Embroidery (Scarf) | Rs.30–50 | 3–4 days (at least 6 hrs/day) |
| Sewing (Clothes) | Rs.35–40 (per outfit) | 1 day (5 hrs) |
| Weaving (*chatai*) | Rs.10 (per *chatai*) | 2–3 hrs |

*Note*: Rs.1 = £0.02

It is at the economic level that the village and the lives of its inhabitants have undergone the most extensive change. The introduction of the cash/market economy and the advent of industrialization have both had their impact on this otherwise isolated village. With the growth of nearby towns, the setting up of industry and the expansion of commerce and trade, the male population has been attracted by the opportunity of extra income. The size of landholdings has therefore declined. A number of villagers have either sold their land or given it out on contract in pursuit of city jobs. Whether this move was imperative for bare survival or for the enhancement of the standard of living for the families concerned needs more investigation, but the fact remains that this process, triggered a couple of decades ago, is continuing. For women, some of whom do not leave the village unless absolutely essential (the floods), the market has come to their doorstep in search of their (underpaid) labour.

Home-based, piece-rate work done by women is almost integral to the manufacturing of a large number of consumer goods in Pakistan, from footballs, sports clothes, and linen for export, to garments, trinkets and scouring brushes for the home market. The phenomenon was initially an urban one, where the formal sector linked with the informal for greater profits, but has now spread to the villages. Thus quite unaware, these women are active (albeit exploited) contributors to the national and the global economy.

## Reproduction, information and knowledge

Social reproduction and servicing of the social collective have been tasks that the women of Sunnakhi, like their sisters elsewhere, diligently perform in all their life stages. Before reaching puberty, the girls look after siblings, help in household chores and assist mothers in the stitching of shoes. Soon after, they are considered ready to take on the burden of physical reproduction. At this stage, perhaps the longest in their lives, they bear children and shoulder major household responsibilities. Finally, at the third stage, a woman's physical workload may decline, but responsibilities remain. Important questions at the core of this research include: how prepared are the women for their roles at different life stages, particularly the reproductive ones? What level of information do they have? What are their sources of information? Some clues were found during the study.

*Life stage one* Menstruation is the watershed between being a girl and becoming a woman. Almost all the women (95 per cent), young and old, when asked about what menstruation represented to them, said it meant being seen as a woman, in other words expected to behave in a womanly manner, i.e. to observe *purdah* and wear a *burqa*, not leave the home, and prepare for marriage.

In Sunnakhi, marriage is usually arranged within two or three years of a girl's menstruation. As births and deaths are not recorded in rural areas, ages are all estimations. According to the women, menstruation occurred between 12 and 14. In one case it did not occur till the girl was 17, causing great anguish and tension for the mother and the daughter (family four). The neighbours, apparently, made fun of her, accusing her of not being a woman. When she finally menstruated there was much relief all round. Most girls are quite unprepared for this change in their lives, while a few have some idea of the impending event.

Socially, a silence is maintained about sexuality; it is not discussed openly even among women. Within the household, if a girl is menstruating, the older women are not supposed to know. If she suffers cramps or pain, then also only those closest to her, like a sister or sister-in-law, are informed. Mothers are told if there is no other person near her age-group. A pretence of illness is maintained for other members of the household. Any information is transmitted either through peers or elder sisters. The information, however, is limited to the fact that menstruation heralds growing up and becoming eligible for marriage. Once menstruation begins, practical information about managing it is passed on by the mother, or, more often, by an elder sister or sister-in-law. In a few instances, young girls reported that their mothers tried to give them nutritious food like milk during their periods.

*Practices related to menstruation*

- Sanitary towels, usually made out of used cloth, not to be thrown out as no one should see them, especially men. These should be reused after washing.
- If disposal is necessary (as it is for the Shias), then the towels should be buried and not burnt, as that would affect the menstrual flow.
- Women are considered *napak* (unclean) during this period. In some families they sleep on a mat on the floor or remove the mattress from the bed; clothes are kept separate.
- Women are not supposed to bathe for the duration of the period, in the belief that they will fall ill with fever or pain. Such beliefs are reinforced by stories like that of a woman who died after a day's illness because she had taken a bath during menstruation.
- Women are advised to refrain from eating certain foods during menstruation, such as yoghurt, pulses or meat, as these may cause cramps or upset stomachs. Cramps during menstruation are common, and

over half the women reported experiencing them. Usually traditional home-brews are used to deal with them. There is a growing number of women using aspirin for relief, which, in their opinion, works faster. Only when the pain is very severe a woman may be taken to the *hakim* (traditional medical man) or a woman doctor. Usually an older woman accompanies them and is the one to communicate the problem.

- Home-brews for cramps: *tarang* (mixture) made of *saunf* (anis seed), sugar and honey; *tarang* made of *saunf*, *desi ghee* (purified butter), and *gur* (unrefined brown sugar commonly known as jaggery).

*Life stage two*  The defining points of this life stage are marriage and childbirth.

The physical side of marriage, which determines a woman's future and defines her role within the family and society at large, is shrouded in mystery. This is not surprising. Sexual relations were an area that the women were most reluctant to talk about; they felt shy and embarrassed when questioned on this subject. The interviewers were not allowed to ask unmarried girls, or even younger married women, questions related to sexual behaviour.

Similarly, the concept of virginity, which is all-pervasive in Pakistani society, was a subject no woman was willing to discuss. Only one woman mentioned her own experience of the practice of checking on a bride's virginity the morning after the wedding (family one). All women reported that they had known very little about sex prior to their marriage. Most learnt about it on the wedding day, through married female relatives: an aunt, a sister-in-law or sometimes a married friend. Some received no information at all; others managed to glean fragments of information from jokes and cracks made by friends and sisters. Not surprisingly, most reported a fear of sex and of not feeling good about it (it could not be ascertained whether enjoyment of sex was genuinely lacking, or something that one is not supposed to admit to publicly).

Women, however, see it as a duty that has to be fulfilled. They feel that they should not refuse to have sex when it is demanded by the husband. Two women did indicate that they sometimes try to refuse by pretending that they are not well, but this ploy does not always work. Only two reported any physical or health problem due to sex. One felt severe pain and the other bled for six days after intercourse (families five and six). Pregnancy is the other unknown for women. They guess that they are pregnant either from sickness or discontinuation of menstruation. The symptoms for confirming pregnancy are learnt from friends and sisters. Older women can predict pregnancy from looking at the face and observing a woman's physical movements. In fact, they claim to know, by looking at the posture, eating habits and expression, whether a woman will have a male or a female child.

Once pregnant, a woman receives a fair amount of advice from women elders of the family and the neighbourhood: about what to eat, how to sit and not to lift heavy objects. If there is a serious problem, women go to the *dai* (midwife, traditional birth attendant) or a female doctor. Regular check-ups are not a common practice. Reported problems during pregnancy were weakness, premature birth, pain and bleeding.

Deliveries usually take place at home with the help of the *dai*. Only in extreme emergency is a woman taken to the hospital, the nearest one being in Muzaffarabad. The lack of access to a hospital (no proper road nor easily available transport) is one reason for home births. Others are lack of privacy in hospital, inadequate and limited facilities for attendants staying with the patient, and above all the cost, which is beyond most.

Once a child is born, the older women of the family – mother or mother-in-law – take charge of the baby, giving the mother a chance to rest. If a child is ill, it is in almost all instances taken to hospital. Some also take children to the *pir* (religious person), largely to protect them from the evil eye. In case of stomach ailments, *desi* (indigenous) treatment is tried, and the infant may be given either a powdered mixture of black pepper, anis seed and extract of seven essential seeds or ground anis seed and salt with a few drops of water. Given the preference for male children and the status the birth of a son brings to a woman, there is a special effort to ensure that the offspring, especially the first one, is a male. Several measures were reported (see below). How successful these are is uncertain. The women from the Shia families stated that they diligently follow the rituals. A number of rituals follow childbirth. There is celebration, revelry and exchange of gifts at the birth of the son. If a daughter is born the gifts exchanged are of half the value.

*Some rituals to ensure male offspring*

- Among the *Shias*, in the seventh month of a woman's pregnancy her husband or eldest son spills a bucket of water over her from the roof while she stands in the courtyard.
- The pregnant woman stands under a tree and drinks either milk or *tarang*, a mixture made of anis seed, cardamom and oil, after her husband has imbibed the same preparation.
- If the hair of a new-born baby is buried the day after its birth, the next one will be a boy.
- Among *Sunnis*, a verse from the *Quran* is recited by the husband

during intercourse to ensure the conception of a male.
• Holy water from Mecca, or water prayed over by a holy man, is taken during pregnancy.

Breastfeeding is common among all women. It is a widespread belief, and also based upon experience, that breastfeeding is the natural way of spacing children. Over half the women reported a gap of up to two years between their children without using family planning measures, and attributed it to breastfeeding. Almost all married women were aware of family planning methods. The main source of information was the Organization. Those coming to the village from urban areas (after marriage) had already heard about family planning, as in towns and cities the media campaigns are more visible and the services more widespread. Women who visited doctors for ailments received information from them. In one case, the husband was the source of information, as he was working with a family planning unit in Muzaffargarh (family five).

Being aware of family planning methods does not necessarily mean that they are widely used. The basic problem is inaccessibility of services and follow-up. Much of the knowledge that the women have is incomplete or inadequate. The more popularly accepted methods are injectables and the pill, the former because they give three months' cover, and the latter because it is easy to administer. About others, there are misgivings that they make one sick or have uncomfortable side-effects. One woman reported practising family planning after the birth of her fourth child and conceiving as soon as she stopped. She did not want another child, so she sought an abortion, which the doctor refused (abortion is illegal in Pakistan unless the life of the mother is at risk). Her mother-in-law then gave her a home-made remedy, of dried dates, anis seed and cardamom boiled in milk, to drink several times during the first three months of pregnancy to induce a miscarriage. It worked in her case, but is not always successful.

It was observed that women practised family planning after having had the desired number of children. Apart from the woman married to the worker in a family planning unit, no one was using contraceptives for spacing children.

Infertility was also reported as a problem, and in a society where a women's role hinges on her reproductive ability, it is a serious one. Initially women go to *pirs* and *mazaars* to pray, in the hope that they will conceive. Some are treated by doctors and reportedly have been helped.

This life stage spans a long period of a woman's life, from 14 or 15 to 50 or more. It also represents her busiest, in terms of workload, bearing and rearing children, and generating income. Beginning with restrictions and constraints, and with no say in domestic or other matters, a woman steadily gains importance within the family. With age, she assumes the responsibility of managing the household, restrictions on mobility relax, and her opinion is solicited on major decisions.

*Life stage three* According to our definition, the third life stage begins with menopause, marking the end of active reproduction. Socially, however, women are treated as having achieved seniority as they approach the age of 50, whether menopause has occurred or not. Most who had reached this life stage reported having had their menopause at 50, but it is again unclear whether they were actually that age, or presumed that the menopause meant being 50 years old. It is the common belief that a woman becomes physically weak and her eyesight is affected. One woman, whose menopause was accompanied by heavy bleeding, believed that this was due to grief over her son's death. Beside the physical change, this stage represents greater authority for women in their households. They are more assertive, manage the household economy, do not need to be escorted outside the home, can go alone to Muzaffarabad, and need not wear the *burqa*.

During this period, their workload varies according to their physical capacity, but women in our sample were going to the fields for fodder, stitching soles of shoes, doing housework and looking after grandchildren.

## Choices and control

When asked how it was to be a woman, almost all those interviewed responded that they felt helpless and deprived; they were not given the opportunity of schooling or employment and were unable to enjoy life like men. A couple of women expressed satisfaction with the way things are, as they do not have to earn or feel responsible for households' needs (families one and five).

The majority, in reality, do carry the responsibility of earning also. In some instances, women of all ages were contributing substantial cash incomes (up to Rs.500 per month or more, if two or more women were working) to the household, with no control over where it was to be spent. Where younger women were earning, all their incomes were handed over to fathers or mothers. In the case of married women, they were allowed to keep a little for personal expenses (cosmetics, bangles, etc.); the rest was given over to mothers-in-law or husbands.

Women's choices and control over their lives range from non-existent to limited. The social fabric ensures that modes of control are reproduced and continued. The system of marriages, within extended family and castes, based on exchanges, leaves little room for any woman to exercise her choice or even voice her opinion. A marriage may be broken as a result of family conflict rather than for reasons inherent to the relationships within it (family eight, for instance). Norms and boundaries have been defined from the male perspective and implemented by both men and women. Women who when young may have resented patriarchal practices become strong advocates when they assume the authority of age.

One of the older women who had been married twice, for instance, snapped at her husband and disregarded his advice against speaking to the interviewers, but did not allow her daughter and daughter-in-law to meet them (family two). In other matters, like marriages and expenditures, he reportedly wielded full control. He broke his daughter's engagement because the other family refused to marry their daughter to him. No woman in Sunnakhi was consulted at the time of her marriage, nor showed any resistance to the decision made for her. Given the young ages at which marriages are arranged, it is unlikely that any of the prospective brides would be in a position to do so. Just as marriages are arranged they may be called off (see above).

The only resistance shown was by the widow, who, because she had some access to independent finance (her husband's provident funds, his pension and a buffalo), withstood the pressure for remarriage (family six). In fact, she took the unconventional step of setting up a utility store in her house, abandoned the *burqa* and made trips to Muzaffargarh alone to acquire stocks for her shop. She also sent her daughters to school. At the same time, the daughters observed strict *purdah* and were restricted from leaving the house without someone accompanying them.

Women seem to have little control over their bodies. To be available for husbands whenever desired is seen as a duty. After having a number of children, and the concomitant passage of time, women can consider choosing and planning any future births. Whether women seek their husbands' consent, or inform them, was not clear from their responses. While the two methods used can be practised without informing husbands, it would only be a conjecture that they do not inform them.

Violence and abuse are weapons often used to keep women under control. In Sunnakhi, domestic violence is fairly widespread, as reported by women who, however, deny being subject to it themselves. There was silence and reluctance to discuss violence; it is viewed as a personal matter, not to be discussed outside their homes. A few women acknowledge being abused and battered, and also report how the mother-in-law or older women intervene on their behalf and try to protect them. The general belief is that violence is a male prerogative, and the best strategy is to remain quiet when men are in a violent mood, for resistance invites greater abuse. Young girls reported battering by mothers and abuse from fathers and brothers.

## Conclusion

The research reveals the highly complex nature of social relations that prevail in Sunnakhi, a village struck by periodic floods and declining land quality, where agriculture is no longer sufficient to sustain the livelihoods of its inhabitants. Each household studied displays the multiple-tiered hierarchy determined by the gender and age of its members. It reaffirms the strong control of patriarchal ideology that defines the strictly imposed parameters of behaviour and roles, and shows that patriarchal attitudes cut across castes in the village, with no strong differentiation evident due to caste groupings. Males, irrespective of age, have more space for exercising options and wielding authority. Women acquire a say in family decisions at the tail-end of their second life stage. Even then, serious decisions regarding changes in behavioural norms (e.g. taking off the veil, going to school) and marriages rest with the men. The extent of unquestioned male authority is epitomized by the twice-married man (family two) who broke off his daughter's engagement because the boy's family was not agreeable to having an exchange marriage of their daughter with him.

It is very clear that the pattern of reproductive decision-making is not in the hands of women, at least not in their early life stages. Interestingly, the study shows that in exceptional circumstances women do assert themselves, for instance the widow (family six) who resists the pressure for remarriage, puts aside mobility restrictions and goes to the nearby town to purchase stocks for a general store that she runs from home (in itself an unconventional activity for a woman). In this case, her independent income was a major factor in her ability to take independent action. Similarly, women in the better-off household (family five) had fewer restrictions relating to mobility and veiling. Women's level of awareness about the outside world is significant, given the remoteness of the village. This is probably due to the presence of the Organization in the village, which has exposed the receptive villagers to outsiders and new ideas.

Knowledge of family planning is also fairly widespread, the information having come from doctors, the Organization and family planning clinics in the towns nearby. Practice, however, is limited. Women turn to family planning when they have had the desired number of children rather than for spacing birth. Information about the methods is inadequate, reflecting poor, unsystematic and inaccessible services (women have to go to nearby towns). The distance from available services means that there is no proper follow-up for contraceptive users, and presumes a high level of motivation to actually make the trip to town. Health and reproductive health information among women was variable and largely fragmented, depending on the experience and level of knowledge of peers, mothers or mothers-in-law.

The transmission of knowledge in this area was found to be both inter- and intra-generational and influenced by the strong silence that shrouds issues of sexuality. Neither mothers nor grandmothers appear as major transmitters of knowledge on menstruation and sex. Sisters and young married women of the immediate family provide information about menstruation, mainly about dealing with the condition. Friends and married sisters-in-law give indirect information regarding sex at the time of marriage. Major gaps exist in the information, and more probing needs to be done to determine the nature of the information required by women in these stages of their lives. Mothers, elders and grandmothers, however, are the source of rich indigenous knowledge for dealing with problems of pregnancy and reproductive health (menstrual cramps, abortion, etc.), of innumerable rituals, and sometimes also of misinformation (menopause results in poor eyesight).

One of the surprising findings of the study was the women's linkage to the modern economy. Working from their homes, the majority of the women in the sample were found stitching soles of shoes in what appears to be a link in an assembly-line chain. They were also producing other marketable goods, based on traditional skills of stitching *parandas* and *chatais*. With reference to the population policy, the study indicates that so far it has focused on services, which are poor in terms of both coverage and content. The services have been incidental and unsystematic, available only to those who manage to reach them. Despite official claims of using a holistic approach and the sustainable development framework for addressing population issues, the research shows that on the ground this is not yet happening.

Necessary elements for women's decision-making, particularly in reproductive matters, are awareness of rights, education, better information on medication and contraceptives to enable informed choices, accessible and improved health facilities, confidence-building measures, among others. Most of these were found to be missing as part of any cohesive policy. Methodologically, the research confirms the effectiveness of participatory approaches for a better understanding of women's perception.

However, it also indicates that sensitive issues, such as sexuality, can be discussed only in privacy and not in a group situation. A problem linked to silence, and not overcome even by this methodology, is the extent to which rules of silence prevent women from admitting knowledge (even if minimal) in the area of sexuality, particularly when physical constraints of limited space (a room usually being shared by the entire family) render privacy difficult, if not unattainable.

To conclude, the study provides a number of pointers towards a viable intervention strategy, the objective of which would be to enhance women's decision-making in reproduction and related health matters. This would require addressing the issue of women's low status. Initiatives could include systematic employment opportunities and training, for increasing women's incomes and raising the standard of living; programmes focusing on men and older women towards attitudinal change; and proper health services so that women can make informed choices.

Strengthening existing channels of information would be the other component of the strategy. Since older women are transmitters of information dealing with pregnancy and health-related problems, their knowledge base may be reinforced; and as young married women are the providers of information to peers on bodily changes (menstruation, marriage), they could be the focus for training in this specific area. Similarly, since women (and villagers generally) were found to be receptive to outsiders (doctors, paramedics and non-governmental organizations), new ideas and information on subjects not discussed in the prevailing socio-cultural context may be transmitted through them. Ongoing interactive processes are essential for identifying needs and designing programmes.

## Acknowledgements

The authors would like to acknowledge the help of Pattan Taraqiyati Tanzeem, the community development organization working in Sunnakhi and the villages around it. Their introduction of the Shirkat Gah team to the village, and their sharing of experience in Sunnakhi is deeply appreciated. Special gratitude is owed to the women in the village for their hospitality, co-operation and lively participation in this unprecedented exercise. Acknowledgements are also due to Farrah Naz and Arifa Nazli, members of the Shirkat Gah field team, whose experience enabled them to handle skilfully and frankly the counterquestions posed by women on issues being investigated.

## Note

1. Shirkat Gah is a national research and policy NGO and resource centre, headquartered in Lahore, Pakistan, focusing on women's rights as human rights, reproductive health and gender and environment issues.

## References

Government of Pakistan (1992) *The Pakistan National Conservation Strategy*, Karachi.

NIPS (1992) 'Pakistan Demographic and Health Survey 1990/1991', Islamabad.

UNDP (1994) *Human Development Report*, New York, Oxford University Press.

UNICEF (1992) *Situation Analysis of Children and Women in Pakistan*, Islamabad.

# 6

## The impact of the global economy: returnee migrant workers in Sri Lanka

SANDYA HEWAMANNE AND
HANS PETER MÜLLER[1]

Most studies on migration in Sri Lanka emphasize the economic aspects of migration, though some do speak of its social consequences. All, though, fail to examine the reintegration process of migrant returnees. This chapter looks at shifts in the attitude of women migrant returnees and their counterparts in their villages towards women's social and economic status and knowledge about reproductive health and sexuality. The study seeks to capture the long-term social and cultural impact of temporary migration on the women themselves, their families and the village environment. The case study focuses on three sets of women in one small rural village, where many village women have migrated, either as domestic servants to the Middle East or as industrial workers to the Katunayake Free Trade Zone. It examines how both the migrants and the women who stay behind perceive the migration experience and the tensions created by the change in economic and social status among and within families. The study looks at the questions that this sudden break in the traditionally tightly controlled lives of young women and wives raises for village morality. It also seeks to monitor the impact of the new knowledge, particularly in the area of reproductive health, on the women and their environment. In general, the study begins to answer how migrant women function as carriers of change and as symbols of the costs and benefits of modern Sri Lanka's entry into the global economy.

### The Sri Lankan context

Sri Lanka is a tropical island of 65,610 square kilometres, situated to the south-east of India. The population in 1994 was 17,800,000, with 8,738,000 men and 8,523,000 women, of whom 4,572,000 were in the reproductive age range of 15–49. Seventy-four per cent of the population are Sinhala (67 per cent are Buddhists) with 12 per cent Tamil and

7 per cent Muslim. The literacy rate is very high, at 82 per cent. In 1991, the life expectancy for men was 70.1 years and for women 74.8 years. In 1992, the infant mortality rate per 1,000 was 0.4. Sri Lanka is one of the exceptional developing countries where female school enrolment exceeds the male in education beyond primary level (see Table 6.1).

**Table 6.1** Enrolment in schools (1988): percentage of females

|  |  |  |  | Science | Arts | Commerce | Total |
|---|---|---|---|---|---|---|---|
| Grades | 1–5 | 6–8 | 9–11 | 12–13 | 12–13 | 12–13 | 12–13 |
| Per cent | 48.2 | 49.4 | 52.2 | 46.6 | 69.5 | 53.2 | 57.9 |

*Source: Annual School Census*, Statistical Division, Ministry of Education, quoted in Jayaweera 1990: 116.

Sri Lankan society operates a strong patriarchal system. Women are expected to stay under the protection of men throughout their lives, to marry young and to have at least one son. Their main role in life is to look after their husbands and children. In addition to household chores, Sri Lankan women contribute to agricultural work, but they have little access to the income, or the power to make final decisions in the household or community. While these values are changing in upper-class urban society, rural society largely upholds them.

Reproductive awareness is high. According to a survey conducted in 1993, 66 per cent of married women in Sri Lanka use contraceptive methods, of whom 43.7 per cent use modern birth control, and 22.4 per cent use traditional methods. In 1993, abortions per 100,000 of the female population were approximately 939.

## Cultural and historical setting of migration

Since the protestant reforming of Sinhalese Buddhist society about a century ago, Sri Lankan gender stereotypes seem to be a mix of local paternalism and British Victorianism. The emerging middle-class intellectuals – Buddhist, Hindu and Christian – still see girls and women as passive, subordinate and confined to nurturing and servicing roles within and outside the home. Educational materials and the 'hidden curriculum' reinforce stereotypes and tend to circumscribe the experiences and aspirations of girls.

This view of female roles lost ground when Sri Lanka's economic liberalization programme replaced socialist and nationalist populism after

1976. The emerging economic, political and social transformation created, for many Sri Lankan groups, living conditions that were incompatible with the traditional value system.

One of the outstanding features of the open economy in Sri Lanka is the mobilization of the female labour force. The process can be observed at two levels. On one hand, a growing number of women are leaving the country to work, mainly as housemaids, in the Middle East; on the other hand, a large number of women are employed in the new international Free Trade Zones (FTZs), particularly in the garment factories producing clothing for Western markets. Statistics that could reflect these processes are few and unreliable, tending to underestimate the dynamic. A government-sponsored advertisement, which appeared in the *Financial Times* in London in 1980, offered an almost unlimited invitation to foreign industrial firms to invest their capital in the newly established FTZs.[2]

The call was not ineffective, although the response was far below expectation. According to Kelegama and Wignaraja (1991), the proportion of Sri Lanka's industrial exports developed as indicated in Table 6.2. In 1990, the garment industry, consisting of about 350 direct export firms and over 500 smaller subcontractors, was the source of Sri Lanka's most successful manufacturing export. 'Between 1977 and 1990, Sri Lanka's garment exports rose from US$12 million to US$604 million (from 13 per cent of Sri Lanka's total manufactured exports to 54 per cent)' (Lall and Wignaraja, 1993: 44).

**Table 6.2** Exports of manufactured goods and garments as percentages of total exports

|                         | 1977  | 1981 | 1985 | 1987 |
|-------------------------|-------|------|------|------|
| Total manufactured goods | 13.08 | 35.6 | 40.0 | 48.7 |
| Garments                | 2.1   | 14.4 | 21.5 | 30.2 |

The disappointment has to do with two facts, quantitative and qualitative:

The IPZ [Investment Promotion Zone] has failed to attract adequate investments and hardly any firm with advanced technology operates in the Zone. After eight years of operation, up to end October 1986, 43,809 jobs have been made available in the Zone and the annual average rate of new employment creation has been about 5,500. (Karunnatilake, 1987: 430)

Many of the jobs created by the attraction of international capital did not compensate for jobs lost due to the abandonment of the import substitution policy:

> The liberalization of the economy in 1977 had a direct impact on local, small industries, many of which collapsed through inability to compete with cheaper imported goods. In the handloom industry, for instance, 40,000 women are reported to have lost their means of livelihood, and the number of looms in use to have declined from 111,000 to 30,000 over two years. (People's Bank, 1980)

The percentage of women employed in the textile industry declined from 70.1 per cent in 1971 to 47.1 per cent in 1981; the number of women declined by 48.1 per cent. Large numbers of rural women from low-income families were therefore displaced as a result of this major shift in national policies (Jayaweera, 1990: 6). In other words, during a period of eight years, fewer than 44,000 jobs were created in and around Colombo, out of which approximately 36,000 were for women, while 40,000 women lost their jobs in and near their homes during more or less the same period, owing to the same open market policy. Hettige (1995) points out that import liberalization virtually wiped out the rural handloom industry, which had employed about 200,000 workers, mostly young women. The 100,000 or so new jobs created in the Free Trade Zone factories absorbed only part of the displaced labour.

Living conditions for the female labour force in the FTZ were bad. The demand for female labour was based on specific gender-role assumptions: that women were expendable, secondary earners, who would accept low wages and be 'pliable' and 'nimble'. Women, particularly young secondary-school-leavers, chiefly from impoverished families, sought employment opportunities in the garment industry. As promised to the foreign investors by the UNP Government, such women earn the lowest wages in Asian Export Processing Zones, while working long hours in monotonous tasks in response to the constant pressure to meet production targets, in a working environment that is often hazardous to their physical and mental health. Patriarchal norms prevail in the workplace, as men predominate in management and supervisory roles. Living conditions are congested and housing ill-ventilated, with practically no facilities and five to eight people sharing a small room.

The loss of jobs and the generally worsening food security for the lowest-income group, after economic liberalization was introduced, combined with the deterioration of the social welfare system and widening income disparities to force many more immigrants than could be absorbed into the FTZs. Eelens et al. (1992) conclude that Sri Lankan migration to the Gulf was a clear case of survival migration by those in the poorest strata of society. In contrast to other Asian exporters of labour, Sri Lankans were predominantly (70 per cent) married females, from the Colombo metropolitan area, with average educational attainment, employed abroad as domestic servants. Fifty-six per cent were unskilled workers, and 24 per cent had been unemployed before migration. The propotion of females among the unskilled workers was as high as 80 per cent (Wignaraja, 1987).

## Case study setting

The case study is of a coastal village in Sri Lanka, where female migrant returnees from the Middle East and factory workers returned from the FTZ live with non-migrants. This village is situated approximately one kilometre from the main Colombo–Galle highway, and displays suburban characteristics. Although data on employment indicate that 53 per cent of workers are employed in the tertiary sector, in administrative identification and in the perception of the inhabitants this is a village.

Galvehera, as it is called, is a Grama Sevaka division, which is the smallest administrative unit in Sri Lanka. It is evident that there are no subsistence farmers. The main reason for this is the flooding of low-lying paddy-fields by sea water in the 1970s. Thereafter most people turned to cinnamon, which is one of the country's leading commercial crops. An enormous amount of cinnamon land in the area is owned by a few villagers and absentee landlords. The majority of workers in the primary sector are labourers on these cinnamon estates. Those employed in the secondary sector mostly work in factories and small industries. The majority of those employed in the area work in the tertiary sector, either as housemaids in the Middle East or in jobs linked to the tourist trade.

Kinship plays an important role in the social structure of the village. Most of the inhabitants living in Galvehera are related, and all are Sinhala Buddhists. To be a descendant of an ancestor born in the village and to have relatives in close proximity is indicative of one's social status. Not only the network of blood relations, but caste relations, which link to networks on the national level, can be clearly seen. There is a caste hierarchy with three main layers. The highest caste, the *Salagama*, is divided into five sub-castes, the first being the soldiers. Another four sub-castes combine to form the second caste. Goldsmiths, drummers, potters, and some considered even lower in the general hierarchy, form the third caste.

This study deals with three migrant and non-migrant environments:

Galvehera village, the FTZ (particularly Katunayake), and the Middle East (particularly Kuwait and United Arab Emirates). Since it is expected that the two environments external to the village, each in its own way, are deviant with respect to the village culture, women are placed in a stressful yet potentially powerful position. They find themselves in a position to compare, understanding certain aspects of the world better than ordinary men and women in the village, irrespective of their educational level. They receive access not only to alternative sources of knowledge, representing different ways of cognitive and normative structuring of society, but also to personal cash income, hence to the power to decide how the money should be spent, for whom and under what conditions. Although we assume that such general consequences can be observed wherever women migrate, there are significant differences between the two migrant groups and the effect the returnees have on the village context.

Even though the proportion of people living from agriculture is shrinking in Sri Lanka, many cultural behaviour patterns, norms and values are still largely inspired by the agricultural past. We think particularly of three characteristics: the role of family and kinship, the dominance of men over women, and the caste structure. The basic objective lies in the long-term reproduction of feudal social relations, and a minimization of economic risks. Conditions in the FTZ and the Middle East are decidedly different.

Irrespective of the geographical distance, the cultural distance from the village to the Middle East environment is probably less than from the village to the FTZ. Though the social relations in FTZs are also hierarchical, the hierarchy is based on different criteria. They are less ascribed, more reflecting the functional necessities of industrial production and the mechanism of exploitation of labour, aiming at the maximization of profit. Race and gender discrimination – unlike class – are not intrinsic to capitalism, but contingent (Meiksins Wood, 1988). If gender discrimination and over-exploitation of women in the Sri Lankan FTZs still describe everyday reality, we explain it by the fact that women are already socially weaker in traditional Sri Lankan society. The most powerful effect of the processes of economic liberalization is the dissolution of kinship and other ascriptive networks of personal obligation (Friedman, 1994: 25). Unmarried women undergo a rapid change in cognitive, social, emotional and moral terms. They live free and isolated from their family's protection and control; they enjoy extensive peer-group contacts; they experience the complete irrelevance of caste in their working positions; they learn to interpret gender discrimination in class terms; and frequently they engage in sexual relations during their five-year term of contract losing their virginity and with it the sense of honour which might have bound them more to traditional discipline.

Compared to the experiences in the FTZs, the migrants to the Middle East are confronted with a very different environment. As a rule, the Sri Lankan migrants are employed as housemaids in Arab households. They leave their families in the village only to find themselves re-integrated into another family. The social relations, compared to the FTZ, are again restricted; satisfaction and dissatisfaction with their behaviour are expressed in personal terms; exposure to sexual risks is a private drama, and not talked about as in the village at home.

The effect of the two forms of migration are quite different on a personal and on a collective level. Young women, after five years of work in an FTZ, have probably developed a kind of proletarian attitude. Comparable to military service, they congregated with very different kinds of peer, all levelled down to the common fate of workers, sharing experiences, fears and secrecies of a kind that non-migrant villagers or migrants to the Middle East can only imagine from hearsay.

Reintegration in the village, marriage, being reduced (or elevated) to the role of loving mother and obedient wife, being disciplined by local gossip and allegations – such a process of getting back to normal seems rather improbable.

On the one hand, daughters who have worked in an FTZ and sup-ported their families and siblings by regular remittances probably receive praise for their loyalty and help. On the other hand, the way the money has been earned is morally disapproved of. The more the daughter was able to save – for a house, for the education of a sister, or for the dowry of her personal marriage – the stronger the allegations.

The same ambivalence may be directed towards returnees from the Middle East, although in the majority of cases they were married when they left. In other respects, the experience must be less disruptive. However, the experience of being able to make a living independent from family support strongly affects the women's attitudes and the social relations in the village. There are also many questions about the women: what kind of mothers and wives will they be? How will they educate their children? What kind of role-model are they for other low-class women? Do the other women fear becoming stigmatized, or do they idealize and imitate migrant women?

## Methodology

The approach of the research was strongly action-oriented. The team tried to find out about the reality of daily life, as experienced and expressed by the women themselves, by studying the women in the village in two stages. In the first stage a survey of the whole village, 232 households, was carried out in order to understand the socio-economic profile of the village and locate the socio-economic characteristics of each household, the level of consumption and the status of the women therein. In the second stage three categories of women were selected from the total population for in-depth interview: 24 Middle-East migrant returnees, 19 FTZ returnees and 24 non-migrant women. It is symptomatic that 24 FTZ returnees were not available in the village, because such women tend not to return.

As a part of our participatory research method we tried to involve women's organizations as research partners, and though this was not very successful, owing to the non-representative and hierarchical character of women's groups in the village, it facilitated the approach to, and generated tremendous interest and support from the village women. Owing to limited time, it was not possible to make the research material available to the village, or to initiate such action as the research results suggest, such as newspaper articles, a radio programme and a self-help forum for migrants.

The data to follow concentrate on the impact of the migration in different fields: the self-perception of the migrants in terms of female identity and role definition; women's health and control over their bodies; personal development. Since the village reality is dynamic and embedded in a changing society, we subsequently asked what kind of knowledge, in a conflicting environment, is considered relevant by which women, and what kind of access they have to such knowledge.

It must be pointed out that most of the migrating women want to migrate. This is not self-evident, since working in the FTZ or in the Middle East means being exposed to extreme exploitation, and often to sexual harassment. Willingness to engage in and even to actively search for such work (often the only work available) seems to support the hypothesis that life in Sinhalese Buddhist villages is less attractive than migration to lower-class women than is commonly assumed. They are not only exposed to the restrictions of their class, but also subdued by the restrictions on women irrespective of their social position. In view of these basic realities, the following questions are raised:

- What role does migration play in women's strategies for emancipation and empowerment?
- What aspects of female existence must be considered in an operational definition of 'improved quality of life'?
- What differences may be expected between migration to the Middle

East and to the FTZs with respect to the alteration of gender roles and the social status of women?

• Is there is enough room for the emancipation of marginalized women within the framework of the dominant middle-class Sinhalese Buddhist ideology?

## The returnee migrant women's experience

When women from the village migrate to the Middle East, they encounter a totally different environment from that of the village. Migrant women live isolated lives, dependent on the families that employ them and restricted in their movements. Occasionally, several Sri Lankan women together are employed as housemaids in one household. They are dependent on their employers to expand their social contacts. Women who work as hospital labourers are not so isolated. The type of social contacts they are able to make influences their situation and expectations on their return.

Women who return after working in the FTZ face a totally different environment from the one experienced during their years in employment. As the migratory worker population began to increase, neighbouring villagers let out rows of rooms with minimum facilities (and security) to migrant women. Women coped with the problems posed by such boarding houses by forming strong bonds among their peers, who were enduring the same conditions. In the boarding room, three to five women sleep, cook, socialize and eat together, and meet other young women who share water and sanitary facilities. Also, in the factory, the women find companionship between themselves as they help each other to cope with the poor conditions. Unlike the Middle East migrants, in this environment the women become more politically aware, and reintegration in the village after such experiences is problematic.

The women who have never migrated hold different beliefs, attitudes and values to these migrant women. Migrant returnees dress and speak in a manner that is perceived by the village community simultaneously as civilized, because it reflects urban life styles, and degrading because it is outside village norms. Most of the non-migrant women interviewed made it clear that the changes in migrants were not a cause for envy. Some, however, though they themselves would be reluctant to migrate owing to family pressure, spoke enviously of the migrant women's economic empowerment, freedom and new experiences.

It is interesting to compare how the three categories of women perceive their and the other groups' environment. While non-migrants perceive their environment as stagnant and devoid of opportunities for upward mobility, they did not approve of migrant women. For the Middle East environment they have nothing but contempt, denigrating it as immoral and dangerous, full of sex maniacs and inhuman employers causing unwanted pregnancies, broken families, veneral diseases and even AIDS.

Middle East migrant returnees, by contrast, regard the Middle East environment as being more protective (and secure) than the village. Domestic servants especially, as they are not allowed outside the home or to have interactions with men, are adamant in this belief, and they themselves, for example, are sceptical about women working in hospitals (there were two such women in the village).

Non-migrants perceive the FTZ environment as alien to village life, permitting too much freedom and interaction with men. To them, it is a physically and morally unhealthy environment for young women. FTZ returnees regard the FTZ environment as physically draining, yet happy and carefree, full of excitement and new experiences, which are shared as a group. Although they had to return to the village, as they failed to find marriage partners, after the freedom of urban life they dislike village society. Seven unmarried FTZ returnees expressed strong feelings that they would like changes in the social and cultural structure of the village. Married returnees showed slightly more ability to reintegrate, though they have a different attitude from non-migrant married women. They showed concern and pity for non-migrants, and thought they were foolish and unfortunate not to explore other life styles. Middle East migrants were harsher on non-migrants, saying that even if their pride kept them at home, they were envious of migrants and trying to under-mine their new status by criticizing the Middle East environment. All migrants agreed that although they may have had hardships outside the village, the economic gain and new experiences helped them to cope better with the exploited and downtrodden life of village women.

As most of the migrant women are from less privileged families, and most of the non-migrants are from families more highly placed in the social hierarchy, some of this mutual distrust is also class- and caste-based.

Migrant returnees are understanding and sympathetic about each other's environments. FTZ returnees think that many of the rumours about the Middle East are malicious, though they are also cautious. While they consider Middle East migration as more rewarding, the basic reason for not going there has been the poor reputation attached to being a Middle East housemaid. Young unmarried women who have to earn their own dowries are reluctant to diminish their marriage prospects by migrating to the Middle East, but many consider going there after marriage. This pattern is now changing, as it is not uncommon for unmarried women to migrate to the FTZ, then to the Middle East, and back again to the garment industry.

It is easier for older married women to migrate to the Middle East, as husbands encourage them to go and are expected to remain faithful, and they settle back more easily into their family lives.

## Changing economic and social status

Women go to work in difficult conditions, leaving behind families with young children or aged parents, because of their poverty and dreams to improve. These women send most of their salaries back home (63 per cent of FTZ workers and 100 per cent of Middle East migrants). They become, in effect, the bread-winners of the families. Husbands, however, are not always reliable, and there are cases where they waste the money on gambling, alcohol and mistresses. The elevated consumption pattern of households, induced by the sudden flush of money, makes it difficult for families to adjust when the woman returns. There are many men (29 per cent) who lost their jobs through negligence after their wives migrated.

The major goal of the migrants is to build a house. It takes around six years to achieve this dream. Only four women had done it. Another four repaired and upgraded their houses, and two had bought land, but will need to return to the Middle East in order to pay for a house. Nine of the Middle East migrants returned to find their husbands had squandered the income.

FTZ migrants receive a smaller salary in rupees. They have to pay for their upkeep and do not benefit from gifts from employers. Their contribution to the village household is less, but they still pay for the day-to-day expenses. In contrast, 15 per cent of the non-migrants interviewed had no income to spend. The amount of earnings is closely related to the women's decision-making power within the family. Thirteen Middle East migrants were the sole decision-makers, while six decided jointly with their husbands. Only one case reported her husband being the sole decision-maker. In contrast to this, only two FTZ returnees have been able to have a say in household decisions. Seven took part in decision-making in consultation with other members of the family, and the other ten were not included in the process. Twenty-one non-migrants stated that their husbands and male kin were the sole decision-makers, and three contributed to making decisions for the whole family.

Of the Middle East migrants, 88 per cent had been married at the time of first migration and had embarked on it with the approval of their respective husbands. The push to migrate had been the abject poverty at home. The decrease in authority of a man at home begins with his wife's migration. Even if he had been a co-earner for the household before migration, during the period of migration he become a spendthrift. The new experience changes the wife too; she becomes aware of her role as the bread-winner, and also that her husband is not a partner in her goal for a better life. In these cases women become the heads of households, taking their own and their household decisions, proud of their own authority and achievements.

FTZ migrant returnees, apart from the three who work in a nearby garment factory, were not able to find a substantial means of income, and have thus lost their brief authority. All but one were unmarried at the time of migration. The social stigma attached to female migration diminished their marriage prospects and, according to them, seven married beneath their aspirations. These seven women see themselves as burdened with young children and deprived of possibilities to engage in income-generating activities. Their experience as garment workers has made them dissatisfied; they do not meekly accept the authority of their husbands, and are frustrated that there are no employment opportunities in and around the village.

Even if most of the migrant women were proud of their independence, their level of responsibility and hard work, all the migrant women interviewed except two stated that marriage and motherhood are essential in a woman's life, particularly for their old age – an unsurprising need given the lack of social security system for the elderly. No preference as to the sex of their children was expressed.

For non-migrants, a sense of pride in womanhood is less clear; rather, they subscribed to the view that a women's identity is an integral part of social and cultural definitions of womanhood: to be an obedient daughter, a dutiful wife and a sacrificing mother. Even in the case of women who worked there is little sense of them as individuals with aspirations, attitudes and values of their own. All expressed their concern at the way some of the migrants, especially Middle East returnees, are treating their menfolk. Migrant returnees, on the other hand, thought that the non-migrants were too obedient and had no self-identity. These two viewpoints express the cultural conflict emerging in the village. Especially for FTZ returnees, who have become accustomed to an urban culture, the conflict is more pronounced. But both sets of migrant women are slowly changing traditional village attitudes towards women.

## The impact on the family

The effect of migration on schoolchildren and infants who are left behind is one of the costs of migration, even if most married migrants make provision for a close female relative to take their place during the period of migration. While more comprehensive research is needed to determine the effect on infants, there is a clear difference between the schoolchildren of migrants and migrant returnees and those of non-migrants. According to the teachers at nearby schools, absenteeism and rowdy behaviour are far more evident in children whose mothers are abroad. Even when their mothers return, the behaviour patterns are hard to change. Standards of school-work are far below the required level, and the mothers' interest in children's schooling (measured by the frequency of meetings with teachers and participation in school functions) is much less than that of non-migrant mothers. From three schools, with around 120 students, only two children with migrant mothers were identified by the teachers as satisfactory students. While some returnee mothers were genuinely worried about the situation, most were indifferent, on the assumption that there is a whole new world out there for the children to explore if they fail in their studies. This is clearly a big departure from the belief that education is the means to social mobility in contemporary rural society.

Returnees showed more concern about the effect of migration on the stability of the family. Among the Middle East returnees, there were three women in the sample who found that their husbands kept mistresses during their absence. The number is said to be far higher throughout the village. There was a clandestine pattern of husbands turning to sisters-in-law for comfort when their wives were abroad and switching back to the old routine as soon as their wives came back. Two marriages ended with one of the women losing the support of her two grown children. In both cases the husbands blamed their migrating wife's immorality. Two other women, however, returned with infants, and were able to reintegrate successfully into their former families. Two women had their young sons and daughters enter early and unsuitable marriages in their absence. Three found that their husbands had lost their jobs, two that their husbands had become alcoholics and gamblers, while four lost a husband, a child or a parent while away.

For unmarried FTZ returnees it is a different situation. FTZ workers return to the village after several years hoping to get married. They find, however, that even if they have gained economically, their marriage-ability has been lowered. Whereas their peer group who remained in the village get married, they find themselves up against social barriers that devalue their mobility and presumed sexual freedom. But even if they are aware of being snubbed by non-migrants, the returnees value the economic benefit to their families, the new knowledge acquired, and their wider circle of friends made during migration.

Men in the village not married to migrants were very critical of migrant women and the effect they are having on non-migrants. In most cases they blamed the male relatives of the migrants for allowing women to leave familiar surroundings. They saw it as an injustice for women to have men depend on them, and were concerned, but did not blame the women, for the women's moral vulnerability. They were critical of the government for not improving economic conditions so that the migration of women is not necessary. Outspoken migrant returnees are perceived as a threat to the familial, social and cultural structure of the village. Such a strong reaction from the men suggests that the balance in gender relations is being shifted by migration. The gender-role reversal in some families will invariably induce a change in people's perception of gender role.

There are new networks springing up among the migrant returnees in the village, who had set up arrangements of reciprocal help during migration and who continue to form a close community. These new networks too are looked on with suspicion, and are a sign of moves away from the family and husbands as the traditional support and sources of knowledge.

## Changes in health and reproductive awareness

That stress and related health problems are experienced by migrant women on their return is evident. For both groups of returnees, the longer the time away the higher the degree of stress. For returnees who are more integrated into village society through marriage before migration, the reintegration is less stressful. Married Middle East migrants are aware that they are helping the family, and do not suffer from the same sense of frustration as the FTZ returnees. FTZ migrants in many instances become accustomed to urban culture, and feel that village husbands are no longer worthy partners. All the FTZ returnees, apart from one, confessed to wishing to marry a person from an urban background and settle in an urban environment. They returned to village life because they could not fulfil that hope. Especially for the eight unmarried returnees, life holds little hope. The village does not offer the chance of a suitable husband. Unhappiness is reflected in poor health. These women complain of feeling tired and exhausted, of sleeplessness, loss of appetite and constant headaches.

Their experience during migration also determines the stress felt on reintegration. If women felt insecure while away, their reintegration is less traumatic, whereas if migrants experienced comfortable family environments with kind employers, their re-entry into drudgery at home is less pleasant.

In the case of FTZ factory workers who became used to their autonomy, they describe the village as stifling and they miss their network of friends. Their physical health, though, did suffer from the exploitative conditions in the factories and the poor accommodation. FTZ returnees are mentally and physically drained, because of constant hard work, and are considered thinner (i.e. not attractive). Most of the factories have an informal mechanism of firing workers after five years, but returnees say that the worker often has to leave the job after two or three years because of poor health and stress. Middle East migrants are, in popular opinion, seen as becoming fairer and fatter, making them more attractive and more marriageable, and no health problems are associated with their period of migration.

*Reproductive health and sexuality* There is a marked improvement of awareness of reproductive health issues after migration. All the returnees know to consult clinics, to have nutritious food, to take special care of themselves during pregnancy and to deliver in a hospital. They all believe that the pregnancy is a joint responsibility, and that pre- and post-natal care is essential. All returnees agreed that abortion is not a solution to unwanted pregnancies and should be avoided.

There are three women who had abortions prior to their first migration. Now all take modern contraceptives. There are seven women (37.5 per cent of migrants) who, after having the desired number of children, have had a tubectomy. This compares with 3 per cent of the non-migrant women. Other methods used in the village are the pill, the loop and injectables. According to the family health workers' statistics, these are used by women who are migrant returnees. Unmarried FTZ migrants, though some were reluctant to discuss their sexual life, exhibited a wide knowledge of contraceptives and also expressed very liberal ideas about love, sex and marriage.

As stated elsewhere, migrants desire fewer children, as they are conscious of wanting to retain their physical health and beauty. Although non-migrants did not wish to have many children, they are either ignorant of, or hold misconceptions about, contraceptive use or are under pressure from husbands not to use them.

Migrants are determined to give equal health care to sons and daughters, and to take care of themselves, whereas the majority of non-migrants think males are more deserving of health care.

Migrants showed marked differences from non-migrants in their awareness of sexual pleasure. While non-migrants saw sexual relations as a duty in marriage, and felt guilty and ashamed of it, migrants desired it with a partner of their choice for the purpose of having pleasure. Three Middle East returnees admitted to having clandestine affairs, and cited dissatisfaction with their husbands as the reason. Unmarried FTZ returnees, however, said that they were constrained by the fact that their behaviour could result in their never marrying within their rural society. It is interesting that, contrary to popular opinion, it is the Middle East returnees who have tended to change their standards of morality. While non-migrants perceived new ideas and liberal behaviour as indicative of the immorality of migrants, migrants pitied non-migrants for their narrow world-view and uneventful life.

On issues such as menstruation, contraception, intercourse, pregnancy, delivery, abortion, lactation, weaning, child care, general health, cooking, specialist skills and charms, Sri Lanka has a long tradition of midwives and other medical specialists. The knowledge that they disseminate is particularly important at ritual events, such as puberty and marriage.

The change in employment opportunities for women, and their new-found independence after the relatively cloistered village life, opens up new access to knowledge, as well as changing the demands for knowledge.

Women in the two age categories under 40 acquire knowledge through friends and magazines. The youngest age-group, between 20 and 25, referred freely to the community services of the Family Planning Bureau. They felt that the information available from the Family Planning Bureau and the prevention units against AIDS and veneral disease was sufficient, and further communication between mother and daughter was not needed. However, they felt that more knowledge on reproductive health should be disseminated through schools. All the women believed that primary responsibility for reproductive health and sexuality should lie with the state education and health authorities, and that parental responsibilities should diminish as the village becomes more integrated into the modern system.

For women over 40, the mass media were not considered a source of knowledge; they relied instead on relatives. Most said that they knew about sexual relations only after they were married. Only two were informed about traditional contraceptive methods by older women relatives, and two others asked friends. The traditional ceremony at puberty and on the night before marriage did not instruct the women in sexual matters. These women see the younger generation as fortunate in being able to attain knowledge through the media (mostly magazines;

radio and television were not cited as sources), and seemed relieved that they were taking less responsibility. They felt that young people were reluctant to discuss such matters with them and that it was much easier to learn from the mass media.

All the women interviewed received knowledge about menstruation, pregnancy, childbirth and child care from their mothers and other relatives. Those with younger siblings learnt child-care skills by assisting their mothers. For young women, mass media – particularly magazines – and formal education in schools and clinics were the major source of knowledge.

In spite of the transition away from older relatives, the traditional source of knowledge, to peer groups, schools and media, family ceremonies around puberty and marriage are still influential in how women understand their own sexual identity as women. The impurity some of them attach to being a woman stems from traditional explanations and traditional attitudes, where menstruating women were barred from certain ceremonies. Most women interviewed suggested that both kinds of knowledge – traditional and modern medical – need to be known. There was considerable embarrassment, though, in speaking about formal programmes of sex education.

Migrant returnees play an important role in transferring new knowledge to other women. But because of the doubts held in general about their morality, the information they pass on about reproductive health and sexuality is stigmatized and not always accepted.

## Conclusion

The study documents how migrant women bring back to the village not only income, but also new knowledge and experience, which are rapidly breaking traditional gender boundaries and shaking some caste and class divisions. The change could not be faster. (No revolutionary socialist regime did it faster!) The women's new-found economic and social position in the family has changed the village to its core, shifting traditional mores and the sense of women's place. Access to different life styles, new friendships and more extensive knowledge of reproductive health and sexuality is shaking the old community order. These changes have also created tensions within marriages, around issues of authority over economic decisions, reproductive choice and care of children. The children of migrants are poor achievers in schools, and some of the husbands have turned to dissolute lives. The shift away from traditional patriarchal values, leading to more autonomy for women, has also caused discord and uncertainty in the community, leading to stress, ill-health and frustration for the women themselves. It is an open question as to whether this pace of change is, in reality, a route to village women's emancipation.

The study breaks new ground in looking at the experience of migrant women in all age-groups. It uncovers rich material, which deserves further exploration and more awareness on the part of the government, whose apparently socially unaware policies rely on women in the migrant trade. The cultural and social disruption to village life, the huge changes wrought in these women's, their men's and children's lives should not be subsumed by the Sri Lankan government's need for foreign currency, or Sri Lanka's drive to enter the global world economy. At the same time, the opening in traditional life to modern knowledge of reproduction and other cultural mores and life styles, which could give women greater autonomy and allow for greater reproductive choice, is also an opportunity that could be guided by services that the women migrants themselves could participate in planning. Their informal support networks, set up after migration, could be valuable channels for new, useful information for all village women, if sensitively handled by outside intervention. Most of all, these women's experience both during migration and afterwards needs to be documented and understood within the social and cultural context of modern Sri Lanka, in order to try and reduce the stress that migrants and their families suffer, and in order to ensure a smooth transition for the Sri Lankan people to a modern economy.

## Notes

1. While Sandya Hewamanne was the main author of the chapter's case study, Hans Peter Müller contributed the section's 'cultural and historical context of migration', 'case study setting' and 'methodology', and supervised the original research.

2. In this advertisement a potential labour force of 600,000 was mentioned: 'As any manufacturer knows, intelligent labor is a boon, especially in labor-intensive industries. Sri Lanka's Free Trade Zone offers manufacturers one of the world's most educated, highly trainable labor reserves: 600,000 men and women who are young and eager to work. Sri Lanka's most valuable natural resource is its educated, intelligent and mostly English-speaking labor ... an unbeatable combination of tax incentives and business-like assistance being offered ... Sri Lanka offers many other advantages: ... Sri Lanka has the most competitive labor rates in Asia. The average monthly wage in manufacturing industries is only US$35. Compare your wage bill with this ...' (Brown 1982, quoted in Hettige 1995: 2).

# References

Brown, M. B. (1982) 'Developing societies as part of an international political economy', in H. Alavi and T. Shanin (eds), *Introduction to the Sociology of "Developing Societies"*, New York, Monthly Review Press.

Eelens, F., T. Scampers and J. D. Speckmann (eds) (1992) *Labour Migration to the Middle East: From Sri Lanka to the Gulf*, London and New York, Paul Kegan.

Friedman, J. (1994) *Cultural Ideology and Global Process*, London, Sage.

Gunnatileke, G. (1991) 'Sri Lanka', in Ders (ed.) (1991) *Migration to the Arab World: experience of returning migrants*, Tokyo, UN University Press, pp. 290–352.

Hettige, S. (1995) *Social Implications of Economic Liberalisations: The Case of Sri Lanka*, New York, Monthly Review Press.

Jayaweera, S. (1990) 'Women and development: a reappraisal of the Sri Lankan experience', in CENWOR (ed.), *The Hidden Face of the Development: Women, Work and Equality in Sri Lanka*, Colombo, Centre for Women's Research.

Karunnatilake, H. N. S. (1987) *The Economy of Sri Lanka*, Colombo, Centre for Demographic and Socio-Economic Studies.

Kelegama, S. (1993) 'Distribution of Income and Ownership of Assets, Trends in Sri Lanka', *Pravada*, 2: pp. 15–21.

Kelagama, S. and G. Wignaraja (1991) 'Trade policy and industrial development in Sri Lanka', *Marga*, Vol. 11, No. 4.

Lall, S. and G. Wignaraja (1993) 'Foreign involvement by European firms and garment exports by developing countries', *Marga*, Vol. 12, No. 4.

Meiksins Wood, E. (1988) 'Capitalism and human emancipation', *New Left Review*, No. 167.

Wignaraja, K. (1987) 'A study of recent trends in Sri Lankan labour migration to the Middle East', Princeton University, Princeton, NJ, unpublished thesis.

# 7

# Two generations of Italian women: shifts in life choices, reproductive health and sexuality

EMANUELA CALABRINI AND
ELISABETTA VACCARO

This chapter describes the evolution of the Italian family and women's status by looking at the socio-economic transformations in Italy since the war. We examine how Italian women adapted to the shift from a rural to an urban industrialized country, by gradually acquiring a higher degree of economic independence and autonomy over their reproductive health and life choices.

Our case study focuses on two groups of women: adult women, who were teenagers in the 1960s, and young women, the teenagers of the 1990s. Adult women and a group of teenagers were selected in Rome, and another group of teenagers in Cuorgné, a small town near Turin. The chapter examines whether these two generations' ideas on marriage, motherhood and work converge or diverge, and what type of communication exists between different generations and among women of the same generation with reference to the transfer of knowledge of reproductive health and sexual behaviour.

The study also aims to assess the present level of communication between women of different generations, and what we believe to be the appropriate means to foster the dialogue and disseminate information on reproductive health and sexuality.

## Geographical setting and population

The Italian peninsula, covering an area of 301,255 square kilometres, is divided into 20 regions, 18 on the mainland and two islands.[1] In the middle of the Mediterranean Sea, the so-called *bel paese* (beautiful country) is one of the most industrialized countries in the world, with strong metallurgical, mechanical, textile, chemical and manufacturing industries and a well developed tertiary sector, with tourism also representing a considerable source of income. The agricultural sector, which was economically important until the Second World War, has been reduced to approximately 8.2 per cent of the economy.

The economic structure of the Italian regions reflects the geographical variety and youthfulness of the country, which was unified only in the late 1860s. Despite its unification, Metternich's definition of Italy as 'more a geographical expression than a country' may still be applied to the extraordinary variety of culture, folklore, languages and mentality coexisting in the Italian boot (Adler Hellman, 1987: 9).

The Italian population is approximately 57.9 million, of which about 29.7 million are women (United Nations, 1995: 23). In the early 1990s, of 15–65-year-old women, 58.3 per cent were either married or co-habiting, 24.9 per cent were single, 14.1 per cent were widows and 2.7 per cent were separated or divorced, whereas above 65 years of age, married women totalled 35.8 per cent, single women 10 per cent, widows 52.5 per cent, and 1.7 per cent were separated or divorced (ISTAT, 1992). From 1960 to 1992, the annual population growth rate was 0.4 per cent. This percentage is now decreasing and it is estimated that in future years there will be a growth rate of nil (UNDP, 1995).

Italy is a Catholic country, with the Pope residing in the Vatican, located in the centre of Rome.[2] The physical presence of the Pope has always influenced Italian history. Before unification, the Pontiff ruled most of the centre of the country, and Catholicism was the state religion until 1985, when the Italian Parliament ratified the new Concordat abolishing compulsory religious education in schools and reducing state financial contribution to the Catholic Church[3] (*The Europa World Year Book 1990*, 1990: 1430). Catholicism in Italy has always been a complex issue, closely intertwined with politics. In fact, the Christian Democrats, the political party that ruled the country from the first post-war elections until 1992, have always supported a policy strongly based on Catholic Church values, family, marriage and motherhood.

## Family evolution from the late 1940s to the early 1990s

The evolution of the Italian family has been greatly influenced by post-war economic transformations. From a predominantly peasant country, Italy has become an urbanized country with an industrially based economy. Many studies have tried to explain the link between industrialization and urbanization on the one hand, and a reduced number of offspring, which is the typical feature of the modern family in Italy, on the other. Francesca Bettio (1988b) states that, whereas in a pre-capitalist agrarian context the family is the true unit of production and children represent a source of labour and income for the whole family, so that the bigger the family, the higher the income, in an urban context this situation no longer holds. As children move away from the family to be absorbed by the new economy, based on commodity production located outside the household, the family is no longer able to control either the income they generate or their services. Parents, therefore, prefer not to invest in offspring, because children's contribution to the family income decreases, and traditional children–parent obligations change accordingly. This explanation can well be applied to the Italian situation of the late 1950s and early 1960s, when the country experienced a period of unprecedented economic boom. This growth led to a transformation of the traditional image of the family – numerous offspring living under the same roof with parents and grandparents – into a modern nuclear family reduced in size, with an accompanying change in children's obligations in kind (assistance to parents in sickness or old age). Another important factor determining the shift from the traditional to the modern Italian family lies in the institutional developments of the early 1960s, when the government passed a law banning child labour for under-14s, and extending compulsory secondary education to 14 (Bettio, 1988b: 199–200).

Urbanization deepened the isolation of the family which, on the one hand, contributed to the family's higher degree of privacy compared to that found in a rural context, and on the other, closed the family in upon itself and made it less open to participation in community life. Urbanization for young family members resulted in a higher degree of freedom both inside and outside the household. Within the family, parental control and authority over children, both boys and girls, lessened, while outside the home new leisure activities began to gain ground, such as meeting friends in bars, playing billiards, listening to juke-box music, riding on scooters, and shopping. Finally, both sexes could mix in meeting places without parental presence and control (Ginsborg, 1990: 243).

These transformations affected the southern regions of Italy to a lesser extent than the centre and the north, given the backwardness of its predominantly agrarian economy. In fact, the *mezzogiorno* – the south of Italy – did not benefit greatly from the economic boom, as industries were concentrated in the northern regions, and were the real engine pushing Italy towards European economic integration.[4] Even the setting up of the 'cathedrals in the desert' – the few state-owned industries created in remote areas of the south – did not have a positive impact on its economy. As a result, this did not lead to profound changes in the traditional southern family structure, characterized by high birth rates and close family bonds. Furthermore, the inefficiencies of local government pushed southerners towards a more closed type of family for protection against criminal organizations such as the Mafia, Camorra and 'Ndrangheta, which the state was not able to eradicate.[5] At the same time, criminality replaced the absent state by providing southern families with illegal job opportunities.

After the economic boom of the 1960s, Italy, like all major Western industrialized nations, underwent a period of social crisis[6] and social turmoil. Some sectors of the Italian population mobilized in order to lobby the government to implement socio-economic reforms to meet the needs of a rapidly changing society. A sense of rebellion against authority spread from universities to factories. Students voiced their dissatisfaction with the poor and backward education system, modern consumerism and the lack of job opportunities. Workers organized themselves to improve their working conditions and salaries. Students' rejection of all levels of authority included the family, which was now seen as an 'oppressive institution', excessively interfering in their private lives. They also questioned 'the modern family closeness, its distrust of the outside world, its predominant values of material enrichment', and advocated 'a greater commitment to their peer group and collectivist ideals' (Ginsborg, 1990: 305). In this period, the most radical left-wingers criticized marriage and opted for cohabiting with their partners.

In the 1980s and early 1990s, family size continued to fall. According to the ISTAT *Annual Report* on the Italian family for 1995, families of three members now represent 69.9 per cent of the population, families of four total 21.6 per cent, and families of five and over, 8.6 per cent (ISTAT, 1995). Yet families seem to be more cohesive than in the late 1960s and 1970s, and certainly the family has returned to the top of the list of commonly held value systems. As Ginsborg remarks,

> [e]ven in urban contexts, Italian grandparents remain closely involved in the care of grandchildren; and once the older generation is threatened by fragility and immobility, it receives considerable assistance and company, especially from daughters and their families. Other relations, too, are frequently involved in the life of the family. (Ginsborg, 1990: 414)

However, Ginsborg also points out that 'any lingering image of the close nature of the Italian family – all work, rest and socializing with relations – has given way to a reality where individual members of the family relate more and more to their peer groups and the outside world' (1990: 417). Therefore, as far as income and overall management strategy of the household are concerned, the family remains united, but as regards consumption and free time, its individual members are autonomous in their decisions. These features may be applied to all the

Italian regions, but certainly in the south larger families with closer links survive. As Ginsborg (1990: 416–17) explains:

> the concept of maximizing the numbers of persons available for the labour market is still stronger than any idea of limiting family size in order to conserve resources. These larger families have to survive in a situation of stagnation on the labour market [ ... ] [In such a situation] it is clear that a majority, not a minority of families still face grave problems.[7]

In ISTAT *Annual Report* for 1995, it emerges that while in the north-west of Italy 43.4 per cent of couples have children, in the south 55.7 per cent of couples have children.

Another feature of the Italian family of the 1990s is that children tend to leave the household later and later, for a series of reasons, including the increase of young people receiving secondary and tertiary education, unemployment, and the high cost of living. Notwithstanding children's autonomy and freedom from parental control, parents tend to continue to be closely involved in children's lives by economically supporting them even when they are earning independent wages. Their behaviour is dictated by an overprotective attitude, because they tend to assume that their children will always remain dependent, needing parents' advice and help throughout their lives. Most of them, for example, assist their children in buying or renting a flat and in bringing up their children's offspring. On the other hand, children themselves somehow take for granted their parents' attitude, and do little to loosen the bonds with their families.[8]

## Women's status in the 1960s

The changes in the family between the 1960s and the 1990s are evident in the changing perceptions of women's status. During the economic boom of the 1960s, the rural exodus to urban areas reduced women's participation in the labour market. In fact, only some of those previously employed in agriculture could find alternative jobs in the cities. Although many women did piece-work at home or in the informal sector, the majority were officially registered as housewives. This status was greatly played upon by the media, which, when advertising products, made use of the image of Italian women devoting all their energies to household chores and caring for their families. Hence the definition of the Italian woman as *tutta casa e famiglia*, or as Ginsborg puts it (1990: 244), '[a] smartly dressed [woman], with well-turned-out children and a sparkling house full of consumer durables'. Such a traditional image of the Italian woman was strengthened by the Church's perception of the woman as a caring mother and faithful wife. Among the features of a marriageable woman, chastity occupied an important place, especially in the south, where the issue of family honour and the traditional concept of morality were strictly linked to a daughter's virginity. In this regard, the society as a whole still retained many taboos, and considered women having intercourse out of wedlock as damnable promiscuity. Men, however, enjoyed sexual freedom, exempt from any social blame if they had pre-marital sexual experiences.

Therefore, the 1960s did not see substantial changes in the Italian mentality with regard to sexual behaviour and women's sexual autonomy. A timid effort to open a debate on sexual matters was made by the publishing of an article and a survey, respectively, by *Oggi* and *L'Espresso*, (two popular, influential national magazines), which dared to discuss sex education and infidelity among Italian wives. Nevertheless, it was not until a decade later that any radical change in Italian sexual mores took place, with an accompanying change in women's status (Ginsborg, 1990: 244).

## Women's status in the 1970s: the importance of the feminist and student movements on women's empowerment and emancipation

Despite the crisis affecting the Italian economy in the 1970s, women entered the labour market in large numbers and found employment, especially in the extensive informal sector. 'In fact the very characteristic Italian response to the recession was to decentralize production as far as possible and to increase the "black" or hidden sector of the economy' (Ginsborg, 1990: 353). In the formal sector, women tended to be employed in labour-intensive jobs, where they were paid less than men, owing to their lack of conventional skills (i.e. skills acquired over a long period of formal or on-the-job training). As a consequence, they were given less responsibility than men, giving rise to a differentiation between female and male occupations (Bettio, 1988a: 82–3).

Women's newly acquired economic independence coincided with their abandoning of the traditional role of housewife and angel of the hearth, which had been greatly emphasized in the 1960s, and with their sexual emancipation. As in many other Western countries, the Italian student and feminist movements played a very important part in questioning traditional sexual mores. While debating fundamental issues, such as women's rights and sexual rights, feminists coined many new slogans – for instance *'l'utero è mio e lo gestisco io'* ('it is my uterus and I look after it') – in claiming women's self-determination over their bodies. Italian feminist groups, which were formed mainly by middle-class women in the major cities, rebelled against patriarchal values and began analysing women's sexual identity and autonomy, as well as women's oppression by men. In addition, they stimulated the discussion on sexual behaviour, helping to eradicate old sexual taboos. By using the slogan first coined by the American women's group NOW, 'the personal is political', the movement stressed the need to address the problems of private life in the realm of formal politics (Ginsborg, 1990: 366–8; Adler Hellman, 1987: 50).

According to feminists, liberation was to start within the family, in everyday relationships between women, men and children, and then spread to society as a whole. The 1970s, therefore, are the years when women began to understand the importance of family planning through contraception, and when the first advisory centres were set up (1975). Several feminist groups raised complementary demands: some denounced marriage and the family as the site of male domination, others requested both 'wages for housework' and state intervention to relieve women's oppression. One of the main Italian feminist groups was the Movimento della Liberazione delle Donne Italiane (MLD), closely linked to the Radical Party. This movement was to become the most influential pressure group for the achievement of civil-rights reforms, including the elimination of sexual discrimination, the implementation of women's right to control their own bodies through free contraception, and the liberalization of abortion (Ginsborg, 1990: 368–9).

The 1970s saw the debate on two crucial issues for women's empowerment – divorce and abortion; these were submitted to national referenda in 1974 and 1981, respectively. The victory of the pro-divorce and pro-abortion factions showed that, for the first time, a majority of Italian society openly challenged the traditional values and teachings professed by the Church. Italian political parties entered the debate on divorce with two different stances. There were those against divorce who, in compliance with the Church teachings, campaigned for maintaining the traditional family. The pro-divorce parties based their views on the consideration that in Italy there were many unsuccessful marriages that needed to be legally dissolved so that newly constituted families could be legalized and safeguarded by adequate legislation (Adler Hellman, 1987: 49). As far as abortion is concerned, the same political divisions were registered. Once again the conservative parties fought for *diritto alla vita* (the right to life), whereas left-wing parties argued that, since abortion was illegally practised anyway, it needed to be legalized, especially to protect women from the working classes who, unlike those of the middle and upper classes, could not afford to travel abroad to end their unwanted pregnancies, and had to resort to illegal abortionists. In this case, feminist groups played an important role in making women aware of their need for self-determination and control over their bodies.

In Italy, abortion was heavily punished by up to five years' imprisonment, but was nevertheless widespread all over the country. It had become a form of birth control, particularly as sex education was prohibited by the Catholic Church, and the distribution of contraceptives and birth-control information was illegal until 1971. Judith Adler Hellman (1987: 42) points out that 'statistics on the number of illegal abortions performed annually [in Italy] ranged from a conservative World Health Organization figure of 800,000 to a widely cited estimate of 3,000,000, with 20,000 women's deaths directly or indirectly attributable each year to bungled backstreet abortions'. The abortion campaign brought out the need for information on sexual matters. This need was finally met by a series of publications by Editori Riuniti, the Communist Party's publishing house, which issued titles on women's topics. At the same time, the party press began tackling several different women's issues, such as sexuality, the sexual division of labour in the home, and sexism in political life (Adler Hellman, 1987: 48).

## Women's status in the 1980s and early 1990s

Another economic crisis occurred in the 1980s. However, women's employment did not suffer at least until the middle of the decade. Ginsborg reports that 'the number of women employees rose by nearly 50 per cent in the period 1970–85' (1990: 410). Automation brought about a decrease in labour-intensive jobs, and women began replacing men in certain areas. 'In the agricultural sector women tended to fill in the positions abandoned by men in pursuit of better opportunities elsewhere in the economy' (Bettio, 1988a: 92). In this period, self-employment began attracting more and more men, while women gained ground by filling traditionally male-dominated positions in banking and public administration (Bettio, 1988a: 92). Italian women, therefore, have achieved a high degree of empowerment, which has resulted in Italy ranking tenth in Gender Empowerment Measure (GEM).[9] As regards women's types of occupation, early 1990s statistics show that 37.6 per cent of women are administrators, managers and clerical workers, and 46.3 per cent are professional and technical workers. After the 1994 elections, women held 13 per cent of parliamentary seats[10] (UNDP, 1995). Women's empowerment can also be explained by the increase in the number of educated women. In the mid-1990s, young women educated at secondary or tertiary level outnumber men, a change from only ten years before. In the 20–24 age-group, 48 per cent of women hold a high-school diploma or a university degree, against 43 per cent of men. In the 30–34 age-group, the total is 39.9 per cent, against 41.9 per cent of men (ISTAT, 1994). However, of the reasons women interrupt their studies, marriage and family still rank first, given by 31.2 per cent of women in the 14–39 age-group. This is a very high percentage when compared to men of the same age-group, who gave these reasons only in 12.2 per cent of cases.

In the 1980s and early 1990s, women's economic independence has brought about a radical change in their role in society. Influenced by the modern prototype of working women, as typified in the United States – competing with men for high-level positions while aiming to appear always young and fit – Italian women have begun devoting their energies to their career and to their looks, body and clothes, but at the same time trying to fulfil their traditional role within the household. In a recent survey published by an Italian Catholic magazine, *Famiglia Cristiana* (1996/18), 47 per cent of women aged 40–45 said they were satisfied with their occupation; 46.8 per cent stated that they mainly work for need, but 53.2 per cent said they were working in order to achieve their ambitions and find fulfilment. This suggests that women no longer find fulfilment only in marriage and motherhood. Nevertheless, they find time to care for their husbands and children. Yet, we should note, as the survey states, that men are also changing and now help women much more than during the past, especially with children.

It is notable that many women interviewed said they were not interested in politics, and claimed to be disillusioned by feminism, seen as 'a half-way completed revolution': 43.2 per cent acknowledged that feminism brought about women's freedom and greater emancipation, whereas 41.4 per cent said feminism created an overlapping of women's and men's responsibilities and a confusion in traditional men's and women's roles. An Italian film director and scriptwriter, Simona Izzo, who was interviewed by the national newspaper *La Repubblica* to comment on the results of the survey carried out by *Famiglia Cristiana*, believes that feminism and political activity have influenced the women of the 1990s who, in turn, have shaped the character of their daughters, the teenagers of today (*La Repubblica*, 1996: 27). From the *Famiglia Cristiana* survey, however, it emerges that 61 per cent of women aged 40–45 believe that a mother should teach her daughter to gain men's respect, and 24.3 per cent that their daughters should aim for equality with men.

Teenagers and young women of the 1990s have grown up with the image of the working woman, able to combine family and job and cope with the inevitable ensuing problems. They enjoy their emancipated status and see themselves as self-reliant women, strong, proud and confident. Girls enjoy their freedom, as reflected in more equal relationships with boys. It is not unusual for girls to make advances to boys or take decisions on what the young couple should do. There has also been a change in sexual mores: all women's magazines and a few TV programmes tackle issues related to sexual behaviour and reproductive health, and disseminate information on contraception and family planning.

## Methodology

In order to look more closely at the socio-cultural changes accompanying the economic transformation of the country in the last thirty years, and in order to study women's current position concerning inter- and intra-generational knowledge transfer as regards reproductive health and sexual behaviour, we have selected two different age-groups of women: the first group is based in Rome, and comprises 14 adult women aged 37–51, who were teenagers in the late 1960s and early 1970s. This sample, therefore, is drawn from that generation of women who fought for women's rights and faced the big social issues of divorce and abortion. The second group consists of 15 young women, aged 15–23, who live in Rome, and 85 teenagers from Cuorgné, a small industrial town 40 kilometres from Turin, one of the most industrialized cities in the north of Italy.

Located in the centre of Italy, with about four million inhabitants, Rome represents a crossroads between the living habits and mentality of the north and the south, and is a pole of attraction for people from all over the country. Regional diversity is reflected in the sample of adult women: some are from Rome and surrounding rural areas, five are from southern Italy, and two from the north. Cuorgné, a town of approximately 10,000 inhabitants, was chosen in order to study the differences, if any, between teenagers living in a large urban area and those living in a small town.

Adult women of the working and middle classes were randomly selected in the Prenestino-Labicano and Montesacro Alto districts, and in more central areas of the capital. Five are housewives, nine work. The working women include: a barmaid, a bilingual secretary, a cleaner, a clerk, a documentalist, an entrepreneur, an interpreter, a porter and a university researcher. This selection was made in order to assess the various ideas and points of views held by women from different walks of life, and evaluate the impact of women's economic empowerment on their attitudes towards sexual matters.

Roman teenagers were selected only in the Prenestino-Labicano and Montesacro Alto areas. Twelve of them attend a secondary technical high school, one attends a graphic arts school, one goes to university, and the other works as an assistant in a sports shop. Teenagers from Cuorgné were selected from three different classes of a technical high school.

To carry out the research, two questionnaires were elaborated for each age-group. They both relate to sexual matters, inter- and intra-generational knowledge transfer on reproductive health, sex education and behaviour. Questions were asked about women's ideas on marriage and motherhood; their level of decision-making within the family; their information on contraceptive methods and attitudes to sexual health; and finally their relationships with parents, relatives, children and friends in relation to these issues. The research team did not include any leading questions, so as not to influence the replies.

In the case of adult women, questionnaires were distributed, telephone interviews were undertaken, or person-to-person conversations were held. The teenagers responded to questionnaires in writing. In Rome, questionnaires were handed out by one of the interviewees to some school-mates and friends. In Cuorgné, questionnaires were distributed to students by their teachers and filled in during religious instruction.[11] All participants are involved in the publication of the findings.[12]

### Adult and young women: a comparative analysis

We report the data on a comparative basis, considering similarities and differences between women of the same age-group, and between the two age-groups.

*Marriage* All 14 adult women in the sample are married, with one separated but living in the same house as her husband. The average age at marriage was 23½; two extremes were represented by the porter, who married at 16, and the documentalist, who married at the age of 35, after cohabiting for ten years. When questioned on the importance of marriage, two tendencies emerged. On one hand, most stressed the importance of marriage as a fundamental element in family cohesiveness: the secretary (47) stated that 'marriage gives security and strength, which are necessary to deal with everyday problems. It gives meaning to a relationship.' On the other hand, both the documentalist and the university researcher thought that marriage *per se* was not important. According to them, a woman may cohabit and be happier because, as the documentalist put it, 'cohabiting is less binding. When one is married one takes for granted one's partner. People get used to one another, they do not stimulate one another any longer, and risk becoming lazy.' When they had to give an opinion on the need to become married, all women, with the exception of two housewives, agreed that it is not necessary for a woman to marry, especially now that most women earn their own living.

When it comes to the younger generation, views of Roman teenagers do not differ greatly from older women's. In fact, 13 of the 15 girls expressed a wish to get married, because they believe this is a fundamental step in a woman's life. They also stated their ideal age for marrying to be between 20 and 30, with four girls choosing the early 20s. As with their older counterparts, all but three claimed that a woman does not need to marry if she does not want to. The 23-year-old shop-assistant argued that 'nowadays women are economically independent and therefore do not need to marry, especially if they do not want to have too close a relationship with their partner'. But one 15-year-old and a 19-year-old adopted a much more conservative stance: the former believes a woman should marry because 'this is what she is made for'; the latter expressed her deep concern about cohabiting.

In Cuorgné, most of the 85 teenagers are more traditional: six girls replied that they do not wish to marry and would be happy to cohabit, the rest would like to marry in their late 20s or early 30s. But all of them agreed that it was no longer necessary for a woman to marry.

When asked whether men should marry, the adult women stated almost unanimously that it was not necessary. However, one housewife and the documentalist noted that men generally want to marry more than women, because 'they may find it difficult to cope with household chores, most probably because their mothers have always done things for them'. The Roman girls and the girls from Cuorgné agreed with the adult women in saying that men do not need to marry if they do not want to. However, five added that men need to marry because they need to be taken care of by women.

Women's economic independence is taken for granted by all the girls interviewed, who stressed their willingness to work after finishing their studies in order to achieve personal economic independence, to have more to spend on their children and families, and to fulfil their personal aspirations. In the Cuorgné sample, nevertheless, four girls said that they would prefer to stay at home and take care of their children if their husbands earned enough money to support the family.

*Motherhood and family planning* Another set of questions for the adult women focused on children and motherhood; specifically, women were asked how many children they have, who decided how many and when to have them, and finally if they thought that being a mother was necessary for a woman. Out of 14 women, only one is childless; the others have either one or two children, some of whom are in their teens. In two cases, women themselves took the decision on how many and when to have children; another eight women decided together with their partners – among them there is one case of pre-marital pregnancy – and the other three did not plan their pregnancies at all. Only one housewife said that she wanted a third child but could not have one because of her husband's objection. All the others said that they chose not to have another child, either out of self-interest, or for economic reasons[13] or organizational problems linked to their paid work.

Five women (four housewives and a cleaner) thought that motherhood was necessary for a woman because of the importance of the family as an institution, and because of the emotion of giving birth. Those arguing that it was not necessary to be a mother claimed that children absorb energy and time, thus preventing women from following their personal interests and sometimes even hindering them in their careers. Even if motherhood is not seen as necessary, the secretary and the entrepreneur point out that women feel it to be important because it 'gives meaning to the couple' and because of 'a woman's inner wish to give birth'.

In the Roman sample, the girls too considered it extremely important to have children, and deemed offspring to be necessary for setting up a family, and for the social and cultural evolution of humankind. However, like the adult women, they would not have more than two children, with the exception of two 15-year-olds and one of the oldest girls interviewed, who would like to have only one child in order to satisfy all his/her needs and spoil him/her as much as possible. For teenagers in Cuorgné, the average number of desired children is two, with 21 of them wishing to have three or more children, four only one child and five none at all.[14]

*Contraception and information on related sexual problems: inter- and intra-generational communication* The average age of first intercourse for the adult women in the sample was 19.8 years, with one woman having had her first intercourse at 15 and one at 27. Some of the women stressed that they had their first sexual intercourse after marriage. As far as contraceptive methods are concerned, and to the question from whom they found information about contraception, five reported no use of any kind of modern contraception but only natural methods, whereas the rest mainly use condoms and intra-uterine devices (IUD). Very few took the pill when they were young. Most women received information on contraception from their gynaecologists and doctors, although other sources of information were friends, mass media and, in two cases, advisory centres. None mentioned either parents or relatives. On sexual health there seemed to be a general awareness of the appropriateness and importance of visiting a gynaecologist at least once a year, although three women reported going to the gynaecologist only if necessary.

Not all the Roman girls openly declared whether they have had sexual intercourse. Most of them replied that there is no specific age for intercourse and that it depends on the girls being ready and sure that they have found the appropriate partner. In Cuorgné, out of 85 teenagers, 30 said they had had sexual intercourse, 44 said that so far they had not, and 11 did not reply. On the question of there being a 'right age' for sex, seven girls affirmed that one should wait at least until 17–18, and another seven stated that a girl should not have sexual relations in her early teens. Three others said that a woman should wait until marriage, and another two, although agreeing with the majority that there is no specific age, stressed that 'girls should have sexual intercourse when they are mature and able to understand the importance of such a step, and not for mere curiosity, because, unfortunately, nowadays too many girls make love too easily and hastily, without really being in love with their partners'.

As regards contraception, in the Roman sample three girls did not reply, eight girls reportedly used them, and four said they had used only condoms. On the question of whether their boyfriends were responsible in the use of contraceptives, two of the youngest girls acknowledged their boyfriends' responsibility, whereas all the others either said no or did not answer. Two of the oldest had decided together with their partners to use condoms, and one stressed the need for individual responsibility in using contraceptives. In Cuorgné, 15 girls reported using or having used condoms, six the pill, four did not explain which method they used, and five did not use any kind of contraceptive. Only one teenager said she used both condoms and the pill. When asked about their partners' responsibility in deciding which contraceptives, if any, the couple should use, most of those having intercourse replied that in their case the decision was taken by both partners. Only a few complained about the irresponsibility of their boyfriends. All the other interviewees agreed that both partners should be responsible in the use of contraceptives.

The adult women thought that nowadays the media generally provided people with more information than when they were younger. Four of them, however, claimed that this information was inadequate and too much focused on AIDS and the use of condoms rather than on general sexual matters.

Teenagers in Rome reported gathering information on contraceptives from peers rather than from parents and relatives. A few indicated the mass media as their main source of information. Five girls said they were not satisfied with the quality of the information: they thought there was too little information on TV and in magazines because sex is still seen as a taboo. Nine of them, however, stated that for the time being, they felt that they did not need further information. Out of the other six, two said they would prefer to receive information directly from their parents, two from mass media, and the other two from school. In Cuorgné half of the interviewees stated that the mass media did not provide enough information on contraception and sexuality and that there were only a few TV programmes dealing with sexual matters. Moreover, the most detailed ones were broadcast late at night. Approximately two-thirds of the interviewees wanted to receive further information, especially from school, parents and mass media; only three mentioned doctors as an appropriate source of information on sexual matters.

All the Roman girls reported talking about contraception and sexual matters with their friends and boyfriends. However, only three girls were satisfied with the information received from their peers. Only two (both among the oldest girls) had been to an advisory centre or to the gynaecologist to ask for more appropriate information.

In Cuorgné, teenagers stated that their main sources of information were school, peers and the mass media. A few mentioned their mothers, and only four mentioned doctors. As far as the quality and completeness of information from peers was concerned, only 20 girls out of 85 were satisfied. When asked if they ever went to an advisory centre or a gynaecologist, only 15 interviewees replied positively.

Almost all the adult women stated that when they were young they had no dialogue with their parents or relatives on sexual matters because sex was considered a taboo. One housewife, from a village in the south, said that in her generation, sex was a taboo subject and that unfortunately she carried this taboo with her until recently, even with her husband. All agreed that they suffered from this lack of dialogue. Only three women used to talk with their mothers, and then only superficially, on general sexual matters. With the exception of three women, who could not tackle these issues with anybody, most said that they discussed sexual matters with doctors or friends, and only two of them with their mothers.

When asked about their dialogue with their children, some women acknowledged speaking with them only superficially or in a 'joking tone'.

Five had a clear and open dialogue. The children's reactions ranged from embarrassment and hostility to feeling at ease when these issues were mentioned.

In the Roman sample, ten girls did not talk with their parents about sexual matters. The other five preferred to talk only with their mothers, either because they were ashamed to tackle these issues with their fathers or simply because they found it more natural to discuss these matters among women. One fears her father's jealousy. Seven did not reply to the question asking whether they were satisfied with the dialogue with their parents. Among the others, only three would like to have a more open dialogue; one of the oldest said that, although she could discuss openly with her mother, she sometimes preferred not to talk to her about her personal sexual experiences because she feared her judgement.

Three out of 15 girls did not reply to the question whether their parents felt at ease when talking about sexual matters. One said they did not speak about these issues at all, another one spoke openly with her parents, and all the others stated that there was embarrassment on both sides when these topics were dealt with at home. This was especially true when discussing their own sexual experiences, or when their fathers were involved in these kinds of conversation. Two girls reported that if on TV there is a sexually explicit scene, their parents always change channels. Communication with grandmothers is non-existent. Three girls said they could talk about sexual matters with their aunts.

The same trend is seen in the Cuorgné sample where, with the exception of three girls, all discussed sexual matters with their peers. Even if some of them talk to their mothers, the majority felt embarrassed when sexual matters were raised within the family. The great majority of interviewees reported that neither their parents nor themselves felt at ease when sexual issues were raised. However, although most of the girls expressed a deep concern for their own embarrassment when tackling these issues, only 29 teenagers specifically advocated better communication with their parents. As in Rome, in Cuorgné, communication with grandmothers is non-existent. However, 21 girls reported talking with aunts of various ages.

*Bodily health* On menstruation, the majority of the women reported that they did not have enough information at the time of their menarche. Most felt embarrassed and shocked because they did not know what it meant. They found it extremely inconvenient because of the towels, which had to be washed and reused many times. Some stated that the only source of information had been older friends and older sisters.

The Roman girls, on the contrary, reported being given information, although not always complete, mostly by their mothers; in two cases by both parents and/or friends; in only one case by an older sister. Despite this, at the moment of their menarche most of them felt strange, one was frightened, another said she was disgusted by it. Six girls reported having enjoyed their first period because they saw it as the entry into womanhood.

Sixty-two teenagers in Cuorgné reported having been informed before the menarche, mainly by their mothers. Only one mentioned her grandmother, three the school, four both their mothers and sisters, and six their friends. Like the Roman teenagers, the reactions of most of them ranged from uneasiness, confusion and embarrassment to fear. Twenty-five reported having been calm and serene. Eight said they enjoyed their menarche because it meant becoming a woman.

*Abortion, AIDS* Only three women openly declared themselves against abortion. One opposed it on religious grounds, but she admitted that in certain circumstances, such as when the mother's life is at risk or when the foetus is malformed, it might be permissible. The pro-abortionists acknowledged that, since interrupting an unwanted pregnancy is a painful decision for women, it should be for them to decide, and not their families or their partners. They advocate women's self-determination and believe that the abortion law in Italy should be respected and safeguarded.

Among the Roman teenagers, six were against abortion, one did not answer, three justified it only under certain circumstances, and the rest saw it as a solution to the problem of unwanted pregnancies.

Among the teenagers in Cuorgné, 39 openly declared themselves to be against abortion, which they described as murder; 20 advocated a woman's right to choose; and 26 said that it depends on the circumstances: some justified abortion in cases of rape, when the foetus is malformed and if the mother's life is at risk.

With reference to AIDS, most of the women considered it the major worry for those beginning a relationship. Even those replying that AIDS is not the major worry for new couples stressed the importance of knowing the partner well before having intercourse with him and, if possible, having a blood test for HIV–AIDS.

Teenagers in Rome reported that most parents fear AIDS, and as a consequence either refuse to tackle the issue, or talk about it in frightening terms. Some advised their daughters not to have sexual intercourse before getting married or before having verified through a blood test whether their partner is healthy. In at least two cases parents said that people should take precautions.

In Cuorgné there is a tendency for parents and children to avoid discussing AIDS and sexual intercourse. In fact, a considerable number of girls stated that their parents do not say anything about these matters to them or they merely advise their children to be careful.

Twelve Roman girls thought that AIDS was the major concern for those beginning a new relationship. For two of them, AIDS was not a major worry. The other stated that AIDS was something that seemed so far away from her and her friends that she felt it would never infect them.

In Cuorgné also teenagers thought that AIDS was a major concern for a couple beginning a relationship. Four of them stressed the need for a blood test before entering into a new relationship, and one girl reported that she and her partner had had a blood test.

*Pregnancy* The adult women were asked what their reaction would be if a daughter were to become pregnant. They all said that they would help her without 'making a thing of it'. The documentalist added that if she had a pregnant daughter she would advise her to abort if she were too immature to bring up a child on her own. Nevertheless, if she were responsible she would support her as much as possible.

The Roman teenagers saw an unwanted pregnancy as a major worry at their age. Five girls were unable to say what they would do; six would have an abortion; three would keep their baby and one felt she would commit suicide. One of the oldest said that she would not know what to offer her child, and another that she would be sorry to deceive her parents.

If they became pregnant, only three girls would tell their mothers, one would not talk with anybody, all the others would talk either with their partners or with their female friends. Generally, the teenagers would prefer to ask advice from and exchange views with their peers, because they fear their parents' reaction. In fact, apart from two who were sure that, although angry at the deception, their parents would help them to cope with their pregnancies, all the others were convinced that their parents would be extremely disappointed and refuse to help.

Girls from the sample in Cuorgné registered the same trend as the Roman girls in considering pregnancy at their age as a major concern. Twenty-seven were unable to say what they would do, 15 would opt for abortion, and 42 would keep the baby. One girl said that rather than aborting she would prefer to give birth and then give up her child for adoption.

In case of pregnancy, most of the girls from Cuorgné would talk first to their partners. Some of them also indicated that they would talk to their peers and parents, preferably their mothers. Two said they would ask their gynaecologist for advice, and one mentioned her aunt. Unlike their Roman counterparts, most teenagers in Cuorgné thought that their parents, after a temporary feeling of disappointment and deception, would help them and give them advice. Seventeen said they had no idea about their parents' reaction, and 26 believed that their parents' reaction would be extremely negative.

*Sex education*  The women in the adult sample believed that sex education should be given to boys and girls in the same way because teenagers from both sexes faced similar problems. School was considered the most appropriate place for sex-related issues to be discussed, owing to teachers' competence and expertise in the scientific aspects of reproduction and on contraceptive methods. Generally speaking, the interviewees saw the need for the family to integrate information given at school, especially from an ethical point of view. All women underlined parents' responsibility in creating an open dialogue with their children, because they know them better than their teachers. There was only one case of a housewife totally acceding responsibility to schoolteachers, since she found it difficult to build an atmosphere of intimacy with her only daughter.

The girls in Rome expressed their desire to have more information on sexual matters from their teachers. Some of them reported having had some discussion at school, but only among students during 'free lessons'. All believed that sex education should be compulsory, at the latest from the last year of junior school.

In Cuorgné, 38 teenagers reported having had sex education courses at school. Among the 48 who had never had sex education at school, a considerable number had asked for lessons without success. Like the Roman girls, however, the teenagers in Cuorgné believed that sex education should be compulsory at school, from either the last year of junior school or the first year of high school.

*Interviewees' remarks*  At the end of the questionnaire, the entrepreneur and the cleaner added their personal remarks. The former said that 'there is still a great difference between the two sexes. The day we speak about ourselves not in terms of different genders will be a great day, because we could probably relate well with men, and sexual divisions will no longer exist.' The latter said that 'although we are at the end of the twentieth century, sex still remains a taboo and unfortunately we are still unable to achieve more sexual freedom and equality within the household'.

Among the younger group, the 23-year-old advocated more open dialogue, without prejudice, about sexual matters with boys of the same age-group. Another asked why homosexuality had not been expressly included in the survey.

In Cuorgné none of the interviewees had further remarks to make.

## Conclusion

In the sample of adult women the most traditional views about the family, pregnancy and contraception are held mainly by housewives, while the paid working women have a more detailed analysis of these issues altogether and are more progressive in their views. In the case of the girls, some contradictions emerge in their replies, so that it is often difficult to understand whether they are conservative or progressive.

On marriage and motherhood, both generations of women converge in considering these important. Despite the many social changes of the 1970s, almost all teenagers express their wish to marry. Probably this is due to the fact that in today's world of insecurity, marriage is still viewed as providing safe boundaries to women and, given the legalization of divorce and women's increasing decision-making in household management, marriage is no longer seen as so oppressive. Yet both groups of women agree that marriage is no longer necessary *per se*, owing to women's newly acquired economic independence. Being single, with or without children, has become more and more acceptable, especially in an urban context. This view is confirmed by statistics reporting that in the early 1990s in Italy there are 2.2 million non-widowed single persons (ISTAT, 1995), and that 7 per cent of Italian women were single women with children, whereas in the 1970s they totalled only 2 per cent (United Nations, 1995: 19).[15]

When discussing the age of first sexual intercourse, inter-generational differences begin to emerge. Whereas some adult women stress that they had their first sexual intercourse after marriage, in Rome none of the teenagers considered it necessary to wait to be married in order to have full sexual relations. In Cuorgné the situation is slightly different, in that three girls plan to have their first sexual intercourse after marriage. The high percentage of teenagers no longer considering it necessary to wait suggests that a shift has taken place in women's views on chastity and honour. Young women now take it for granted that decision-making in sexual relations is an individual's right, and it is not to be dictated by parental ethical codes or religious teachings. They prefer to have sexual intercourse when they are young because they wish to have their own experiences, and virginity is perceived as a burden that may prevent them from having a successful and happy relationship.

The questionnaires confirm the transformation in Italian women's status from the 1970s to date. Economic empowerment is considered fundamental for a woman's independence by both women and girls. In fact, all the teenagers interviewed, with the exception of four girls in Cuorgné, replied that they wanted to work after school. The 1960s myth of the good housewife, therefore, has definitely collapsed, because women no longer consider the care of children, husbands and house as a woman's sole aim. In addition, the fact that more and more women are working outside the home has made men more responsible towards household management and child rearing, thus reversing the trend of the past, where men were the sole bread-winners and women were mainly housewives. The questionnaires reveal that most women are helped by their husbands in household management and child rearing. In two cases, husbands and wives are considered interchangeable at home. Nevertheless, the percentage of husbands co-operating in house-hold chores is still low, either because of their job, which prevents them from staying at home and doing housework, or because, in women's opinion, they have no inclination for such things that traditionally belong to a woman's domain.

There is now a greater degree of inter-generational knowledge transfer on bodily health and reproduction than there was in the past. In the 1990s, mothers inform their daughters about menarche, menstruation, giving birth and other related matters. The questionnaires reveal that both groups openly discuss these matters. This is certainly a positive shift, when we consider that in the 1960s mothers could not broach these issues with their daughters.

On the other hand, personal sexual experiences and behaviour are still marked by inter-generational silence. Despite women's emancipation brought about by feminism, this silence may be explained by the fact that the majority of adult women have been brought up to see sex as an issue to be carefully avoided, surrounded by taboos and silence and have, therefore, instilled in their daughters the same feeling of unease in speaking about these issues. It is also likely that the excessively motherly attitude held by Italian women towards their offspring does not help frank discussion on sexual matters, given the fact that daughters are always considered as little children. As a consequence, notwithstanding their apparent open-mindness and self-confidence, young girls still find it difficult to discuss sexual matters with their parents and relatives. They prefer to talk with their peers, exactly as their mothers did when they were young.

Notably, adult women state that they long for a more open dialogue with their daughters. At the same time, however, they declare their inability to create an atmosphere of intimacy, which would certainly help to build such a dialogue. Among the reasons listed by the daughters themselves are their embarrassment and unwillingness to disclose their inner feelings and talk openly about their sexual experiences for fear of being judged and reprimanded by their parents. Unfortunately, this silence has brought about a mutual feeling of uneasiness and mis-understanding between the two generations. For example, in the case of pregnancy, Roman teenagers think their parents would scold and heavily punish them, whereas the adult women say they would be willing to help their daughters in their choice of either aborting or keeping the baby.

In Cuorgné, teenagers do not seem so concerned about their parents' reaction, although their disappointment is seen as inevitable. They think that, in the end, their parents would help them and advise them.

Unlike their mothers, young girls are advantaged in having a greater access to information on contraception, family planning, sexual health and sexual behaviour because of today's mass media interest in sexual matters, and the fact that talking about these delicate subjects is no longer considered scandalous. However, it seems that women's magazines are mostly read by women over 20, and not so much by teenagers.[16]

In order to spread more information to teenagers, it would be advis-able to include columns or specific sections on sexual matters in national and local newspapers on a regular basis; the information would then be accessible to a wider reading public, made up of both adults and young people.

Information on contraception has certainly increased in the last 10–15 years, and probably contributed to the decrease in abortions; in 1980 there were 209,000 abortions, in 1995 only 124,500 (ISTAT, 1996). Certainly, making contraceptives more accessible to all could help reduce abortion further. Advisory centres could distribute them free to teen-agers. In addition, the number of automatic condom machines could be increased, and condom costs lowered, in order to avoid the embar-rassment associated with buying them either at the chemist's or in supermarkets, and allow anybody who chose to make use of them.[17]

Among the institutions that could play a leading role in providing correct and more appropriate information on contraception, bodily health and reproduction are advisory centres and schools. Services offered by advisory centres should be advertised at cinemas, discos and at school in order to make teenagers aware of how they could be helped. The school as a source of information has been explicitly mentioned in the questionnaires by both adult and young women. Adult women think that schools could foster the dialogue between children and parents on this delicate issue, and certainly provide children with more adequate information. Teenagers themselves ask for compulsory sex education courses at school from the early teens.

To conclude, we think that, despite a marked improvement in women's status over recent years and a greater access to general information on sexual matters and related issues, in Italy sexual behaviour is still surrounded by deeply rooted taboos and a certain form of hypocrisy within the family, which should be dismantled in favour of a more liberal discussion between parents and children. Running sex education courses at school, designed to involve not only schoolteachers and students but parents as well, with the support of a team of psychologists, could certainly help to remove parents' and children's fears and mutual mistrust when dealing with sex-related issues.

Another powerful means to disseminate information on sexual matters is television. Appealing educational programmes on reproductive health and sexual behaviour should be created for both young people and adults. Unfortunately, only a few Italian television programmes analyse sexual matters in detail: they mainly focus on AIDS[18] and contraception, or give information in bits and pieces.

Frank discussion, stimulated by school and adequate television programmes, could certainly help to bridge the gap between the generations, demolish false assumptions and beliefs surrounding sexual matters, and give appropriate advice. This open debate, as our survey has shown, is deeply needed and would be welcomed by both generations of women interviewed. In fact all adult interviewees appreciated discussing these topics during the interview and also volunteered with enthusiasm for more in-depth interviews. Teenagers reported having found it interesting to contribute their views on such an important debate.

There should be a wider public debate, stimulated by the mass media, on such issues as sexual identity, reproductive health and women's life choices and rights. The feminist debate on these issues seems to have stagnated in the 1990s, as economic worries crowd out social and cultural concerns. Given the close link between reproductive and productive work for women, this is short-sighted. It is also a pity that the opportunity afforded by the WCW in Beijing in 1995 was missed by the Italian press, and that the many crucial issues for women worldwide reached only a very few women in Italy. Italian women would benefit from looking afresh at their lives from an international cross-cultural perspective. The opportunity to share their worries and hopes with women of other cultures and similiar ages would be an eye-opening and strengthening experience. Too often in the area of development we look at how to intervene and assist Southern women's situations, blithely ignoring similar issues for women in the North. We hope that this study is a modest contribution to opening out the debate, so that the silences among generations of women are replaced by constructive dialogue, which will help young women to make their choices in life with a sense of security in their own knowledge and community support.

## Acknowledgements

We would like to thank all the people who helped us in writing this chapter, especially all the interviewees who gave their time to answer the questionnaires that were the basis for our study. Particular thanks to Veronica Rossetti in Rome for facilitating the distribution of the questionnaires to her colleagues in the technical institute 'Di Vittorio', and to Piera Bitti, also in Rome, for distributing them to friends living in her neighbourhood. In Cuorgné, thanks are due to Alba and Gabriella Vaccaro, Don Franco Peradotto and all the teachers of the technical Institute 'G. Jervis' who handed out and collected the questionnaires. Finally a special thank-you to Wendy Harcourt for her initial encouragement to us to undertake the Italian case study, and for her suggestions and invaluable assistance in writing up the chapter.

## Notes

1. Italy can be divided into three main areas: the North, the Centre and the South. The northern regions are: Aosta Valley, Piedmont, Lombardy, Veneto, Liguria, Trentino-Alto Adige, Friuli-Venezia Giulia, Emilia-Romagna. The centre is made up of: Tuscany, Umbria, the Marches, Latium, Abruzzi and Molise. The south includes: Campania, Basilicata, Calabria, Apulia, and the two islands of Sicily and Sardinia.

2. More than 90 per cent of the Italian population are adherents of the Roman Catholic Church. There are also several protestant churches with a membership of about 50,000, and a small but strong Jewish community (*The Europa World Year Book 1990*, 1990: 1430).

3. The New Concordat signed in February 1984 between the Prime Minister Bettino Craxi and the Papal Secretary of State Cardinal Agostino Casaroli replaced the first Concordat signed in 1929 when Roman Catholicism was recognized as the official religion of Italy. Yet, the Vatican City's sovereign rights as an independent state under the terms of the Lateran Treaty of 1929 were not affected.

4. The late 1950s, in fact, had seen a remarkable expansion in international trade, which contributed to the take-off of Italian industry in the north, whose development was already in progress in the immediate post-war period. Italian employers and policy-makers were clever enough to realize that the newly developed northern industry, by marketing a sufficiently diversified range of products, could take advantage of the possibility of open trade within Europe.

Within a few years Italy became one of the major industrial nations in the West.

5. We are referring to the Mafia, which in the south of Italy replaced the often absent or inefficient state; as a consequence, Mafiosi were seen as providing security and jobs to the people working for them. It is notable that the Mafia itself is organized in a family structure, with the older members receiving a higher level of respect and being honoured the most. In our study, however, we will not focus our attention on such a complex issue, for a detailed analysis of the Mafia requires a study of its own.

6. In 1973, in fact, the Western industrialized countries went through a period of stagflation (stagnation and inflation) due to: the decisions taken by OPEC countries to reduce oil exports by 10 per cent and to increase oil prices by 70 per cent; the break-up of the Bretton Woods system; the dollar devaluations; the rise in European wage rates; over-accumulation in relation to the labour supply; and the sharp decline in profitability (Ginsborg, 1990: 351).

7. For a detailed analysis on the Italian family in the 1980s, see Ginsborg 1990: 412–18.

8. For different reasons, both authors of this chapter still live at home with their parents. Elisabetta earns her own living, but cannot afford to buy a house of her own. She is not the only child in her family still living under the same roof as her parents: her elder brother, who is 29, lives at home because he has not yet found a job. Elisabetta could afford to rent a flat, but given current Italian rents this is not at all convenient. Paying rent is a waste of money that could be invested in buying a house. In addition, her family would not accept her cohabitation with her partner; it would lead inevitably to a breach with her parents. Emanuela, on the other hand, does not have a permanent job and cannot afford to rent a flat as she would like to do, having lived on her own for five years when she attended university in Britain. She is 26 and is the only child living at home since her elder brother (29) moved out when he married two years ago. He was financially helped by parents and parents-in-law to buy and refurnish a flat.

9. 'The Gender Empowerment Measure (GEM) examines whether women and men are able to actively participate in economic and political life and take part in decision-making' (UNDP, 1995: 73).

10. Statistics for the years 1990–92 show that women, with 9 per cent of jobs in the agricultural sector, 32 per cent in industry, and 59 per cent in services, represent 43 per cent of the labour force. Figures for 1994 reveal a drop in women's employment in both the agricultural and industrial sectors (respectively, to 6 per cent and 26 per cent) and an increase in the tertiary sector (rising to 68 per cent) (UN, 1995). After the 1996 elections, only 8 per cent of parliamentary seats are held by women, 25 in the Senate and 60 in the Chamber of Deputies.

11. Debating sex-related issues during classes on religion is certainly a shift from the norm of religious instruction 30 years ago, when such classes were given mainly by clergy and focused on religious matters. Nowadays it is more common to have religion taught by lay people, and for discussion to focus on cultural, ethical and sociological matters.

12. The research team noted that it was easier to gather information from the adult women who were directly interviewed; the women felt at ease and seemed

to enjoy the conversation, to the extent of accompanying the answers with original considerations and personal remarks. On the other hand, those replying by writing went less into detail and sometimes gave only short answers or brief elaborations. Some teenagers told us that they had already been quizzed on such issues at school, but they enjoyed co-operating with us. Not all the girls signed their questionnaires, showing once again that, when it comes to personal matters, they do not trust unknown people and prefer to remain anonymous. They may fear their parents finding out about their replies, and interfering in their personal life experiences.

13. Interestingly, working women cited economic reasons for not having another child.

14. That teenagers in Cuorgné express their wish to have numerous offspring could be explained by the fact that there is a high number of southern families in the town, who migrated in the early 1960s from Calabria. The southern family pattern is to have large numbers of children and to be patriarchal and conservative in outlook, a model that they still look to at this stage in their life cycle.

15. This percentage is still low compared to other Western countries, probably because it takes time for the deeply rooted Catholic mentality to loosen.

16. In a recent survey carried out by CENSIS (a national statistics institute) and Premio Grinzane Cavour (a Torinese foundation), it was found out that the main weekly women's magazine read by male and female teenagers aged between 14 and 20 is *Donna Moderna*.

17. In Italy condoms are expensive for young people who want to have a regular sexual relationship.

18. In Italy there are approximately eight cases of HIV infection per 100,000 people (UNDP, 1995: 199).

## References

Adler Hellman, J. (1987) *A Journey among Women*, Cambridge, Polity Press.

Bettio, F. (1988a) 'Sex-typing of occupations, the cycle and restructuring in Italy' in J. Rubery (ed.) *Women and Recession*, London, Routledge and Kegan Paul.

Bettio, F. (1988b) 'Women, the state and the family in Italy: problems of female participation in historical perspective' in J. Rubery (ed.) *Women and Recession*, London, Routledge and Kegan Paul.

*Europa World Year Book 1990, The* (1990) London, Europa Publications Limited, Vol. 1.

*Famiglia Cristiana* (1996), 'La Quarantenne Donna di Frontiera', No. 18.

Ginsborg, P. (1990) *A History of Contemporary Italy*, London, Penguin Books.

ISTAT (1994) *Indagine multiscopo sulle famiglie, anni 1987–1991*, Rome.

— (1995) *Rapporte Annuale*, Rome.

*La Repubblica* (1996) 24 April.

United Nations (1995) *The World's Women 1995 Trends and Statistics*, Social Statistics and Indicators Series K, New York, No. 12.

UNDP (United Nations Development Programme) (1995) *Human Development Report 1995*, New York-Oxford, Oxford University Press.

# 8

# Motherhood in Switzerland: a rational and responsible choice?

VERENA HILLMANN AND
THERESE VÖGELI SÖRENSEN[1]

This chapter examines the impact of modernity on Swiss women's reproductive choices. Following a brief survey of demographic, economic and reproductive changes in modern Switzerland, the chapter turns to biographies of three modern Swiss women, to test the concept of rational choice for women choosing to have children for the first time. As one of the richest countries in the world, with high per capita income and access to the latest medical technology, it would appear that women in Switzerland are free to choose to have children when they wish. They should be able to act as autonomous individuals, rationally selecting the moment when it is best for themselves and their partners to have children. As the case studies show, this is an assumption that hides the many complex decisions that the responsibility of modern motherhood entails. The low fertility rate in Switzerland since 1975 – around 1.6 – suggests that few women are choosing motherhood.[2] Motherhood for many Swiss women means a loss of economic independence and social status, and unwanted dependency on their partner. Mothers with small children are generally excluded from the working world and limited in participation in the sphere of politics. Rearing children is seen as a private affair, with the mother as the key person responsible. She is meant to find her own way, calling on her own resources, to balance work, child care and community responsibilities.

Our study examines the ideological, social, economic and physical environment that influences young women's decisions to have their first child. In what way is it possible – if at all – to come to a rational and responsible decision to have a first child? The three case studies offer an insight into the complex reasons behind young Swiss women's choice to have or not have their first child. The three women selected are between 24 and 34 years old. The youngest is a student who is choosing to be a single mother, without the father's but with parental and state support.

The 27-year-old is married and living in a stable relationship, has no particular career goals and is the closest to the norm of young women having their first child. The 34-year-old is near the expected upper age limit for women to have their first child, and the child has been planned and conceived following the establishment of her career. She exemplifies means to make a rational choice with financial security and strong support from her partner. All of the women are tertiary educated, live in Zurich,[3] the biggest city in Switzerland, and are in stable relationships. They are not representative of Swiss women in general, but they do illustrate some of the dilemmas modernity presents for women. Their stories help us to come closer to understanding the negotiations of modern women in exercising their reproductive choices.

## The Swiss context

Historically, the state of Switzerland was formed by a coalition of mountain farmers and pastoralists 700 years ago. Divided into four language zones, Switzerland has 26 cantons, each assuming a degree of autonomy in education, health, social security, and canton politics. Only 60 per cent of Swiss live in urban zones (small and medium towns, and cities). The landscape is formed by a patchwork of small industries intermingled with agricultural production shaped by its local ecological, political and socio-historical environment.

One of the richest countries in the world, Switzerland has a typical post-modern economy, with 4 per cent working in the agricultural sector, 30 per cent in the industrial sector and the bulk of the population employed in the service sector. The Swiss natural environment, of mountains and abundant rains, favoured industrialization based on hydro-power, which led to Switzerland's strong economic position in the nineteenth century. In the twentieth century, Swiss neutrality through the two world wars enabled a strengthening of its economic position, with an expansion of its international trade and later the tourist and the service sectors.

After the Second World War, the Swiss economy is characterized by a rapid downturn in industrial production. While Switzerland still leads in some industrial sectors, the overall rate of employment in industry has decreased. The industrial sector demands increasingly high specialization, and technological innovation now seldom creates employment (robot technology, computers and new information systems actually displace jobs).

Switzerland's demographic development is typical for Europe (Höpflinger et al., 1991). Life expectancy is 75.1 for men and 81.6 for women.

There is a low fertility rate of 149:100 women (below reproduction level) and the average age for women having a first child is 27.8 years (1994 figure). The population increase of 0.2 per cent is 60 per cent due to the naturalization of migrants. (The entry of migrants and the naturalization of foreigners is a major concern of Swiss demographic policy.) The majority of the population increase is occurring among people over 79, whereas the smallest is among children and adolescents, who make up 25 per cent of the population.

There has been a decrease in the fertility rate (2.1 in 1970, 1.5 in 1994). The recession (following the 'oil shock') in the 1970s, after two decades of economic boom, together with governmental migration policies, determined population growth (see above). Some authorities (Höpflinger *et al.*, 1991) also point to the influence of feminist politics on demographic development in the 1970s and 1980s, mainly in the change in marriage patterns and reproductive behaviour. In this period, women achieved higher education, the age of having a first child increased, more men and women remained single or cohabited, and the divorce rate increased. In 1994, one-third of households are inhabited by one person alone and the only increase in population growth is from migrants (in 1993–94, 13,739 migrants became Swiss citizens).

In comparison to other European countries, Switzerland has a high number of single households, a low rate of single mothers, and a large number of women working in part-time employment. The decreasing fertility rate has been paralleled by a feminist movement for institutional, economic, political and legal changes in gender-biased regulations, accompanied by the fight for empowerment and autonomy for women in determining their individual life path.

## Gender, demography and poverty

Gender-differentiated statistics on wealth and property are not available in Switzerland. However, studies on poverty provide some indication of the relation between poverty and gender. A 1989 study considered 2.7 per cent of the population as poor, half of them temporarily. Among these, single parents, single women, widowed men and the self-employed were grouped together with illiterates, disabled, ex-prisoners and older people. According to these authors, poverty is increasing in Switzerland. Later studies state higher figures for poverty. The national report on women for the United Nations Fourth World Conference on Women (WCW) in Beijing 1995 indicates that 10–25 per cent of the population in Switzerland is living in poverty. According to this source, single parents and women are the most affected. Among women, the main factor leading to poverty is the break in their working careers due to motherhood; low education and low social security rates are interdependent factors. Income studies indicate a dwindling middle class, and an increase in the rich and the poor in the country. Unemployment statistics show that women are more affected by economic structural changes than men. Some sociologists foresee a 'two-thirds' Swiss society in the future, in which only one-third of the people are permanently employed.

## Reproduction and development in Switzerland

Since the nineteenth century, the feminist movement in Switzerland has been involved in issues related to reproductive rights and wage labour security, campaigning for maternity leave, old-age pension, childcare facilities and other initiatives to allow women to combine their productive and reproductive roles. Swiss fathers contribute little to household chores; 96 per cent work full time all their lives, while mothers interrupt their working careers to have children, and constitute only 28 per cent of the overall work force.

Family patterns are also changing. Between 1980 and 1990, the number of persons without children living in *de facto* relationships increased by 53 per cent; *de facto* couples who lived with children increased by 44 per cent (Lüscher and Thierbach, 1993). Hungerbühler (1989) and Ley and Borer (1992) researched the diversity of families. The majority favours marriage and having children, particularly as it offers tax breaks (Ryffel-Gericke, 1979: 46). Of couples living with children in 1990, 83.8 per cent were married, only 2.4 per cent of them lived in *de facto* relationships, and 13.7 per cent lived as single parents (Lüscher and Thierbach, 1993). Increasing numbers of marriages ended in divorce: 20 per cent in 1975 and 33 per cent in 1984.

Besides the fact that maternity leave is not yet secure, the tax system and the social security system discourage double employment among married couples, and part-time working mothers generally belong to the better-off segments of the population, while among the less fortunate, full-time employment, with motherhood or childlessness, dominates.

Political movements against the participation of mothers in the workforce and against single women were formed in the 1930s, during a phase of convergence of economic crisis and negative fertility rate, demanding the implementation of family policies which discriminate against single women (based on the pre-industrial paternalistic family model). But, before any family policies were implemented, the fertility trend in Switzerland changed and the movement lost its strength. Currently the conjuncture of economic decline, increasing joblessness and the fall in the fertility rate gives rise to new versions of pro-natalistic, pro-family and anti-single-woman policies, supported by some church groups, who problematize equity in wages between mothers and single women and the provision system of social security for all. The pro-natalistic movement in the 1930s was a political reaction to a long struggle of feminists and socialists for the implementation of a general social security and pension system. Possibly the current family and pro-natalistic movement can also be interpreted as political reaction against some of the achievements of the feminist movement and a broad base of different socio-political forces in Switzerland.

In the 1980s important legislative improvements for married and single women were achieved or fought for, such as 'equal pay for equal work' (achieved in 1988), the new marriage law and new inheritance law (achieved in 1987), paid maternity leave (not yet achieved), and a social security reform (in preparation), all of which improve partnership between men and women in the productive and reproductive fields, at least on paper. Beside these improvements at the legislative level, the feminist movement endorsed the right for free reproductive choice, including abortion. While contraception is freely accessible, abortion during the first twelve weeks of pregnancy is allowed only on medical grounds, and is governed by criminal law. However, statistical estimations indicate that the number of illegal abortions is very low, and the number of legal abortions has decreased in the last ten years (Federal Commission for Women's Issues, 1995).

Another area of reproductive politics for the Swiss feminist movement was the protest against rape and violence against women, leading to the creation of houses for women threatened by violence and their children. With the creation of autonomous preventive health centres, a range of successful health projects were achieved by the feminist movement to enhance women's autonomy and competence in health and reproductive issues, rooted in a critique of the medicalization of women's bodies, and expressing concern about the increase of cancer in women (ranking among the three most frequent causes of death for women in Switzerland).

One area of public concern and political debate linking reproductive health and the environment is the rise of new reproductive technologies. Medical research advances rapidly in the development of reproductive pre-natal technology (*in vitro* fertilization), which raises the hopes of sterile couples for parenthood, and provokes fear in others of the unethical use of these new technologies. Reasoning on ethical grounds, three feminist NGOs (Antigena, NOGERETE, Basel Appeal against

Genetic Engineering) opened a public debate on human dignity, research ethics and the application of these new technologies. The main current concern of these groups is the Bioethics Convention 1994, currently under discussion in the Council of Europe, which 'legitimizes' the use and development of genetic engineering and human organ transplantation. Ethics, individuality, human dignity and a requestioning of what is nature, self and identity are elements of the cultural discourse around the newest developments in reproductive technologies, which bear the potential of challenging fundamental social, kinship and ethical considerations related to gender and reproductive issues, nature and culture.

## Ideological background

As well as this historical background, in order to understand the situation in which young mothers find themselves, we also need to look at some common beliefs held in modern Switzerland. As in most Western economies, the most pervasive ideology is the belief in the 'autonomous individual', able to make rational choices that lead to his or her happiness. This concept is summed up in the saying '*Jeder ist seines eigenen Glueckes Schmid*' (everybody is the architect of his/her own fortune).

The belief in the autonomous individual starts from the assumption that a person creates her or his well-being through his or her own abilities with the assistance of modern science and technological progress. Social success is gained through personal performance, and it is possible for every individual to climb the social ladder. The autonomous individual behaves rationally to achieve his or her goal of measurable social and economic success, which is the guarantee of happiness. The emphasis on work in order to achieve economic success generates an increase in individualism that is devoid of a sense of community values or responsibility. Ultimately this produces insecurity and a loss of direction: one of the common maladies of modernity.

Gender relations in modern Switzerland also require an explanation. Feminine or masculine identities in a society with so many different life choices and family arrangements are no longer derived from rights and duties. Instead, characteristics are assigned to men and women's 'nature'. Women are passive, dependent and virtuous, whereas men are seen as active, autonomous, rational and honourable (Hausen, 1976: 368). The modern family (from the 1950s onwards) reflects these assumptions. The family provides a private space where women are primarily responsible, owing to their nature, for child care, nurturing and education as well for the physical and spiritual well-being of the whole family. The man negotiates the public space as the primary bread-winner. Marriage in this type of family is no longer the partnership of women and men to satisfy their sexual needs, to rear their children and to pool their economic interests. It is a bond based on love with a gender complementarity. In this romantic idealization of marriage, the family becomes the refuge and place where the man can come home, after his battle in the competitive outside world, to the care and human concern provided by his wife.

In the 1970s this romantic view of marriage was challenged by the women's movement. Women fought to replace this vision of the family and woman's natural role in it with equality between men and women in the sense of the 'autonomous individual'. The battle cry was for self-determination and autonomy over their bodies (abortion was a rallying point) where the 'personal is political'. Taking this ideological background into account we can see that a 'rational and responsible choice of parenthood' is different for women and men. For a man, his professional career is predominant and it determines the social status of the family. His chances of improving his career, and therefore his family's income and happiness, depends on the quality of care provided in the family by his wife. The woman's individual choice is subsumed to the family needs, which are ultimately determined by the husband's requirements to perform well in the workplace. The question we are asking in our study is whether the decision to have children can be seen as a rational and responsible choice, as implied by the feminist concept of self-determination.

## Methodology

Our research sets out to answer this question by looking at the reasons for women to have a child, and whether they perceive themselves as planning their family in a rational and responsible way. The methodology we adopted was on three levels. We first examined existing studies, on reproductive choice, changes in family patterns and women's paid and unpaid labour, undertaken in Switzerland over the last decade. Secondly, we interviewed a number of professional women working with mothers-to-be: a gynaecologist, a psychologist, a social worker, a youth counsellor, and women working on family planning phone-lines. The third stage was to conduct two in-depth interviews with three young women from different social and economic backgrounds on their choices to have children.

The methodology for the interview was the 'process-oriented-systematic-think figure' approach developed by Silvia Staub-Bernasconi for social counselling, which builds self-confidence in their clients to seek their own solutions. This method aims to help the client to map out what are her or his resources and problems. Applying Staub-Bernasconi's model allowed the interviewees to explain the areas of tensions around their decisions to have children and relate the problems not only inward but also outward to the social environment. This enabled us, with the women, to identify the desires and anxieties, and the real environmental conditions that determine a 'rational and responsible' choice or an 'irrational' and 'irresponsible' choice.

## Clara: the child as a joyful event

Twenty-nine-year-old Clara and her husband Karl, who is five years older, have been together for ten years. They live in a three-roomed flat in a municipality near Zurich. Clara works in a co-operative travel agency, and Karl has, after a time being paid unemployment benefit, found a job as a chauffeur. Two years ago they married with the intention of working in order to begin a family. They intended to take their time over having children. When Clara became pregnant it came as a surprise, but they both agreed it was not unwanted.

After the birth, Clara plans to take leave for one year, with six months on paid maternity leave. After that she will work half-time in her former job. Karl plans to set up his own business as a chauffeur and also work part-time. They aim to share housework and child care.

Clara describes herself as someone who was naturally destined to have a child. 'It is within me, it's my personality.' However, she waited a while to realize this wish. After their marriage – she married only because she wanted to have a family – she had intended to wait one more year when she fell pregnant. But she was not really taking full precautions; they 'chanced it'. Clara recalls:

One year ago I went off the pill after nine years. [...] Somehow I developed an increasing aversion to taking those little pills every day. We discussed that I would stop taking the pill and we then would wait a little longer to have our first baby. We were quite careful. He was on the dole for two years and financially it was going downhill. We reckoned that in this situation it would not be a particularly good idea to have a child, though if it comes to that point, it must be right and so be it. In that sense we tempted fate. [...] We are very much looking forward to our child. Of course, we were bothered with the question of how to justify a baby at a time with so many doubts about the future. [...] But I think too, that our child might be able to do a better job than we did. And somehow it might also be a kind of egotism in the sense that I really wanted to have this kind of experience and nobody had the right to take that from me.

The basic requirement for having a child is, for Clara, a good and stable relationship with her partner. If this situation is created, the wish to have a child follows as a natural consequence:

> To me it is the way things are, if you stay together for so long. If you are still young you can't imagine that you can tie yourself to somebody else and have children and be responsible for everything. But if you have a relationship of eight or ten years and it is a good relationship this comes naturally. I find it difficult to express how this comes about. It is simply right because it harmonizes.

Clara thinks of herself as an easy-going person with few worries, and considers these qualities important. Her own childhood, and especially her mother, played a very important role in arriving at this perception of life. At first sight there might seem little reason for such a positive attitude. Her father left the family when Clara was 10 years old. She had very little contact with him before he left. Her mother always tried to keep problems from her and her sister and worked hard to bring up her daughters on her own. She created an atmosphere of harmony and security. Sexuality and contraception were not problems for Clara, and her first menstruation she experienced as an exciting and joyful event. She describes the atmosphere in her childhood as 'everything was like looking through rose-tinted glasses'. Reflecting on the past, she comments: 'My mother was an ideal. However there were drawbacks. By avoiding conflicts we never learnt to cope with them in a positive manner. We lacked that experience. I become stressed if I cannot control things.'

Although she does not complain about her childhood, she wants to promote a different pattern in her own family. She places a stable and harmonious relationship with her partner at the top of her priorities, and emphasizes the importance of both father and mother spending time with the child in order to build up a close relationship. Both partners must share paid labour and housework. However, she holds herself primarily responsible for the child after birth: 'There shouldn't be too much change in life for my partner. I must look after both of them.'

There is no question about whether Clara goes back to work after the child is born. This is not because of professional self-fulfilment or the economic benefits, but because she values the work atmosphere and requires a job that allows her to work part-time. As this also requires that Karl work part-time, and part-time work for men is difficult to find, he has had to plan his own business. The economic costs of their choice is high. Clara's salary is low. Karl's self-employment plans are economically uncertain.

Clara's example illustrates how the modern Swiss couple expects little support from the relatives. Despite the fact that all relatives look forward to the baby, the couple does not expect practical support: Clara's sister works at night, her mother is still fully involved with her job, and her parents-in-law live too far away.

To Clara, motherhood is a natural part of her way of life, built on the basis of her long and satisfying relationship with Karl. It is interesting that she acknowledges that to Karl personal freedom and money are more important than a family. This suggests that she describes the timing of pregnancy as fate in order to avoid conflict with Karl. She can fulfil her wish to have a child without having to face potential opposition from Karl. This is a common strategy of women who claim that their pregnancy was an accident (but are careless with contraception). Her taking responsibility for the well-being of her partner after the baby is born could suggest a hidden feeling of guilt that she exercised her power to become pregnant without Karl's express support.

## Margrit: the child as a stroke of fate

Margrit, who is 24 years old, and her friend Hans were both half-way through their degrees at university, when out of the blue she became pregnant. They had been friends for several years, living in neighbouring flats (which they shared with other people). They had agreed on a common future together without having children. Hans, particularly, relishes his freedom and independence and is not interested in change. He in fact favoured abortion. Margrit then faced the difficult decision of whether she should carry her child to full term or not. She decided in favour of the child, and they have agreed to remain a couple, but only she will be responsible for the child. Though Hans will support her financially, he is not prepared to have any emotional ties with the child. Margrit has interrupted her studies at university for one year, and then plans to finish her postponed degree.

She states that it was a difficult decision:

> I decided on the life of a child. Still, at this point I don't know whether my decision was the right one. [ ... ] And I decided for Hans. And with this the feeling is inevitable that my decision to have the baby is bad for him. When I tried to decide for myself, I found that I had no idea.
>
> Constantly, I asked myself 'is it a living being or not?' And finally I have

decided 'yes', it is a living being. The pictures that one can see of a foetus in the eighth week, where the tiny hands of a little being are clearly visible, made me believe this. Certainly, that has influenced me. Another influencing factor was that my little brother died and I often visited his grave; even after his death he belonged to our family. For instance, if I painted the family as a child I always painted everybody, including him. My feeling that something can be here despite its invisibility certainly plays a part. I have to say that I have always tried to feel the soul of this little child. But as a matter of fact I did not experience feeling it. [ ... ] I have a friend and she also wanted to feel the soul of her little unborn child. She didn't feel anything and so decided to have an abortion. [ ... ] Despite my experience, I had the feeling, my little child was there. [ ... ] I am fond of it already. To me as a human being it would be much more difficult to live with the death of this child.

Margrit has a very positive view of life and self-trust because, she says, she had a secure childhood. Her parents were practising Catholics and Margrit went to a Catholic school:

I believed, as a child, that whatever happened my parents would never with-draw their love. [ ... ] If I do something wrong, I can always put it right again. That is something I feel very deeply within myself. I believe that this is connected to my religious values, the school I have attended and the things I have heard in church.

The family lost not only one son when he was a baby, but Margrit's older brother died when he was 16, from meningitis. 'We lived with this death in such a way, that something new could emerge out of it. [ ... ] Something really terrible can happen, but you still have the love. You have the support of a strong network of friends.'

Margrit knew about contraception. At school, sexuality was a topic in biology and religion classes, and her mother talked with her about contraception and openly answered Margrit's questions. She gained additional information from television, magazines and through talking with her peer group. Her first menstruation was not a happy event and she later dieted severely to be fashionably slim. 'The boutique clothes were perfect for me because I looked like the mannequins in the windows. It seemed ideal.' The price of this dieting was that she suppressed her menstruation. 'That was the contradiction – to be beautiful and fertile.' She went to see a doctor and he recommended the pill in order to reactivate her cycle, and advised her to put on weight. 'It was quite important to me to menstruate again. The thought that I couldn't have children, that I literally didn't belong to womanhood occupied my mind for quite a while. [ ... ] The menstrual cycle belongs to a woman's life.'

From time to time, Margrit stopped taking the pill to find out whether her menstruation would reappear. Although menstruation did not return, she did become pregnant. She blames herself for irresponsibility. This leads her to think that you cannot divide, as she had done, sexuality and fertility. She reflects: 'Deep down there always was the wish to have a child. However, I did not really acknowledge that fact while we slept together. This was the reason, that I didn't realize fully that I had to do something against it.' As mentioned before, she regards this as inappropriate behaviour.

> Hans has blamed me and says I made an appalling mistake with contraception. I see it as a big mistake myself. I have noticed this before, that often I switch off the brain and act out of the belly. [ ... ] But in this situation it was a matter of life or death; hence it was an existential thing, something I hadn't really thought through. For me it is a true mistake. The decision in favour of the child was simply because I had a certain trust that even out of a mistake something might emerge.

She is prepared to be responsible for this mistake herself. This means that the decision for or against the child is entirely hers. Furthermore, Hans, if he chooses, is not obliged to have anything to do with the child.

There were also practical considerations that played a role in the decision to have the child. How could she pay for the child's keep? Who would look after the child while she was finishing her degree, and later when she was earning her living? Would she have to move house? With the support of her parents, various counselling offices and social aid, she feels she has found a solution to these problems. She has secured support from her family and a wider social network. Additionally, she is confident that other men around her will take the role of 'surrogate fathers'. Despite all this, her visions of the future include fears: she might fail to provide the right support for her child; one of her greatest fears is that, despite the common agreement with Hans, he could reject his child.

Even before the pregnancy, Margrit and Hans were aware of the fact that they had differing views. While she emphasized sharing things in common, mutual support and security, his priorities were independence and personal freedom. Margrit's wishes, which do not correspond with the rational autonomous individual, seemed not to have much space in their relationship. With the child, Margrit's position becomes stronger and Hans has to deal with this. She compromises in order for their relationship to continue. Margrit concentrates on her role as mother, with everything that goes with it, and Hans carries only a certain financial responsibility. The agreement seems to be constructive in the sense that they find common ground at least theoretically in their contradictory demands, even if Margrit's emotional needs and wishes are not met.

Margrit expects from herself that she be able to plan consciously and rationally to have a child. The fact that she became pregnant without planning she interprets as a self-inflicted mistake, a mistake that might be the source of something good. However, it is her mistake and she is responsible for it. There she concurs with Hans's view: that he was misled, and against his own will suddenly confronted with fatherhood. This view legitimizes for both of them his rejection of any future role as father.

From Margrit's point of view the practical problems and changes that go with motherhood are not serious obstacles, though she will depend for longer on her parents and the state, her living conditions will be modest, and her future career uncertain.

The story of Margrit is an example of a modern woman's struggle to reconcile different values, ideologies and choices. There are no coherent ideals and marked paths to follow, and the realization of this is very personal and individual. She demands from herself that she not limit Hans's freedom at any time.

## Monika: the child as a project

Monika is 34 years old and grew up in a small town. Her mother was a housewife and her father worked away and was with the family only during weekends and holidays. Monika went to commercial college, where she met, at 18, her husband Frank.

After her course they worked and travelled together. They retrained as hotel managers after their marriage in 1992, with the dream of managing a guest-house together. After their retraining, they both decided to stop using contraceptives, and Monika fell pregnant soon after. They now live in a municipality just outside Zurich, in a large flat. In winter, after the birth of the child, Frank will leave his well-paid job, and they plan to move to a health resort in the mountains, where they will both work in a small hotel attached to a seminar centre, marking the first step of their dream to run their own hotel.

Monika and Frank do not consider having a child as inevitable, even after 15 years of being together. They are aware that other couples do not choose children. Monika explains that they married 'in view of the fact that we wanted to stay together and children belonged to a common future'. However, they postponed children in order to retrain. 'Somehow I still wasn't ready for it. [ ... ] Taking into account my feelings, I noticed that I wanted to do something else first. I wanted to prove [ ... ]

that I had the power for something new, I mean professionally. And then I noticed that this was much stronger than the wish to have a baby.' After completing the course, they re-examined the question of whether they should have a baby or not.

> We spent our holiday in a nice place together with many families and little babies. It was really cute. And we looked around and talked about our future. Is a childless future an option for us? Is having children? We truly have a good friendship and we found that we could have a good time without children. [ ... ] Our dream to have our own pension went with our wish to have our own children. With all those children around, naturally, I think we were quite influenced. [ ... ] And then I personally felt that I didn't want to wait too long. On the one hand there was my age, on the other I wanted to know whether I could become pregnant or not.

The couple agreed that both would like to share equally paid labour, housework and child care. Monika did not see herself as a housewife. The experience of her original family has influenced her own ideas considerably, and is very important to her, even if she and her partner have decided, relatively late, to begin a family. Her mother's life as a housewife was a negative experience:

> I saw how she stayed at home on her own. She was waiting for my two brothers and me to return from school. [ ... ] She waited for us as the only thing that would fulfil her day. She could stay in the house for days simply knitting. And I saw that she was very sad and that she didn't really live. This was the point where I said to myself, no, not that way, never. If I have children at all I would never simply sit at home.

Actually, her mother did want to take up a profession. But her low education would have allowed her to take only a low-paid and low-status job. Her husband and her children were against it, with the result that she stayed at home. Monika therefore values her professional activities highly. The frequent absence of her father she did not experience as a problem; she has happy memories of holidays and weekends. For her own family, though, she wants to have equal commitment in terms of child care.

Up until the pregnancy Monika and Frank had separate incomes; now Monika will be dependent. Money, though, she felt was not an issue, as long as she has financial security.

Monika holds a very egalitarian model of gender relations. It is important to her to maintain a balance of commitment concerning the spheres of personal education, professional activities, the sharing of housework and family life. Furthermore, mutual confidence and obligation are a very important ingredient in her relationship. To Monika it is decisive whether her partner is in favour of children: 'together with Frank or not at all' is the basic line. Contemplating the sources of her ideals of equality and partnership, Monika comments:

> I didn't have a role model. At least there was no such thing as a feminist example in any way. It was far more that I listened to what I really wanted. Perhaps there was a some egotism involved: I have had a good education and I have an equal right to work like Frank. If both of us want to have a child, both have to be responsible for it equally. I did not take this idea from anybody else, but I sense that the example of my mother is in the background.

During their relationship, Monika and Frank have successfully used different forms of contraception. More problematic was when to stop. A key factor in the timing of the child was Monika's age. She considers herself at the end of the biological spectrum to give birth, mirroring a view widespread in Switzerland that 35 marks the border between a 'normal' and a 'risky' pregnancy. Another important reason was to confirm her fertility. As she would not have resorted to medical intervention, she was relieved that she so quickly became pregnant.

Monika is an example of a modern woman. She has clear ideas of how she wants to live and she is convinced that she can put those ideas into practice. Her education has enabled her to make her own life together with a strong relationship with her husband. She plans a family with both her professional and her partner's needs in mind. 'Life is what you make it' is her ruling principle.

Interestingly, it is Frank rather than Monika who has had to change his working life, as he has to leave a well-paid job to accommodate the new baby. Monika's pregnancy has forced the decision to go and work in the hotel trade. She states: 'If I hadn't have become pregnant we would have postponed that for a while. This just put some pressure on us to do something about it.' It seems that the child is a catalyst, in terms of a common professional future and their move from the city to the mountains.

To Monika the child is something like a luxury; she expects a bonus with great emotional gains: a confirmation of her fertility, the chance to experience motherhood, and a new dimension in her relationship with Frank.

## Tensions between traditional and modern values

The portraits of these three women raise some interesting issues. Unlike couples in traditional family arrangements, modern couples have to take into account many different possibilities. Individual aims in terms of education, professional choice, social experience and travel now determine choices. A rationally justified decision is demanded, although many factors for women cannot be determined rationally (Höpflinger *et al.*, 1991: 188). This brings us to ask whether this autonomous individual is not gender neutral but a decidely male individual. It seems hard to reconcile being a working woman and a sexually free woman (and autonomous individual) with being a mother. There is a basic incompatibility between family life and working life. The competing value systems in an unstable environment cause insecurity, contradictions and tension. In the legal system and the education system, the demand for equality of the genders is to a large extent already realized, and feminist ideals concerning relationships and the division of labour have had an impact on private life. Nevertheless, the myths of the self-conscious, autonomous individual, a love-marriage and an idyllic family life as a refuge of security and happiness are still powerful and effective (Wahl, 1989: 93).

All the women in the case studies strive to work within these myths, despite the contradictions. Monika emphasizes equality, and claims full participation in the public sphere in order to avoid repeating her mother's life. This meant postponing a family, until she found herself up against nature's clock, and she and her husband had to change their life style radically in order to accommodate a child. Clara is closest to the norm, as she fits the average age of Swiss women having a first child, and her aim is not professional fulfilment. Nevertheless, in order to have a good family life in partnership with her husband, they have to juggle shared child care and part-time paid employment. Margrit, in contrast, is coping with an unplanned pregnancy on her own. Her essentially individual choice to have a child leads her to put aside her education, with the support of her religious values, family and state funding. Margrit's voyage into anorexia nervosa shows the contradiction between the ideal body and fertility. The increasing emergence of anorexia nervosa and bulimia among modern women is disconcerting.

All of these women have based the decision to have children on their family background and individual needs. To have children is felt as an exclusively personal matter, for which only personal motives and interests are taken into account. Although we did not look closely at the relationship between generations, we do glimpse how all of the women are reacting against the mother's life choices, as divorced mother bringing up a child singled-handed, or as bored and unvalued housewives. It is not economics or social pressure that determine these modern women's choices, but the way they see themselves as women and their vision of the family. It is striking that two women describe their wish to have a child as egotism. It is interesting that the decision to have a child is made in the abstract; there exist very few points of contact beween the world with and that without children. 'Here (in Switzerland) somebody can become an adult without even once having held a child in her/his arms.' Parenthood brings – especially for women – literally a change in worlds.

The transfer of knowledge relating to sexuality and contraception is secured through the school, the peer group, the mass media and, depending on the quality of the relationship, the mother. But transfer of information on child care is clearly not happening. Another gap is that parenthood has a different meaning for men and different consequences, but fatherhood is not a matter of public debate or research. The Straub–Bernasconi model employed by us could be used to capture and analyse the relationship and conditions of power between the two genders. One aspect worth looking at is the different meaning of fertility to the genders, in relation to the way they see themselves.

Fertility and motherhood, as close as they may be to each other, are not equal in terms of what they acutally mean to women. Our study shows women trying to control how motherhood shapes their lives. For Clara, a child is simply a desired part of a woman's life. Margrit needs to experience herself as a fertile woman. For Monika a child is a bonus, desired but not necessary, to her full professional and marital life.

We need to recall that these women are only conjecturing. As all parents know, it is only after the child is born that the full impact of their choice can be understood. These portraits suggest that the women are not aware of these realities, and it would be interesting to revisit them a few years later to see if all their plans were successful.

## Conclusion

To our question 'is motherhood a rational and responsible choice?', it is clear that children are not compatible with the concept of the autonomous individual, the maximization of profits and of prosperity. This confirms that the individual is decidely a male individual. Despite the attempts of the feminist movement, the areas that women need to weigh up in order to come to a decision are not openly voiced. It is essential that society takes up greater responsibility to assist women in making a fulfilling choice that takes into account women's new role in the family and workplace.

The negotiations these women make suggest that the history of modern sexuality, love, marriage and fertility moves us away from the right to parenthood. The political and ethical questions of parenthood need to be on the public agenda, as they are in these women's decisions. It is only then that it will be possible to lead a public discussion of how to divide the labour of parenthood between the two genders, and of the private and the public spheres.

A starting point would be to encourage discussion between couples, or simply between people who are interested in the question of whether to have a child. How to redistribute the 'joys' and 'burdens' that children bring could be looked at, in order to plan motherhood and fatherhood according to personal and collective needs.

These women, compared to many women in other societies, are in a privileged position of choice. They have partners beginning to share child care, parents who are not hindering and a society that provides some facilities. This environment allows them to choose, but they feel the decision is essentially an individual one, which expresses some deep sense of feminine identity that appears to be in contradiction to what a modern woman should also be doing – having a career. The contradictions they see not as structural but as part of their personal ability to cope or not. It is important to break these myths of autonomous individual and rational choice, in order to give public voice to the doubts these women face. Undertaking this research in a North–South context helps to put the dilemmas into an international context, which highlights that reproductive choice for women is not just a matter of medical technology or economic security, but has to be negotiated through complex historical and culturally bound gender relations.

## Acknowledgements

First of all, warm thanks are owed to the women who were ready to share with us their very personal experience of their way into motherhood. Resource persons of various organizations and institutions have been very helpful and offered important insights for our work. We profited from the warm interest and critical comments of the members of the international research team. We are most grateful to Wendy Harcourt for her sustained support, assistance and friendship. A special vote of thanks is due to our families, who accompanied us with great patience throughout the ups and downs of this project.

## Notes

1. This chapter was translated by Heinz Jufer.
2. The low rate of pregnancy among teenagers, 0.6 percent of all Swiss

women who give birth to a child for the first time, and the increasing age of women who give birth to a child for the first time (in 1993 there were 43 per cent over 34 years old), the increase of childlessness from 10 per cent of women who were born in 1936–40 to 18 per cent of women who were born 1950–55, as well as the diminishing size of the family from three to two children, are indicative figures.

3. The population of Zurich is 342,518: 14 per cent are below 19 years of age; 66 per cent between 20 and 64; and 20 per cent aged 65 and over.

## References

Federal Commission for Women's Issues (1994) 'Great achievements – small changes? On the situation of women in Switzerland', Bern.

Hausen, K. (1976) in C. Werner, *Sozialgeschichte der Familie in der Neuzeit Europas*, Stuttgart, Klett-Verlag.

Höpflinger, F., M. Charles and A. Debrunner (1991) *Familienleben und Berufsarbeit. Zum Wechselverhältnis zweier Lebensbereiche*, Zürich, Seismo.

Hungerbühler, R. (1989) *Unsichtbar – Unschätzbar. Haus-und Familienarbeit am Beispiel der Schweiz*, Grüsch, Rüegger.

Ley, K. und C. Borer (1992) *Und sie paaren sich wieder. Ueber Fortsetzungsfamilien*, Tübingen, Edition Diskord.

Lüscher, K. und R. Thierbach (1993) 'Die Vielfalt privater Lebensformen im Spiegel der Volkszählung', *Neuer Zürcher Zeitung* (13 December).

Meyer, Th. (1989) *Fundamentalismus. Aufstand gegen die Moderne*. Essay, Haburg, Rororo 12414.

Ryffel-Gericke, C. (1979) 'Die Geburt des ersten Kindes. Erste Ergebnisse aus Tiefeninterviews mit Zürcher Ehefrauen', *Schweizerische Zeitschrift Soziologie*, No. 6.

Statistique du Mouvement de la Population, 1979, 1990 und 1993, Tables No. 2.01.041. Bern, Bundesamt für Statistik.

Straub-Bernasconi, S. (1995) *Systemtheorie, soziale Probleme und soziale Arbeit: lokal, national, international oder: vom Ende der Bescheidenheit*, Bern, Haupt.

Wahl, K. (1989) *Die Modernisierungsfalle. Gesellschaft, Selbstbewusstsein und Gewalt*, Frankfurt a. M., Suhrkamp.

# 9

# Conclusions: moving from the private to the public political domain

WENDY HARCOURT

These case studies from Tanzania, Ghana, Brazil, Pakistan, Sri Lanka, Italy and Switzerland present changes in women's 'reproductive lives' in diverse cultural contexts. They are necessarily partial and incomplete. The information and analysis continue to be gathered and the lives will continue to change. This conclusion records the historical shifts in reproductive health issues for these women in recent years, as a contribution to accelerating those changes that will open up political space to the recognition that women's reproductive lives have public as well as private significance.

There are three overarching, interlinked themes in the discourse on reproductive health, which we can discern in each case study, despite their diverse manifestations in the different cultural contexts: the growing influence of modern economic and social trends; the change in the knowledge of the body; and the change in sexual practice and behaviour.

## The influence of modern economic and social trends

As stated in the introduction, modern economic and social trends brush the lives of all these women in varying degrees. Our study does not aim to measure quantitatively the impact of these trends – for one thing, we look at only a tiny fragment of each of the country's women – but it is clear that, qualitatively, modern trends are a powerful influence. The case studies each bring out similar modern factors at play, which impact on the women's reproductive lives: the global economy, schooling, mass media, the struggle for women's rights (feminism), and the process of Western medicalization of birth and health services. As the case studies show, such trends are multi-faceted and have a different level of impact according to the cultural context. There is no sense in which there is a linear, progressive line from traditional to modern. Instead, each situation registers varying mixes where traditional and modern trends compete, not always clearly to the advantage of the women involved.

One of the most surprising finds is that even women living in seclusion in rural Pakistan are touched by the global economy, with some cash-earning capacity, rudimentary education and changes in women's status beginning to be introduced into the village of Sunnakhi. In Ghana, women's buoyant economic activity, greater access to schools and family planning have led to shifts in their status and expectations within family and community. Such shifts indicate that modernity is unsettling traditional roles even as women struggle with polygamy, for rights to equal access to education, land and a stronger say in national decision-making. In Dar es Salaam, there is a break away from traditional family ties to a greater reliance on schools, state and medical institutions. This leads to considerable uncertainty as to who takes authority in reproductive life, and to what the outcome of new life styles and life choices will be for young women. In Rio de Janeiro, women working in domestic service are struggling for better status in a vastly inequitable society, and for access to knowledge on reproductive health through mass media and publicly available medical technology. Their questioning of the benefit of partnerships with men is indicative of an emerging new sense of self. Sri Lankan migrant women's even more rapidly changing lives, owing to their rude entry into the global economy, are exposed to more knowledge of the outside world and non-traditional sexuality and mores than their village lives had prepared them for, leading to major shifts in their position in village life on their return. Italy, a wealthy and decidedly modern society since the 1950s, continues to live with the contradictions of what is said in the media and in schools. Though progressive expectations exist, young women are still constrained by family expectations and conditions, and, lingering in the background of Italian cultural and political life, by the Church. The complexity of relations that determine young women's reproductive decisions indicate how reproductive lives have not yet been fully taken on board by public institutions and discourses. Zurich, at the opposite end of the scale from the rural and poor Sunnakhi, represents the most affluent society in the study, with high levels of education, possibilities for the participation of women in the paid economy, awareness of women's rights and men's responsibilities for the family, and access to information-age services and technology. Like Italy, however, once the surface appearances are challenged, the modern Swiss woman faces contradictory and conflicting life choices.

Modern society provides greater access to resources, education, new knowledge and technology, offering potentially great benefits to women.[1]

As the case studies show, in recent years there have been positive changes for most of these groups of women in the growing knowledge, services and options available in the area of reproductive health. However, the cultural, political and economic structures in which women's reproductive lives are shaped are rarely publicly acknowledged or debated in a way that helps women to find autonomy and self-affirmation in these choices. Instead, most of the women are facing contradictory messages, silences and gaps in knowledge over what is a valid reproductive health choice.

This dynamic is evident if we look at the changes in the knowledge of the body, and in sexual practice and behaviour, as documented in the case studies.

## Changes in knowledge of the body, sexual practice and behaviour

In Sunnakhi village, there have been some shifts in women's social status, particularly in families headed by a woman who has broken away from traditional male authority to become economically independent, supporting her family and herself without male support. The changes in reproductive lives are more difficult to measure. Exposure to the NGO working in the village, new income-generating opportunities, the possibility of girls receiving some basic education, and some rudimentary awareness of family planning for older women have begun to make some changes. But this is only marginal. In terms of knowledge of bodily health, young girls are not well informed, and there are few places within the home where they can find information. Unmarried women are basically ignorant of their maturing body and sexuality, and kept so as a sign of their chastity, which is strongly linked to family honour and therefore to their marriageability. This changes as women grow older and they play a role in transmitting knowledge to younger women on issues such as menstruation and pregnancy. Menstruation is not discussed even within the family, and the pretence of illness during menstruation is maintained, with women expected to hide all signs of bleeding.

Sexual practice and behaviour are much more closely shrouded in silence between genders and generations and within the community, both chosen silence, as part of the need to preserve honour, and also the silence of ignorance, particularly of what type of contraception is available. Young women are completely silent and silenced on this issue; they have no control over their lives and there is no acknowledgement of their sexuality, indeed their non-awareness is imbued with great sexual significance, but they are objects not subjects of this discourse. Girls enter young into arranged marriages, and are expected, as are older women, to obey their husband's desires. Older women are equally reluctant to discuss sexuality. Feminine sexual pleasure is denied by older women, but whether as a sign of their feminine chastity it is not clear. Reproductive choice is also not in the hands of women, in two senses: their husbands determine sexual relations, and their status depends on them producing children (sons). Therefore, in order to fulfil their role as women, they are obliged to have children at whatever personal health risk. Contraception is used once the woman considers she has reached the end of the child-bearing period, and not for child spacing.

The NGO working in the village, and also the research carried out for the book, open up some room for at least the older women to express what they might need in order to improve their reproductive health, if not their reproductive choices. An important strategy, which the case study highlights, is the need to work with older women as the transmitters of information, and through men who have access to doctors, paramedics and NGOs. A multiple strategy is needed to improve women's rights, including education and information that is culturally sensitive to women's experience in *purdah*, and that aims to reach the different generations.

In Ghana, the information available on bodily health is much more closely linked to sexual knowledge and practice. There has been a shift away from the traditions that link women's status to their reproductive life cycle through rites and rituals. Family planning is becoming more widely known about, if not always practised, delinking women's sexuality from their reproductivity, even if there is not always much choice and accurate information about the different technologies. Similarly, some practices that women themselves identify as oppressive, such as polygamy, are declining, and women in urban areas are able to resist what the study identifies as 'troublesome' husbands. Some women also feel that the move away from tradition helps women to move away from the traditional prejudice inscribed within the old rituals of women as unclean or polluting men. Women also indicate that they are being able to choose their partners more easily. However, there is a disruption of family life in a way that is not always constructive for women's reproductive lives, particularly for young women. Parental authority and, even more, grandparents' authority, is declining with the growing influence of school and state services. This shift creates some unfortunate gaps in the transfer of knowledge of bodily health, menstruation, childbirth and sexual activity, which had been imparted during traditional rites and ceremonies, sometimes involving the whole family. Instead, a mismatch of moral judgements and misunderstandings between generations emerges which, without the support of good education or medical services, results in a deteriorating level of reproductive health for many women. Combined with increasing economic hardship and family responsibilities, women's burdens are in general increasing. Sexuality, instead of being something that can be spoken and learnt about within traditional rituals, is tabooed, leading to a confusion in the information that young people are able to glean from their peers, the mass media and schools. Inevitably this leads to an increasing number of unwanted pregnancies, as women continue to be sexually active at an early age even if they marry later.

The tensions between modern social and economic trends and traditional practice have to be resolved by looking at the particular needs of Ghanaian women in their different situations, in rural and urban areas and different religious practices. This means that strategies to improve women's reproductive lives have to take what is good from old and new, and try to resolve problems of communication between generations and genders, in order to build on and not detract from the many strengths that Ghanaian women show in their business acumen and organizational skills. The family planning services already well established in Ghana have to look at why women and their partners are failing to take up these services, and work with women in the community to design more appropriate health assistance.

The study in Dar es Salaam focuses on the shifts in social and normative knowledge and technical and practical knowledge, and, as in the Ghana study, shows that the result is a disruption of traditional knowledge, leading to a very incomplete knowledge of reproductive lives on the part of teenage women. In terms of bodily health, young girls no longer have clear channels of information; instead of learning from grandparents or aunts, they receive partial information from schools and medical services, but rely largely on peer groups and mass media. Institutions seem reluctant to fill in the gaps, and parents themselves no longer wish to take on the responsibility. In discussions on sexual knowledge and practice, there is a major divide between generations. Parents see the problem as adolescent sexual activity, whereas the adolescents identify the problem as unwanted pregnancy and therefore insufficient accurate knowledge and access to contraception.

There seems to be a disjuncture in knowledge and practice brought about by the traditional understanding of the regeneration of life, once a recognized social and cultural practice, being subsumed under the medical concept of health, which ignores the complex issues of social and cultural power, which reproductive health necessarily involves. Solutions to these problems and the alarming rate of teenage pregnancy would be to acknowledge the different actors involved (male and female teenagers, parents, grandparents, teachers, public health authorities and media) and to try and support young people's choices and life options. The plea is to try and separate out moral issues from health needs, not in order to ignore them, but to create the most appropriate forums to address these issues while still meeting the immediate education and service needs of young women.

Changes in values, exposure to new knowledge and ideas, changes in family patterns, increase in age of marriage, and greater education for girls should be opportunities to enrich, and not, as at present, debilitate reproductive lives. A too technical and mechanical approach by health services is not able to bring this about. The case study outlines several strategies that the different actors involved suggested, which help to bring the debate into the open, making it socially and culturally more acceptable to take advantage of introduced medical technology and information on reproduction and sexuality, while at the same time recognizing that what was valuable in traditional customs should not be lost.

In Rio de Janeiro, for women working in domestic service, their reproductive choices and autonomy lag behind their productive lives, which the case studies suggest are steadily improving. Knowledge of bodily health is regulated through the medical services, which young women feel are inaccessible. In the case of older women who seek out contraception, because of their recognized need to control fertility, the service is limiting as it is not patient-oriented, so that women do not choose so much as submit to the choice of the doctor (irreversible contraception is very common among these women). Most information is picked up through the mass media, usually soap operas and popular shows, or through government anti-Aids campaigns. The information received does not always enable women to make informed reproductive choice, and thus enjoy their reproductive lives. Two outstanding findings of the case study are that these women are choosing non-biological motherhood as a life option, where they care for others' children and do not have a family life of their own, and that they perceive the men in their lives increasingly as oppressive and a burden. For the mature women among them, the economic independence afforded by paid domestic work means freedom from men, and an end to active sexuality and fertility. This is a very negative picture of women's reproductive lives, compounded by the silences on sexuality between generations (what the study identifies as 'classes of age').

Teenage pregnancy in Rio is on the increase, as is AIDS. Even if mass media are breaking some of the silences, there is a need for women to be enabled to talk more openly about sexuality, gender relations and their life choices, in order to take control over their own bodies, relationships and lives. More high-quality medical care is needed, along with more informed media that promote reproductive rights and choice and male responsibility for their sexual behaviour. The public debate needs to recognize women's need to lead full productive and reproductive lives. National women's organizations, such as CEPIA, which carried out the research, are creating such forums (often with substantial support, through networking and collaboration with the international women's movement) among poor women in urban centres. These initiatives need to be more strongly supported by the government.

The study of returnee migrants in Sri Lanka focuses mainly on changes in sexual mores, brought about by women's entry into the global market place as domestic workers or factory workers. Here the rapidity of the change leads to tensions and challenges within and among families in the village, with returnee migrants placed in an ambiguous position, as bearers of new knowledge and representatives of new life styles, which are treated with suspicion. The ambivalence these women experience, the silences, pressures and difficulties they find on their return home, is indicative of how damaging such changes can be. At first glance, opening up to a new way of life and to possibilities of receiving income appear beneficial. However, because these changes have been brought about by economic need, which cuts across social and cultural mores, and does not take into account the importance of women's reproductive lives (their role as mother, wife and daughter is subsumed to the economic possibility to gain income), the gains in the long term are more doubtful.

In terms of changes in sexual knowledge, there is an uneasy mix of traditional and modern. Young migrant women are more knowledgeable and more likely to be sexually active: women's own sexual pleasure is even mentioned during the interviews, something unthinkable for their village counterparts. They represent a modern sexuality, and are therefore considered unmarriageable in the village context (whether or not they experience premarital sexual relations). It is interesting that whereas all groups of women see the advantage of non-traditional sources of knowledge (mass media, clinics and school) on reproductive information, the knowledge of the women themselves who venture beyond the village is stigmatized. (It was suggested by the researchers during discussions, but not elaborated in the chapter, that class is a strong factor here, with the lower-caste and poorer working-class women forced to migrate, and the middle-class women staying in the village; hence, the stigma could also be attached to class prejudice.)

It is clear from these women's lives – the stress they feel and the disruption to their families and communities – that they are paying a high price for Sri Lanka's entry into the global economy. Their reality needs to be reassessed in future development policies, with a sensitive reading of their reproductive and productive futures.[2]

The two Northern case studies throw up different questions from the Southern case studies, regarding the change in knowledge and practice in bodily health and sexual matters. In Italy, information and discussion on bodily health has improved markedly for young women, in comparison to their mothers' generation. There is more open discussion about menstruation, and young girls are aware of what services are available. Their mothers now also are knowledgeable and able to seek advice on a regular basis. Women are choosing to take up contraception, plan families, decide on their future partners and to monitor their own health. Abortion, even if controversial for practising Catholics, is available. Nevertheless, there is an express lack in the services available to support women's choices, particularly in relation to easily accessible youth- and women-oriented medical care, child care and sufficient housing for young people.

Silences and difficulties come with issues of sexuality. Here there is less knowledge and knowledge-sharing within and between the generations. There is a mixture of conservative and progressive thinking, but fear and uncertainty are prevalent about the space in which young women have safe sexual practice and identity. It is not a question of legal rights, but rather cultural and social acceptance within and outside the family. It appears that schools, health and media are the institutions defining the discourse on sexuality, even if the family is still defined as the grounds in which it can be safely practised. The strong recommendation is for the media and schools to work with parents and children to help break down the barriers that still exist between the different public and private expressions of women's reproductive lives.

In Switzerland, services, education and media are as open to issues of reproductive health and sexuality as in Italy, perhaps even more so, as the culture of alternative life styles is well established, at least in Zurich, the town studied. Homosexuality is more openly acknowledged, and cohabitation and divorce are more the norm than was found in the towns studied in Italy. The research looks in depth at how individual needs in a consumer society have eclipsed community needs, leaving women feeling individually responsible for their choice for motherhood. The case study questions just how much autonomy women really do have in choosing to have a first child. The issue here is not the legislation, information or technology required, but the type of cultural and social support, which is at best ambiguous. On choosing motherhood, the women, brought up to see themselves as independent autonomous individuals, become dependent on spouse, family and society. When faced with the realities of child-bearing, they find they have to reorganize their entire lives, and those of their partners, in order to create an environment that would earlier have been part of the traditional family and community domain. They ask that the political and ethical rights of parenthood are placed on the public agenda, as a way of finding what new social and cultural institutions are needed for modern parenthood, for both and their male partners to lead fulfilling reproductive lives.

## Redefining the reproductive health agenda

What do these studies suggest for our original concerns – the transfer of knowledge within and between generations, the concepts of life stages, and the shifts in understanding of the role of motherhood?

In all cases, the inter-generational transfer of knowledge on reproductive health and sexuality is not the key area where young women find out about reproductivity and sexual practice. Other institutions are more important, either traditional institutions (rites and ceremonies) as in Ghana and Africa (now breaking down), or schools, clinics and media. Grandparents, parents and children look to these public domains for instruction, even if children would like to discuss it more openly within the family. It is these institutions, currently unable to do more than inform on reproductive health problems, that need to take up the more complete agenda sketched out in each of the case studies.

Intra-generational knowledge is very important in all cultures. The participants are aware that if it is not the most reliable of sources, it is certainly the easiest way to acquire knowledge. Knowing this, policies need to take advantage of peer-group solidarity and support, particularly for adolescent women but also for older generations confronted by doubts about self-worth, pressures of work and social changes in a rapidly changing world.

Inter-cultural knowledge, although not originally included in the research problematic, emerges as very influential. Essentially, the flow of cultural exchange is one-way, with Northern models of reproductive knowledge and behaviour being transmitted to the South. The transfer of knowledge through medical services, schools and media, based on copies of Western models, is predominant, often debasing local traditional knowledge. What is missing, in using these channels of information, is a way to validate traditional approaches to reproductive practice. This more culturally sensitive approach is necessary, not only in order to unsettle the hierarchy of Western knowledge, but also to design more accessible information programmes that reflect different women's realities.

'Life stages' is confirmed by the study as a key concept. In all cases, it is crucial to look at the different knowledges and practices of women according to their age. Reproductive health and sexuality for adolescents need much more understanding within each cultural context, not as a problem but as a reality which will determine future generations of women's life choices. The change in women's productive activity, with more women entering the work-force and taking up a more public position, needs to be recognized and understood when looking at information, support and health services required for reproductive-age women. The pressures facing women at this age have to be much more publicly discussed, not as medical concerns but as cultural, social and ethical concerns, particularly in relation to the shared responsibility of partners for family and community life. Our book does not look carefully at changes in older women's reproductive lives, rather it monitors the change in their family status due to modernity devaluing the knowledge gained by older women (with the exception of Pakistan where older women still assert more power). The needs of these women, as an age-group destined to become a majority in future communities, need much more public recognition.

The different age-groups need very different reproductive health policies and approaches. Most critically, policies need to move away from the developmental and medical approach, which tends to treat all women as the same.

The book steers away from a central focus on motherhood, in order not to fall into stereotyping women's reproductive health as only connected to their function as mothers. Nevertheless it is obvious that the role and importance of motherhood too is shifting. In all cases, including in the case studies in the North, motherhood remains an important concept in defining women's sense of self, in both the private and public domain. However, there are many more variations in the role now, as it is in competition with other aspects of women's lives; from Zurich to Sunnakhi, modern economic and social trends are disrupting traditional expectations of motherhood. This is an ambiguous shift, as motherhood is expected to be managed privately, even if women's growing public productive role is diminishing their ability to handle their responsibilities as mothers. In all cultures, the role of motherhood is uneasily balanced between the two domains, creating stress and dissatisfaction for women's reproductive lives.

What also emerges as an uneasy factor in women's reproductive lives is the silences: between mother and daughter, between genders, between cultures; about sexual pleasure for women, about homosexuality and, perhaps surprisingly, about AIDS and sexually related illnesses. As stated in the introduction, the researchers find themselves reluctant to break down barriers that they recognize, particularly among poor communities, to be necessary for survival. Nevertheless, it is many of these silences, particularly in the first four areas mentioned above, that fascinate and that point to ways to open up a debate that could lead to safe, self-determined reproductive lives in a modern era. Essentially this is a feminist political agenda, culturally and historically defined, which we need to embrace. We hope that the information we have shared and the questions we raise are one step in the direction of defining that agenda.

What this book makes clear is that we should not be afraid of either modernity or tradition, but should look carefully at what is useful for women in different cultural contexts to balance their productive and reproductive lives. We cannot hide behind the concept of the private as if it is of no concern to the public; it all too evidently is, and our world economy runs on the pretence that social reproductive work is not a concern of the community, or of national or international institutions. But nor can we expect all cultures to take up confidently the feminist slogan, 'the personal is political'. We have to respect different political agendas, and while some can accommodate this plea, others would only twist it to oppress women more. In a reproductive agenda we need to redefine 'public' and 'private' to accommodate the need to support women's and men's social reproductive functions. Perhaps we need to create multiple public spaces so that we have recognized institutions outside the family where it is safe to discuss intimate relations and sexuality in such a way that the results of those discussions become linked to national decision-making.

The same considerations apply to the appeal of both technology and the natural world. We cannot afford to romanticize either. Current reproductive technology is useful, but it needs to be separated out from today's medical and bureaucratic organizations. Currently, these are regimes which make knowledge and decision-making inaccessible to those subject to the technology. We need to be careful to see the politics behind how a technology is conceived and practised, and separate out what women, in their specific cultural context, understand and therefore would find useful when exercising their choice. In some cases this could mean rejecting today's reproductive technologies in favour of less inter-ventionist tools. But it should not mean a return to a completely non-technological world of childbirth. This, in any case, no longer exists. We have to take on board the social transformation of health and medical institutions to incorporate social and cultural requirements as defined by women at the local, national and international levels. This political strategy will no doubt lead to a varied number of reproductive life patterns, reflecting not only Western medical technology but also traditional practices that women feel are adaptable and still useful.

A reproductive health agenda would therefore do the following: value different women's histories and self-perceptions based on age and cultural experience; remove the tensions women experience from the contradictions in their reproductive and productive lives; open up the possibilities for women to take advantage of what modernity offers in terms of the freedom to choose motherhood and to experience self-fulfilment and sexual pleasure; enable women to share the joys and burdens of children with their partners, families and communities; acknowledge the past role of the family, community and individual in reproductivity while producing possibilities for new knowledge; and work creatively with new technologies as tools to create choices, not as controlling mechanisms.

This agenda goes beyond what a health service or mother-and-child development strategy could hope to provide. Instead we need to create new conditions through new political institutions and theories. This need takes us back to the ambitious goal we set ourselves to link the local with the global, as stated in the first chapter. The case studies set out what is happening at the local level, but we need also to see how it is linked to the global quest for justice.

It is important not to take the reproductive health agenda as a separate women's agenda but to tie it closely to the international agenda for global justice. Such an agenda needs to be delinked from the predominant development agenda, which fails to take into account the complexity of inter-cultural relations and gender relations and the tensions between productive and reproductive lives.

The search for justice in a globalized world moves us beyond the polarities of North and South. On this journey the international feminist movement has already embarked. In breaking down the myths that this book challenges about reproductive rights for women in the North and South, the population problem and sustainable development, women have evidently moved beyond traditional North–South divides. Women in the international feminist movement, while acknowledging their differences, do combine to forge more democratic ways of working and new political institutions. In continuing to push the agenda forward, the divisions between traditional and modern, private and public, and technological and natural worlds also have to be reworked.

To begin with, we have to foster self-esteem, asserting the value and potential of women in making their own choices, in order to open up

the path to creativity and action in both their reproductive and productive lives. We also have to create conditions for women to select
from outside influences. Outside intervention should not be overwhelming but enriching. Women have to be able to select what is useful for
them and reject what is damaging. Outside information and technologies
have to be accepted by the women and adapted to the local environment,
with their own experience and culture as the basis for their selection
and order of priority. They would therefore also have the right to resist
what is harmful to themselves and their community. This resistance has
to be discerning and clear-sighted, based on self-esteem, knowledge and
a capacity to select. It also demands a sense of direction and purpose
that is not solely an individual but a community one. Essentially this
means that reproductive health has to be part of a political agenda that
determines how we live together successfully in just and equitable social
relations. To adopt Ricardo Petrella's concept, we need to move today's
development agenda away from a 'culture of the object' to a 'culture of
the subject' (Verhelst, 1996: 21) – a desire at the heart of the international feminist movement.

This book is one step towards mapping out the terrain for a
reproductive health agenda. The second step will be how to develop it
theoretically and politically with the participation of the women who are
the subjects of our case studies. We look forward to working with them
locally, nationally and internationally to resolve some of the dilemmas of
how to produce feminist knowledge and practice that can constructively
break the silences around reproductive health and sexuality.

## Notes

1. For Western feminists working in international development there is uneasiness in proclaiming the benefits of modernity. First, because you are aware
of the attacks, in the name of modernity and progress, on many social and
cultural traditions, which, when interpreted differently, are not necessarily
oppressive to women. Secondly, you become uncomfortable with the imposition
of Western feminism on the international movement; this can be culturally
insensitive (and has been accused of being a form of cultural imperialism).
Nevertheless, in working with Southern feminists on the book (and in other
areas of my work with SID), I am now more confident that feminism has been
adopted and adapted by women in non-Western cultural contexts so that it can
be seen, more or less unambiguously, as a vital force in opposing women's
oppression. These women can claim as feminists what they regard as the benefits
of modernity, while retaining a healthy scepticism of some aspects of Western
culture.

2. One of the best studies I know about on the 'maid trade' in south-east

Asia is by the Asian and Pacific Development Centre, co-ordinated by Noeleen Heyzer and Vivienne Wee in 1993. Five years of research came up with some important policy recommendations and also documented the lives of these women in detail (Heyzer *et al.*, 1994).

## References

Heyzer, N., G. Lycklama à Nijeholt and N. Weerakoon (eds) (1994) *The Trade in Domestic Workers*, London and New Jersey/Kuala Lumpur, Zed Books/Asian and Pacific Development Centre.

Verhelst, T. (1996) 'Cultural Dynamics in Development', *Cultures and Development*, n. 24, 4/1996.

# Index